John Cowley

Communications and Networking

An Introduction

 Springer

John Cowley, BA, Dip TEO, MSc, MEd,
Faculty of Computing, Engineering and Technology
Staffordshire University
College Road
Staffordshire ST4 2DE
UK

British Library Cataloguing in Publication Data
A catalogue record for this book is available from the British Library

Library of Congress Control Number: 2006926824

ISBN-10: 1-84628-488-0   Printed on acid-free paper
ISBN-13: 978-1-84628-488-5

Printed in the United States of America   (TB/EB)

9 8 7 6 5 4 3 2 1

Springer Science+Business Media, LLC
springer.com

Communications and Networking

Contents

1
Introduction

This short chapter starts by considering how we can define what a network is. Next there is a short discussion of different types of networks. This is followed by an account of the reasons why networks are used. Communication between computers is then discussed. Several basic terms used when discussing computer communication are introduced.

1.1 What Is a Network?

A network consists of a number of interconnected, autonomous computers. Being 'interconnected' means that the computers can send information to each other. We need to include the word 'autonomous' in our definition so as to exclude *distributed systems*. These consist of many processors linked together, but acting as one computer under the control of one copy of the operating system. In a network, however, all the computers have their own operating system and can act independently. The hardware and software of which a network is composed are considered in later chapters of this book.

1.2 Types of Networks

Local area networks (LANs) are limited to a small geographical area. LAN data transfer rates tend to be very high. The whole LAN—computers, cables and all other components—is usually owned by one organisation, for example, a business. Further details of LAN technologies are given in Chapter 4. Figure 1.1 shows a LAN.

Wide area networks (WANs) connect computers over long distances, even right round the globe. WAN data rates are typically lower than those of LANs. WANs are normally used to interconnect LANs. It is uncommon for an entire WAN to be owned by one organisation. Almost always, third-party telecommunications carrier companies will provide the long-haul links. Further details of WAN technologies and services are given in Chapter 5. Figure 1.2 illustrates a WAN.

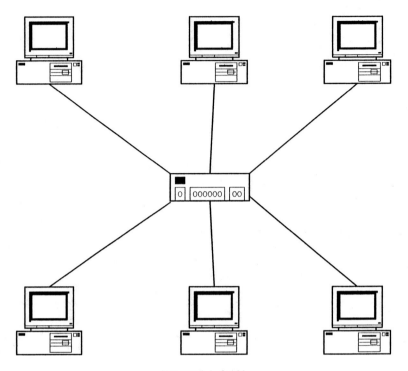

FIGURE 1.1. LAN

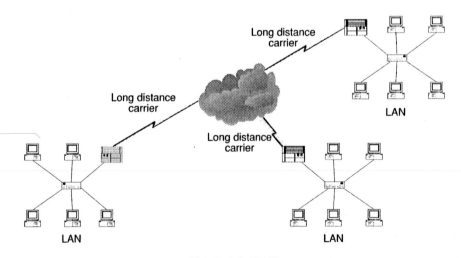

FIGURE 1.2. WAN

You may also encounter the term *metropolitan area network* (MAN). MANs are a halfway house between LANs and WANs. They can span an entire city and its suburbs, but their reach is not as great as that of WANs.

Personal area networks (PANs) and *home area networks* (HANs) are very short range networks. These are described in Chapter 10.

1.3 Reasons for Networks

LANs make it possible to share computer hardware, software applications and data files. They also make communications such as e-mail or instant messaging possible. WANs enable the same possibilities as LANs, with the added advantage of a worldwide reach.

1.4 Communication Between Computers

1.4.1 Source, Destination and Transmission Medium

As shown in Fig. 1.3, whenever information is sent through a network, there is always a *source* (the sending computer), a *medium* along which the data travels (often, but not always, a cable) and a *destination* (the receiving computer). Further information about transmission media is given in Chapter 2.

1.4.2 Packet

As is shown in Fig. 1.3, the data is usually sent in a *packet*, a unit of information suitable for travelling between one computer and another. In addition to the data itself,

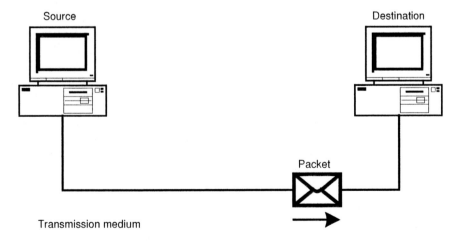

FIGURE 1.3. Source, destination and transmission medium

the packet will contain *addressing* information. The source address in a packet identifies the sending computer. The destination address identifies the receiving computer. Besides address information, the packet will also contain other items that are needed to facilitate communication. Details of the structure of various kinds of packets will be given later in this book.

1.4.3 Protocol

When we want to send a packet of data from one computer to another, it is vital that the source, the destination and any other devices on the network all use the same *protocol*. A protocol is a set of rules. These rules make communication via a network work satisfactorily. Outside the field of computer science, one meaning of the word 'protocol' is a code of conduct. We find the word used this way in the phrase 'the protocols of the Geneva convention'. An explanation of how various protocols work together to facilitate communication can be found in Chapter 3 (Section 3.1).

1.5 Summary

This introductory chapter started by considering the definition of a network. Next, different types of networks were briefly discussed and then some reasons why networks are used were given. Finally, computer communication and some of the basic terms used were introduced.

1.6 Questions

1. What are the differences between WANs and LANs?
2. What benefits do networks offer?
3. Why do data packets need to include addresses along with the data?
4. What is a network protocol?

2
Communications Technologies

In this chapter, we look at some of the technologies that are used for computer communications. The chapter starts with an explanation of the differences between serial and parallel data transfer, asynchronous and synchronous communications and duplex, half-duplex and full-duplex communications. The distinctions between data rate, bandwidth and throughput are then explained. Modulation and encoding, error control methods, switching and multiplexing are then discussed. The topologies used in networking are described. Finally, network transmission media are explored.

2.1 Serial and Parallel Communications

Inside the case of a computer, data is often moved around on parallel pathways. Multiple wires are used to transfer whole units of data simultaneously. Parallel transfer is used inside the processor, for example. Outside the processor itself, in a data bus such as peripheral component interconnect (PCI), 64 parallel wires can be used to transfer data between components. If we want to transfer, say, 8 bytes of data, with a 64-bit parallel system, all 8 bytes can be transferred at once. An 8-bit parallel transfer is illustrated in Fig. 2.1. A whole byte of information is transferred at once, with each bit of the byte moving along its own wire.

Even inside the computer case, parallel data transfer is not always used. For example, a serial advanced technology attachment (serial ATA) cable may be used to attach a hard disk drive to its controller. It is possible to use parallel connections over short distances to external peripheral devices, for example, a parallel printer. Usually, however, serial connections are used for external connections. In serial transfer, only one wire carries the data and only one bit is transmitted at a time. Figure 2.2 illustrates serial transfer.

One vital piece of hardware for communication over a network is the *network interface card* (NIC, pronounced nick). Inside the computer, the NIC sends and receives data via a parallel connection; outside the computer, the NIC is connected in serial fashion to the network. These connections are shown in Fig. 2.3. NICs are covered in more detail in Chapter 4.

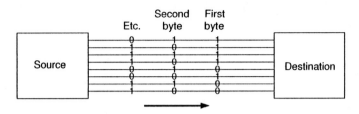

FIGURE 2.1. Parallel data transfer

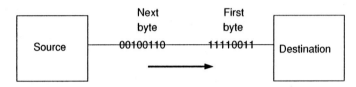

FIGURE 2.2. Serial data transfer

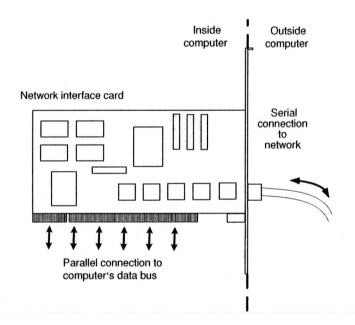

FIGURE 2.3. Serial and parallel data transfer to/from a NIC

2.2 Asynchronous and Synchronous Communications

In serial transmission, the receiving device has to know when a new character begins. This can be done using either asynchronous or synchronous transmission.

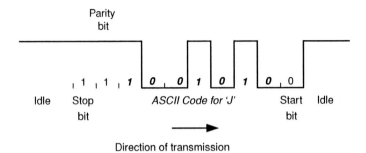

FIGURE 2.4. Asynchronous transmission

2.2.1 Asynchronous Transmission

Asynchronous transmission is used in low-speed applications where communication is only sporadic. An example of this kind of situation is the connection of a console (terminal) to a router. In an asynchronous transmission, a special bit called the 'start' bit is sent before the bits that make up the character and one 'stop' bit (or possibly two stop bits) is sent at the end. For this reason, an alternative term for asynchronous transmission is start–stop transmission. The start bit alerts the receiving device to the fact that a character is about to be transmitted. The stop bit tells the receiver that no more bits will be sent for a while.

Figure 2.4 illustrates asynchronous transmission. In the diagram, the transmission of the capital letter 'J' is shown. A 7-bit ASCII code is being used (1001010). The diagram should be read from right to left. The communications line is initially in the idle condition—nothing is happening. Then, out of the blue, a start bit arrives. This warns the receiver that the next bit will be the least significant bit of a character. The remaining bits of the character follow. The 0s and 1s are represented by different voltages on the communications line, for example, +5 and 0 V.

After the most significant bit of the character, there is a parity bit—a check for errors. In Fig. 2.4, even parity is being used. This means that over the whole of the character and the parity bit there is an even number of '1' bits. If the received bit pattern does not accord with this, then it is assumed that there has been a transmission error. Alternatively, odd parity could have been employed, in which case with no errors there would be an odd number of '1' bits over the whole of the character and the parity bit. An 8-bit code could have been used instead with no parity check. There is further coverage of error control methods later in this chapter (see Section 2.6). After the parity bit, there is a stop bit to tell the receiver that transmission has ceased for the time being. EIA/TIA-232 (RS232-C), mentioned in Section 3.2.1, is an example of an asynchronous protocol.

2.2.2 Synchronous Transmission

In asynchronous transmission, roughly 30 per cent of the bits that have to be transmitted are not data bits. This is a rather large overhead and so for high-speed

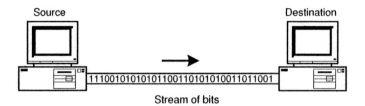

FIGURE 2.5. Synchronous transmission

transmission, synchronous transmission is used instead. In synchronous transmission, data is sent as a continuous stream at a constant rate, making maximum use of the available line capacity. To achieve this, the clocks on the transmitting and receiving devices are synchronised by sending synchronising bits. Once the sender and receiver clocks are synchronised, the receiver can distinguish the beginning of the data stream and can pick off each byte by counting the number of bits. Figure 2.5 illustrates synchronous transmission. High-Level Data Link Control (HDLC) is a typical synchronous protocol. A description of HDLC can be found in Section 6.3.

2.3 Simplex, Half-Duplex and Full-Duplex Communications

Simplex transmission is transmission that can take place only ever in one direction. An example of simplex communications is a household radio set, which can receive data from radio stations but cannot transmit. In half-duplex transmission, data can be transmitted in either direction across a communications link, but in only one direction at a time. A walkie-talkie radio is an example of a half-duplex device because only one person can talk at a time. In full-duplex transmission, data is transmitted in two directions at the same time. A telephone is an example of a full-duplex device because the people at both ends of the line can talk at the same time.

In computer communications, simplex is less common than either half- or full-duplex working. Many fibre optic systems are simplex, with a different strand of fibre having to be used for each direction. Many satellite services are also simplex. In such systems, a satellite is used for downloads and some other system—a dial-up modem, for example (see Chapter 5)—is used for communication in the other direction. Satellite and optical fibre are covered in more detail later in this chapter. Simplex transmission is illustrated in Fig. 2.6. In computer communications, half-duplex and full-duplex working are more commonly found, however.

Half-duplex working is fine for transferring files between computers when most data is flowing in one direction at a time. However, when used for other applications, it may cause delays. When low-speed versions of the popular LAN protocol Ethernet are used with a hub instead of a layer-2 switch (see Chapter 4), they can use half-duplex transmission only. Two computers connected to a half-duplex

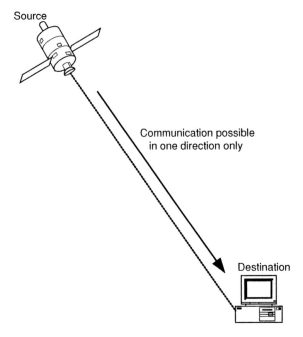

FIGURE 2.6. Simplex transmission

Ethernet LAN must take turns to send information to each other. A computer has to wait for the transmission that it is sending to end before it can receive data. Full-duplex working removes this restriction. Half-duplex transmission is illustrated in Fig. 2.7.

Full-duplex transmission is illustrated in Fig. 2.8. Full-duplex working is ideal for interactive applications because it eliminates the waiting time referred to in the previous paragraph. Ethernet used with a layer-2 switch is an example of full-duplex transmission. The switch can automatically sense whether the device at the other end of the wire, for example, the NIC of a PC, has a full-duplex capability. If full-duplex transmission can be used, this has the effect of speeding up the operation of the LAN.

2.4 Data rate, Bandwidth and Throughput

The terms data rate, throughput and bandwidth are related but not synonymous.

2.4.1 Data Rate

The data rate is the amount of data transferred per second. This term is used to describe the performance of many different kinds of computing device, for

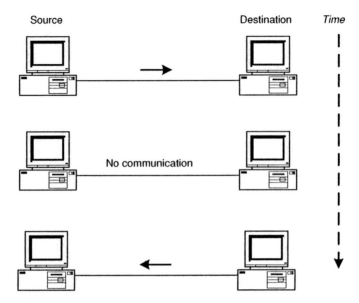

FIGURE 2.7. Half-duplex transmission

example, disk drives, as well as networks. Data rates are expressed in bits per second (bps). For example, 2 Mbps is 2,000,000 bps. The units used to express data rates are shown in Table 2.1. Note that the meaning of the prefixes kilo-, mega- and so on differs from the meaning when these are used for storage units. When indicating the capacity of storage units such as hard disk drives, these prefixes stand for powers of 1024. For example, 1 kbyte of storage is 1024 bytes.

2.4.2 Data Transfer Calculations

A formula for calculating how long a data transfer takes is as follows: time taken = file size/data rate. How long will it take to transfer a 600-kbyte file over a network

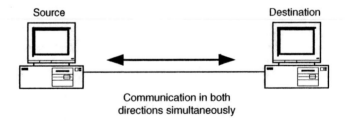

FIGURE 2.8. Full-duplex transmission

TABLE 2.1. Units used to express data rates

Unit	Equivalent in bits per second
Bits per second (bps)	—
Kilobits per second (kbps)	1000 (10^3 bps)
Megabits per second (Mbps)	1,000,000 (10^6 bps)
Gigabits per second (Gbps)	1,000,000,000 (10^9 bps)
Terabits per second (Tbps)	1,000,000,000,000 (10^{12} bps)

running at 100 Mbps?

Time = total number of bits/data rate

File size = 600 kbytes = 600 × 1024 bytes = 614, 400 bytes = 614,400 × 8

= 4,915,200 bits

So, the total transfer time = 4,915,200/100,000,000 s = 0.049152 s.

This result is only an estimate. In practice, the file would not be transferred in its raw form but would have to be packaged up into the right format to travel over the network. This would involve extra, non-data, bits being added. Also, as we shall see in the following section, the data rate would not be at its ideal maximum.

2.4.3 Throughput

In a real network, various factors militate against the theoretical data rate of a channel being realised. The devices attached to the network (user workstations, server computers, switches, routers and so on) will all affect throughput to some extent. The layout of the network, the characteristics of the data being sent and how many people are using the network will also affect throughput. We can define throughput as the actual amount of data successfully transferred from one place to another in a given time. This figure is unlikely to be as high as the notional data rate (see the last sentence in Section 10.4.3 for an example).

2.4.4 Bandwidth

The term bandwidth is used in two different ways for analogue and digital communications. Let us first have a brief look at bandwidth as used to describe analogue signals.

Analogue data transmission is performed by manipulating electromagnetic waves. These waves vary continuously and they can be sent over various kinds of media, for example, copper wire. Figure 2.9 shows an analogue signal. The variation in the waves directly mirrors (is an analogue of) the variations in the light or sound waves that a transmitter produces. For example, a modem (see

FIGURE 2.9. Analogue signal

Chapter 5) produces shrieking sounds, which are sent over the analogue sections of the telephone network as continuously varying electrical waves. The bandwidth of an analogue signal is the difference between the highest and lowest frequencies contained in the signal. The frequency is the number of times the wave goes up and down per second. Frequency and analogue bandwidth are measured in cycles per second or hertz (Hz).

Digital transmission, on the other hand, is done with a series of electrical (voltage) pulses. Figure 2.10 shows a digital signal. With digital signalling, the information that is being sent out over the medium is turned into a stream of bits. A digital signal is not affected by noise (interference) or attenuation (weakening of the signal) as easily as an analogue signal. In the digital context, the term bandwidth is commonly used to mean the same as data rate and is expressed in bits per second. It can be argued that this is an incorrect use of the term bandwidth, but in computer networking, it is very frequently encountered with this meaning. So the phrases 'a data rate of 100 Mbps' and '100 Mbps of bandwidth' can be taken to mean the same thing.

2.5 Modulation and Encoding

2.5.1 Amplitude Modulation, Frequency Modulation and Phase Modulation

The term *modulation* refers to ways of encoding information onto a carrier signal. The device that carries out modulation is called a modulator. For example, we may need to turn a digital signal from a computer into an analogue signal in order to send it out over a network. At the other end, conversion from analogue to digital will be carried out to give the original digital signal. The device that does these conversions is called a *modem* (see Chapter 5) because it is both a modulator and demodulator.

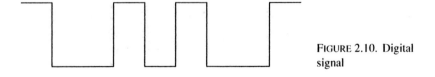

FIGURE 2.10. Digital signal

FIGURE 2.11. AM, FM and PM

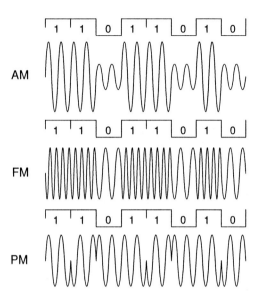

There are three fundamental ways of altering the carrier signal: *amplitude modulation* (AM), *frequency modulation* (FM) and *phase modulation* (PM). In AM, the amplitude of the carrier signal is manipulated, changing the height of the wave. In FM, the frequency of the carrier signal is manipulated, altering how many waves there are in a given time. In PM, the phase of the carrier signal is manipulated: The wave is made to start at a different point in its cycle. These three different modulation methods are illustrated in Fig. 2.11. A combination of AM and PM works well in modems and combined with other techniques such as echo cancellation can give remarkably high speeds considering that the analogue phone system is being used.

2.5.2 Codes for Transmitting Digital Data Using Digital Signals

If we want to send digital data using a digital signal, the most obvious way of encoding the bits would seem to be simply to use a high voltage level to represent a 1 bit and a low voltage level to represent a 0 bit. However, if this were done, the receiver could misunderstand the significance of a low voltage. Such a voltage might signify a 0 bit, but it might alternatively mean that nothing were being transmitted. This form of encoding is called non-return-to-zero (NRZ) and is illustrated in Fig. 2.12.

There are many different coding schemes, but we shall look at just one other besides NRZ. As can be seen in Fig. 2.12, Manchester encoding uses a transition in voltage to represent 1s and 0s. A transition from low to high (representing a 1 bit) or high to low (representing a 0 bit) voltage occurs in the middle of a bit

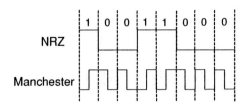

FIGURE 2.12. Encoding schemes

time. One advantage of such a scheme is that the receiver has only to look for a change in voltage (easier to detect than voltage value). Furthermore, always having a transition in the middle of a bit time provides a clock signal as well as data. Manchester encoding is used in 10 Mbps Ethernet (further details of Ethernet are given in Chapter 4). More complicated encoding schemes than Manchester are used in higher speed versions of Ethernet.

2.6 Error Control Methods

Signal impairment can lead to errors in bit transmission. Data error rates are usually defined in terms of a ratio. For example, 1/1000 means that for every 1000 bits, one bit will be transmitted in error. This can also be represented as an error rate of 10^{-3}.

Finding out whether errors have occurred (error detection) and correcting these errors (error correction) can be important because of the potential cost of data error. As a simple example of this, consider the following: A figure representing a bank balance is sent over a network. An error occurs in only one digit of this balance, but that is enough to make the received figure differ by thousands of euros from what it should be.

All error control methods involve adding extra, redundant bits to the message that is to be transmitted. We can classify these methods into automatic repeat request (ARQ) and forward error correction (FEC).

2.6.1 Automatic Repeat Request

The idea behind ARQ is for the transmitter to add enough redundant bits to the block of data that it is sending out to make it possible for the receiver to tell if there has been an error during transmission. The receiver cannot correct the error itself and so it asks for a retransmission of the data block that contains the error.

Parity (see Section 2.2.1) could provide a simple form of ARQ. A parity failure would provoke the receiver into asking the sender to resend the data block in question. However, if there were more than one error, such a simple system might fail to detect any error. For example, let us imagine that even parity is in use. The data that the sending computer transmits is 1010111. To give even parity it adds a 1 bit, making the message 10101111. During transmission, two bit errors occur and the bits get changed to 00100111. But when the receiver checks for parity, it finds an even number of 1 bits and is satisfied that there have been no errors. For this reason, simple parity is not used for ARQ in practice.

A more satisfactory alternative to simple parity is the *checksum* method. Here, the sending computer adds up all the data bytes of the message to be transmitted. The resulting figure, the checksum, is transmitted along with the data. At the other end, the receiver performs the same operation on the data and compares the checksum it has calculated with the one that the sending computer included in the message. If these two checksums are not the same, the receiving computer concludes that there has been an error during transmission and asks for a retransmission. The size of checksums is kept within reasonable bounds by, for example, the sending device throwing away any carries beyond 8 bits. One protocol that uses checksums is TCP (although the calculation involved is slightly more sophisticated than that described here). The TCP protocol is explained in Chapter 6.

The *cyclic redundancy check* (CRC) is a more sophisticated error detection method than checksums. This technique lends itself to implementation in hardware, which is fast, since it requires merely a shift register and an exclusive-OR (XOR) function. The transmitting device divides the outgoing block of data by a certain number (chosen because it gives good results). It is the remainder that results from this division that is sent out with the data. At the other end, the receiver does a similar calculation and compares the result it gets with the CRC that the sender has sent it. If there is a discrepancy, then the receiver assumes that there has been a transmission error and asks the sender to retransmit the data.

As can be seen in Fig. 2.13, the division is actually carried out modulo 2 in binary. In modulo-2 arithmetic, there are no carries and no borrows and there is no difference between addition and subtraction. When done on paper, the calculation is a binary 'long division sum'. However, it is easier to do than a normal long

Divisor = 1101
Data = 101010
Bits transmitted = 101010011

```
            110111
      _____
1101 |101010000
      1101
      ____
       1111
       1101
       ____
        1000
        1101
        ____
         1010
         1101
         ____
          1110
          1101
          ____
Remainder = 011
```

FIGURE 2.13. CRC calculation

division sum because instead of having to perform subtractions and use borrows, we can utilise XOR. See, for example, the first stage in the division process in Fig. 2.13, where we take the XOR of 1010 and 1101, giving a result of (0)111. In CRC division, one number is said to 'go into' another merely by virtue of having the same number of digits. Before starting the division, some zeros need to be added to the end of the data. We add the number of digits in the divisor (four in this example) minus one (that is, three zeros). When we finish, the result (the remainder) must be one digit shorter than the divisor. That is the reason for the leading zero in the remainder in Fig. 2.13. We then append the remainder (011) onto the end of the data (101010) and transmit 101010011.

CRCs are very good at detecting burst errors (most data transmission errors occur in bursts). There are several international standards for CRCs. A prime example is the 32-bit CRC, which is used for error control in the Ethernet frame (see Chapter 4).

Automatic Repeat Request Mechanisms

We shall now look at two different ways of organising ARQ: *idle RQ* and *continuous RQ*. In idle RQ (or *stop-and-wait RQ*), the transmitter sends a block of data and then waits for an acknowledgement from the receiver. The receiver checks what it has received. If there are no errors, it sends back a positive acknowledgement (ACK). If the receiver finds an error, it discards the block and sends back a negative acknowledgement (NAK). If the block is completely lost or destroyed, there is no ACK. If the transmitter receives an ACK, it sends the next block. If it receives NAK, it sends the previous block again. (It always keeps a copy of the block that it has just sent out, in case it is needed.) If the transmitter does not receive an ACK within a given time, there is a timeout and the block is resent. The idle RQ system is illustrated in Fig. 2.14.

It can be seen in Fig. 2.14 that time is wasted while the sender waits for the receiver to acknowledge receipt of a block. As the term idle RQ suggests, the transmitter is idle while awaiting an acknowledgement. Continuous RQ is a way of increasing efficiency over what idle RQ offers. The aim of continuous RQ is to transmit data blocks continuously so that there will be no idle time. The sender sends off several data blocks in succession, without waiting for an acknowledgement. The sender gives every block that is transmitted a *sequence number*. Every acknowledgement uses the correct sequence number such that the sender knows which block is being acknowledged. Continuous RQ is illustrated in Fig. 2.15.

FIGURE 2.14. Idle RQ

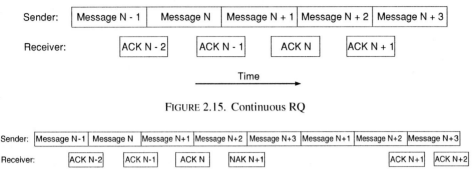

FIGURE 2.15. Continuous RQ

Sender: | Message N-1 | Message N | Message N+1 | Message N+2 | Message N+3 | Message N+1 | Message N+2 | Message N+3 |

Receiver: | ACK N-2 | ACK N-1 | ACK N | NAK N+1 | | | ACK N+1 | ACK N+2 |

FIGURE 2.16. Go-back-*N*

Automatic Repeat Request Retransmission Mechanisms

If an error occurs when continuous RQ is in use, there is a choice of ARQ retransmission mechanisms. These mechanisms are *go-back-N* and *selective retransmission*. In go-back-N, after an error, the receiver sends a NAK. This means that the block having that sequence number should be sent again. The sender sends that block again and then sends the following blocks, even though these may already have been transmitted successfully. In Fig. 2.16, block N is positively acknowledged but block $N + 1$ is negatively acknowledged. By the time the NAK for block $N + 1$ arrives, the sender has already sent out blocks $N + 2$ and $N + 3$. Since blocks $N + 2$ and $N + 3$ are out of sequence, the receiver ignores these and waits for block $N + 1$ to arrive again. Having retransmitted block $N + 1$ (which this time is received with no errors), the sender retransmits blocks $N + 2$ and $N + 3$.

Selective retransmission is illustrated in Fig. 2.17. When selective retransmission is in use, the sender's response to a NAK for block $N + 1$ is to retransmit block $N + 1$ only, but not blocks $N + 2$ and $N + 3$. Despite the fact that blocks $N + 2$ and $N + 3$ are now out of sequence (because block $N + 1$ has not arrived intact), the receiver accepts them. When the sender has retransmitted block $N + 1$, it sends blocks $N + 4$ and $N + 5$ and so on.

The disadvantage of the go-back-N method is that some blocks will be retransmitted unnecessarily. This is a waste of bandwidth. The disadvantage of selective retransmission is that the receiver needs plenty of buffer (temporary storage) capacity in order to store temporarily data blocks that have been received out of sequence. Go-back-N is the more popular of the two methods, since buffer capacity is finite.

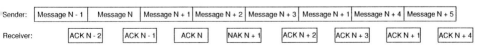

FIGURE 2.17. Selective retransmission

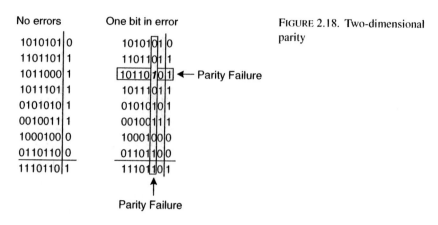

FIGURE 2.18. Two-dimensional parity

2.6.2 Forward Error Correction

The idea behind FEC is to add enough redundant bits to the data block to be transmitted so that the receiver can correct errors without having to ask for a re-transmission. It is, of course, essential to use FEC instead of ARQ if only a simplex link is available because in such a situation it is impossible to ask for a retransmission. When there is a duplex link, FEC is often used in combination with ARQ.

Two-dimensional parity offers a very simple form of FEC (see Fig. 2.18). In two-dimensional parity, we not only add a parity bit to each character but also add a row of parity bits after a block of characters. The row of parity bits is actually a parity bit for each 'column' of characters. The row parity bits plus the column parity bits add a great amount of redundancy to a block of characters. Unfortunately, such a system can correct only single-bit errors. So, in practice, we need a more sophisticated system, as it is quite possible that there will be more than one error in a block.

Usually, special error correcting codes known as Reed–Solomon codes are used for FEC. The applications in which these codes are used include wireless and mobile communications and digital subscriber line (DSL) modems. The sophisticated mathematical techniques used by Reed–Solomon codes are beyond the scope of this text. Please refer to the following Web site if you need further information: http://www.4i2i.com/reed_solomon_codes.htm.

2.7 Switched Connections

Switches are devices that can make a temporary connection between other devices. A switched network is shown in Fig. 2.19. As can be seen in Fig. 2.19, the computers have been given numbers and the switches letters. Each of the switches makes a connection between two of the links to which it is connected. There are three kinds of switching: circuit switching, packet switching and message switching.

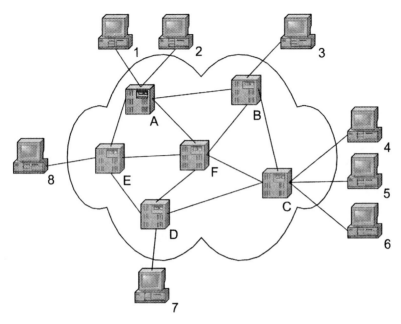

FIGURE 2.19. Switched network

2.7.1 Circuit Switching

Circuit switching is used in the public switched telephone network (PSTN). Circuit switching has three stages. Firstly, a circuit is set up from one end device to another. This circuit may involve several switches along the route. Next, the data is transferred. Finally, the circuit is disconnected. In circuit switching, there is a dedicated path between the end devices.

Setting up the circuit before any data can be sent takes some time. Let us assume that circuit switching is in use in the network shown in Fig. 2.19. If computer 8 needs to connect to computer 7, the complete circuit between them needs to be set up. Computer 8 will send a request to switch E to be connected to computer 7. Switch E will have knowledge of available routes and will be able to choose the best one. A dedicated path is set up between switches E and D. Switch D then asks for access to computer 7. If computer 7 permits access, then an ACK will be sent back to computer 8. Only now can the data be transferred. When the data is being sent, the only delay involved will be the time taken for it to propagate through the network. When data transfer is finished, more signalling takes place to 'tear down' the circuit (get rid of it) and make all the links that have been used available again for future use.

If there is only a little data to transfer, circuit switching is inefficient because of the time taken to set up the circuit. Also, a transfer will hog a transmission path that no other devices can use until the circuit is released. Despite these disadvantages, circuit switching has been very successfully used for voice transmission.

2.7.2 Message Switching

In message switching, the circuits are permanent but it is the data that is switched. There is no need to set up a dedicated path before sending the data. If an end device needs to send a message, it adds the address of the destination to the message before sending it off. At every switch in the communication path, the message is briefly stored before being passed on to the next switch. For obvious reasons, this technique is known as *store and forward*.

Let us assume that message switching is in use in the network shown in Fig. 2.19. Computer 3 wants to send a message to computer 7. Computer 3 appends the address of computer 7 to the message. The message is stored briefly by switch B, which then forwards it to switch F. After having briefly stored the message, switch F forwards it to switch D. Switch D stores the message before forwarding it to computer 7.

For computer data transfer, message switching is more efficient than circuit switching. However, it is no longer used because of the large amounts of storage space required on the switches. Furthermore, the delays involved are unacceptable today.

2.7.3 Packet Switching

This technique is similar to message switching, in that addressing, storing and forwarding are all involved. What is different is that, instead of complete messages being forwarded between switching devices, the source divides the data into much smaller packets before it is sent off. It is these packets that are given addresses and then sent through the network.

There are several advantages to sending packets rather than messages. Firstly, there is much less delay, since the packets are short. The small size of the packets means that less storage is needed in the switches compared with message switching. We have already discussed the concept of sequence numbers (see Section 2.6.1). When combined with addressing, sequence numbers permit the interleaving (multiplexing) of packets from more than one source (multiplexing is explained in Section 2.8). When this is done, the communications channel can be used more efficiently. Packet switching is a very popular method of communication. There are two variants: *datagram* packet switching and *virtual circuit* packet switching.

Datagram Packet Switching

In datagram packet switching, each packet contains the destination address. The route that datagrams take between the same source and destination can vary. For example, let us assume that datagram packet switching is in use in the network shown in Fig. 2.19. Computer 3 sends two successive datagrams to computer 7. The first datagram travels, say, via switches B, A, F, E and D. The second travels via B, C and D. It is possible that the datagram that was sent out first will arrive after the second one because the route it took was shorter. This problem is taken care of by each datagram having a sequence number. The datagrams can be reordered at the destination using the sequence numbers.

Virtual Circuit Packet Switching

In virtual circuit packet switching, a route from sender to receiver is set up before any transfer takes place. This is not the same as the dedicated path that is set up in circuit switching. The physical path along which successive packets travel may vary. Addressing of the packets is carried out by means of virtual circuit numbers, which indicate the virtual circuit a packet belongs to. Virtual circuits come in two forms: switched virtual circuits (SVCs) and permanent virtual circuits (PVCs).

Switched Virtual Circuits

An SVC is set up temporarily whenever it is needed. The virtual circuit does not persist when the data transfer is finished. For example, let us assume that computer 8 in Fig. 2.19 is going to send some data to computer 3 using an SVC. Computer 8 sends out a set-up call to computer 3. The virtual circuit is established automatically with no human intervention. When all the data packets have been sent, the virtual circuit is automatically torn down.

Permanent Virtual Circuits

As the name suggests, a PVC is somewhat longer lasting than an SVC. It has to be set up by a network administrator. There is no need for a set-up call; the virtual circuit is always available whenever it is needed. We will mention PVCs again when X.25 and Frame Relay are discussed in Chapter 5.

2.8 Multiplexing

In multiplexing, signals from several sources are sent down one long-distance channel at the same time. At the destination, these signals are separated again. The advantage of this is that an expensive WAN link can be used very efficiently. There are two major varieties of multiplexing: *time division multiplexing* (TDM) and *frequency division multiplexing* (FDM). A third kind of multiplexing, *wavelength division multiplexing* (WDM), can be classified as a variant of FDM.

2.8.1 Time Division Multiplexing

The idea of time division multiplexing (TDM) is to interleave bits (or bytes) from several sources. Figure 2.20 shows how it works. In the diagram there are eight low-speed channels feeding into the multiplexer. The multiplexer takes a bit or a byte (depending on the system in use) from each low-speed channel in turn and outputs it onto the high-speed communications link. The multiplexer cycles

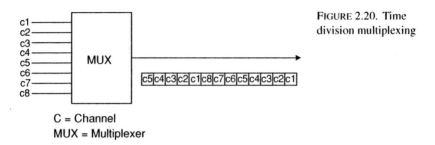

FIGURE 2.20. Time division multiplexing

C = Channel
MUX = Multiplexer

through all the eight channels on a round robin basis. What is not shown in Fig. 2.20 is that there is another multiplexer at the destination, which demultiplexes the multiplexed data into low-speed channels. Simple TDM is a fairly efficient way of using a high-speed, long-distance communications link. However, it is wasteful if low-speed channels have nothing to send when it is their turn. A more complicated technique called statistical multiplexing gets round this by filling the slots on a first-come-first-served basis, rather than using a round robin system.

2.8.2 Frequency Division Multiplexing

In FDM, a high-speed link is divided into several bands of frequencies. Each channel is carried within one of these frequency bands. This is an analogue technique, whereas TDM is digital. FDM is illustrated in Fig. 2.21.

2.8.3 Wavelength Division Multiplexing

WDM is similar to FDM in that multiple signals are sent simultaneously over one transmission path. However, instead of electrical signals being sent, light signals are transmitted. Data from different channels (different colours of light) is carried at very high rates over a single strand of optical fibre. (For a discussion

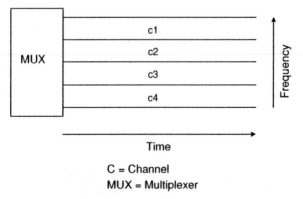

C = Channel
MUX = Multiplexer

FIGURE 2.21. Frequency division multiplexing

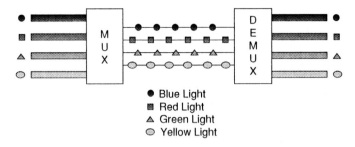

FIGURE 2.22. Wavelength division multiplexing

of optical fibre, see Section 2.10.2.) The sender multiplexes the source channels before they are sent over the long-haul link; the receiver demultiplexes these. WDM is illustrated in Fig. 2.22. For the sake of simplicity, only four colours are shown in the diagram, though many more are possible. Dense wavelength division multiplexing (DWDM) allows even greater bit-rates than does simple WDM.

2.9 Topologies Used in Networking

The term *topology* as applied to a computer network refers to the structure of the network. A distinction is drawn between the physical and logical topologies. The physical topology is the way in which the network is laid out. The logical topology is concerned with how the transmission medium, for example a cable, can be accessed by the computers attached to the network. In this section, the discussion is confined to physical topologies. Logical topologies will be covered later (see Section 4.2.3).

2.9.1 Bus

Outside the computing context, the term *bus* can be used to denote an electrical conductor that is used to connect several circuits together. Inside a computer, a bus is a common path for moving information about, for example, a data bus. In a computer network, a bus is a single piece of cable to which all the computers are attached. At the two ends of this cable, there are resistors that absorb unwanted signals so that they are not reflected back along the bus. If the bus fails, communication ceases. A physical bus was used in old types of Ethernet LAN (further details of Ethernet are given in Chapter 4). The bus topology is illustrated in Fig. 2.23.

2.9.2 Ring

As the name suggests, in the ring topology the computers are laid out in a ring. An endless cable (ring) connects the computers together. If the ring fails, there can

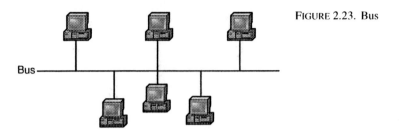

FIGURE 2.23. Bus

be no further communication and so sometimes a double ring is used. The ring topology is illustrated in Fig. 2.24.

2.9.3 Star

As shown in Fig. 2.25, the star topology looks rather like a wheel without a rim. The devices at the ends of the spokes of the wheel can communicate with each other only via a central hub. Originally, this central hub was a computer and the other devices were usually dumb terminals (devices with a keyboard and screen but no processing power). In modern star networks, the devices at the outer ends of the spokes are computers but the hub is a device that will not necessarily have any intelligence. Irrespective of how much intelligence it possesses, if the hub fails this has a catastrophic effect on the functioning of the network. Despite this, the star topology is a very popular one for LANs.

2.9.4 Tree (Hierarchical)

The tree or hierarchical topology is illustrated in Fig. 2.26. The computer at the root of the tree (shown at the top of Fig. 2.26) controls all the traffic in the network.

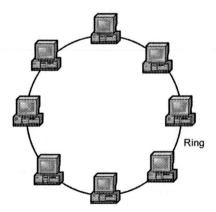

FIGURE 2.24. Ring

FIGURE 2.25. Star

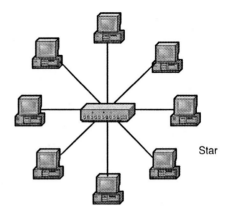

Star

2.9.5 *Mesh*

In the mesh topology (Fig. 2.27), every computer is directly connected to every other one. If one link between any two computers stops working, an alternative route will be available. A topology such as this is expensive, but it may be necessary for applications where it is vital that computers do not lose contact with each other. An example of such an application is controlling a nuclear power station.

2.10 Network Transmission Media

The word *media* is the plural form of *medium*. As we saw in Section 1.4.1, in networking these terms are used to refer to the pathways along which data travels.

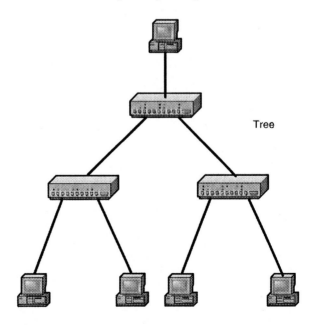

Tree

FIGURE 2.26. Tree

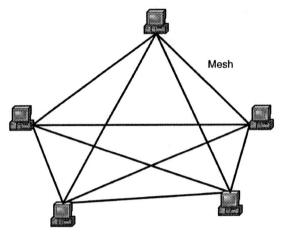

FIGURE 2.27. Mesh

Mesh

The pathway is often a cable of some kind, but not always. There are three classes of media: copper cable, fibre optic cable and wireless media.

2.10.1 Copper Cable

Copper cable is the most common kind of cabling in LANs. There are several different forms of copper cable, each with particular advantages and disadvantages. All these forms carry an electrical current that represents the data.

Coaxial Cable

This cable consists of two copper conductors, one inside the other, separated by plastic insulation. The inner conductor is a thick copper wire. The outer conductor is a cylindrical mesh of thin copper wire. This layer also acts as a shield for the inner conductor, helping to cut down on electromagnetic interference from outside the cable. A plastic sleeve protects the cable. A coaxial cable is illustrated in Fig. 2.28. As can be seen from the illustration, the kind of coaxial cable that is used for computer network installations is very similar to a television aerial cable.

A coaxial cable has some useful features. Fewer repeaters are needed to boost the signal than with twisted pair cable. It is less expensive than fibre optic cable. It was used for cabling Ethernet LANs. However, for some years it has not been used for new Ethernet installations as it is expensive to put in compared to twisted pair cable. It is also tricky to connect the outer conductor properly. A coaxial cable is commonly used for carrying cable television signals (and computer data as well if a cable modem is in use) into the home.

FIGURE 2.28. Coaxial
cable

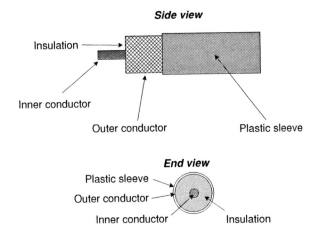

Unshielded Twisted Pair Cable

As the name suggests, in a twisted-pair cable pairs of copper wires are twisted together in a helix. This is done to cut down on *crosstalk* (electromagnetic interference between the signals carried on adjacent wires). Most twisted pair cables are unshielded twisted pair (UTP). In UTP cable there are four pairs of wires. Each individual wire is covered with plastic insulation. The most common form of UTP cable is Category 5e (CAT 5e). A UTP cable is shown in Fig. 2.29.

UTP cable is very popular in LANs for several reasons. It is cheap, easy to install and small enough to fit into wiring ducts easily. The main disadvantages are susceptibility to electrical interference and the short distance that is permissible between repeaters.

Shielded Twisted Pair Cable

In shielded (STP) or screened (ScTP) twisted pair cable, shielding or screening is added to a four-pair cable to give more protection from interference, both from inside and outside the cable. In STP cable, each pair of wires is surrounded by a

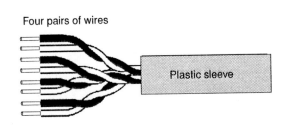

FIGURE 2.29. UTP cable

Four pairs of wires   FIGURE 2.30. ScTP cable

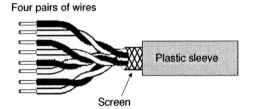

metallic foil and then the whole bundle of wires is shielded. In ScTP the individual pairs of wires are not shielded. An ScTP cable is illustrated in Fig. 2.30. The shielding/screening makes ScTP and STP cable much more difficult to install than UTP but interference is greatly reduced.

Straight-Through and Crossover Cables

Normally, computers on a LAN are connected together via a hub or switch. In this case the type of cable that is needed is a *straight-through* cable, in which the transmit pin at the computer end is directly connected to the transmit pin at the hub or switch. The respective receive pins are also directly connected to each other. The use of a straight-through cable is illustrated in Fig. 2.31.

However, if we wish to connect two computers directly to each other without using a hub or switch, we have to connect the transmit pins at each end to the receive pins at the other end. The kind of cable that is necessary in such a situation is called a *crossover* cable. The way in which a crossover cable is used is shown in Fig. 2.32. Both these kinds of cables would normally be UTP, but STP or ScTP could be used instead.

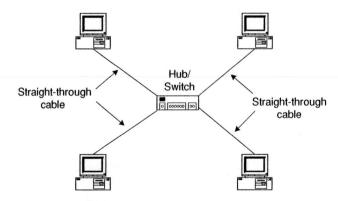

FIGURE 2.31. Straight-through cable

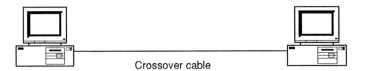

Crossover cable

FIGURE 2.32. Crossover cable

2.10.2 Fibre Optic Cable

Instead of using electrical currents to represent data, optical fibre carries a beam of light. The fibre cores are made of glass (or plastic). Cladding, consisting of glass (or plastic) of a refractive index different from that of the core, surrounds each fibre. The cladding stops the light beam getting out of the fibre, relying on the principle of *total internal reflection*. There is a buffer layer (usually plastic) around the cladding to protect it from damage. Finally, a plastic jacket surrounds the other layers. A cross section of a fibre optic cable is shown in Fig. 2.33. The cables are often used in pairs, with a fibre for each direction.

Fibre optic cable has several advantages over copper. It offers higher data rates and needs fewer repeaters. It is light and occupies little space. It is completely immune to electrical interference. It is difficult to tap, which gives greater security. The disadvantages are that it is more difficult to splice than a copper cable and, crucially, is more expensive. Fibre optic cable is commonly used for trunk telephone lines and for 'vertical' cabling for LANs. For connections to LAN desktop computers, however, copper still predominates.

The diameter of the core of *single-mode* fibre is just sufficient for one wavelength of light. The light source is a laser diode and the light travels in a straight line along the fibre. Few repeaters are needed to transmit signals for long distances and data rates can be very high. *Multimode* fibre has a greater diameter, which allows multiple wavelengths of light to take multiple paths through the fibre core. Multimode fibre uses a cheap light-emitting diode (LED) as the light source. Both single- and multimode fibres use a photodiode, which generates an electrical pulse when light falls upon it, to detect the received light signal. Single- and multimode fibres are illustrated in Fig. 2.34.

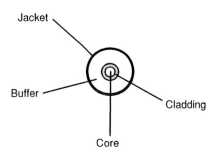

FIGURE 2.33. Cross section of fibre optic cable

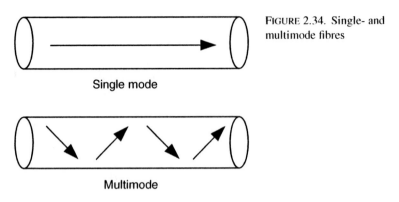

FIGURE 2.34. Single- and multimode fibres

Single mode

Multimode

2.10.3 Wireless Media

Laying a cable can often be difficult, expensive or inappropriate. In such circumstances, wireless media can be used instead. For example, if a temporary link is needed between sites it may not be worth laying a cable and a wireless network may be the answer. If a deep ocean trench separates an island from the mainland, laying a cable might be impossible and so a wireless link can be installed instead. Any kind of mobile computer system will need a wireless link. Compared to wired links, wireless links tend to have relatively low capacity and high error rates. They tend to be affected by weather and installation is often highly regulated. Despite these disadvantages, wireless transmission is very popular (see Section 10.4.1 for some of the advantages of WLANs).

Microwave Radio

Microwave radio is the commonest form of transmission without wires. Two places where it is used are 802.11x LANs and mobile telephone networks (see Chapter 10). The information is carried through the air by ultra-high, super-high or extremely high-frequency radio waves. Microwave signals (unlike ordinary radio signals) can be aimed to travel in a particular direction and so the signals can be targeted precisely at those who need to receive them. Microwave transmission offers high bandwidth. A line of sight is preferable between transmitter and receiver because buildings have an adverse effect on the signal. For this reason, high towers are commonly used to relay microwave transmissions (see Fig. 2.35). Rain can interfere with microwave signals. Various ways in which microwave transmission can be used are explored in Chapter 10.

Satellites

Microwave signals can be sent over very long distances using satellites. Although the cost of launching a satellite is high, it can carry a vast amount of traffic. It carries

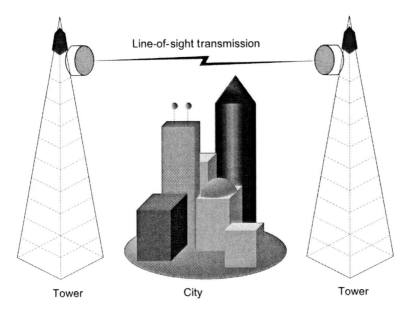

Line-of-sight transmission

Tower   City   Tower

FIGURE 2.35. Line-of-sight microwave transmission

a number of *transponders* (transmitter/responders). These listen for incoming radio signals, boost them and then retransmit them at a different angle from the angle at which they arrived. Each transponder works on a different frequency.

Communications satellites are usually in a *geosynchronous* orbit, 35,785 km above the earth's surface. At this distance, a satellite is synchronised with the rotation of the earth: To an observer on the earth, it does not appear to move in the sky. A geosynchronous satellite is illustrated in Fig. 2.36.

An alternative to the geosynchronous satellite is the *low earth orbit* (LEO) satellite. The orbit of a LEO satellite is much closer to the earth's surface than that of a geosynchronous satellite. This means that it appears to move relative to the earth's surface. An array of 64 LEO satellites is sufficient to cover the whole of the earth's surface.

Infrared

Infrared signals can be used for networking over short distances. Whilst a line of sight is merely preferable for microwave communications, for infrared this is absolutely essential because the signal cannot pass through solid objects well. This is both an advantage (because of lack of interference with other systems and good security) and a disadvantage (because of shortness of range). With no need for aerials on the devices, an infrared system can be very successful at linking together small, portable devices within a room. Unlike microwave, no spectrum licensing is

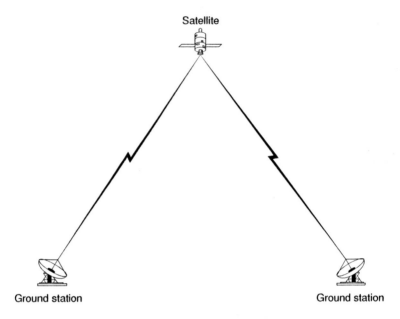

FIGURE 2.36. Geosynchronous satellite

needed. However, infrared networks are much less popular than microwave-based networks.

Free Space Optics

We have already seen (Section 2.10.2) how light signals can be used to transmit data when constrained within fibre optic cables. It is also possible to use lasers for computer communications without a cable. This is known as *free space optics* (FSO). In FSO, light beams are transmitted from one transceiver (transmitter/receiver) to another using low-power lasers. A line of sight is essential. Fog and snow can impede the light beam, which is a serious disadvantage. Despite this, FSO is often used for connecting LANs together across a street, using equipment such as that shown in Fig. 2.37. FSO systems can work over distances of several kilometres. The transceivers will work through windows and so it is not even necessary to mount them on the roof of a building. As with infrared systems, no licensing is necessary.

2.11 Summary

This chapter has looked at some of the technologies that are used for computer communications. The chapter started with an explanation of the differences between serial and parallel data transfer, asynchronous and synchronous communications

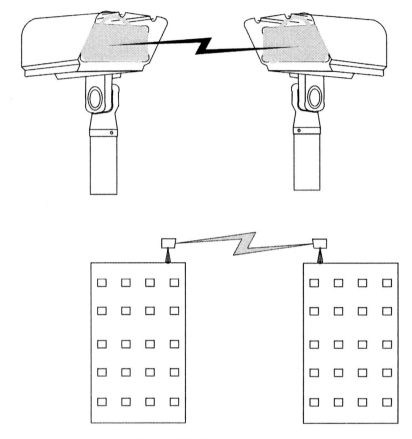

FIGURE 2.37. Free space optics

and duplex, half-duplex and full-duplex communications. The distinctions between data rate, bandwidth and throughput were then explained. Modulation and
encoding, error control methods, switching and multiplexing were then discussed.
The topologies used in networking were described. Finally, network transmission
media were explored.

TABLE 2.2. Two-dimensional even parity

0	0	1	0	0	0	0
0	0	1	1	0	0	0
0	1	0	0	0	1	1
1	0	0	1	0	0	0
0	0	0	0	0	1	0
1	0	0	0	1	1	1
1	1	0	0	0	1	0

2.12 Questions

1. The lowercase letter 'w' is being transmitted using asynchronous transmission. The 7-bit ASCII code for 'w' is 1110111 (77 hexadecimal). Even parity is being used and there is one stop bit. Draw a timing diagram illustrating this. Base your diagram on Fig. 2.4.
2. Describe hub-based Ethernet LANs in terms of the following dichotomies: serial/parallel transmission, synchronous/asynchronous transmission, full-duplex/half-duplex transmission. In addition to reading this chapter, you may have to do a bit of further research to answer this question.
3. How long, in theory, will it take to transfer a 1-Mbyte file over a network running at 1 Gbps?
4. Explain the difference between analogue and digital transmission.
5. Investigate the 8B/10B encoding scheme that is used in gigabit Ethernet. In addition to reading this chapter, you may have to do a bit of further research to answer this question.
6. (a) If even parity checking is in use, what are the parity bits assigned to the ASCII characters capital 'B', 'F', 'J', 'P' and 'W'?
   (NB: The ASCII code for capital 'A' is 41 hexadecimal, i.e., 1000001 binary. The other codes can be worked out by counting on from 41 in hexadecimal and then converting to binary.)
   (b) What are the parity bits if odd parity is used?
7. A message is transmitted using cyclic redundancy coding to check for errors. The message is 101011. The divisor that is used for the CRC is 1101. Give the total bit pattern that is sent (see Fig. 2.13 for an example).
8. Two-dimensional even parity is being used. Fill in the column and row check bits for the block of data in Table 2.2.
9. Explain the differences between TDM and FDM.
10. Distinguish between physical and logical topology.
11. Distinguish between UTP, single mode and multimode optical fibre.
12. What kind of cable would be best for the following applications?
    (a) horizontal wiring in an office
    (b) vertical wiring in a building
    (c) a connection under the Atlantic ocean
13. Describe the physical form of a coaxial cable.
14. In what circumstances would a crossover cable be needed?
15. What are the advantages and disadvantages of infrared transmission?

3
Networking Models and Standards

In this chapter we look at layered models, which are standard ways of organising networks. The chapter starts with an explanation of network layering and its advantages. One of the most important networking models, the open systems interconnect (OSI) 7-layer model, is then explained. This is followed by an explanation of the principles of data encapsulation. Another important networking model, TCP/IP, is then explained and compared with the 7-layer model. Finally, several important networking standards bodies are described.

3.1 Layering of Networks

Most networks are organised as a series of layers or levels. At the lowest layer, physical communication takes place; at higher layers, virtual communication happens. At the higher layers, *peer processes*—the entities comprising the corresponding layers on different machines—appear to communicate directly with each other. For example, in Fig. 3.1, layer 3 at the source and layer 3 at the destination are peer layers.

In reality, these peer processes communicate via protocols. The protocol at a particular layer carries out a sequence of operations on the data. Next, this protocol passes the data to another layer and there a different protocol carries out a different sequence of operations. Thus, the data gets passed down from layer to layer at the source until finally it is ready to be sent over the physical network medium, for example, a cable, to the destination. At the destination, the data gets passed upwards from layer to layer through the *protocol stack*. At each layer, a protocol performs operations on the data that reverse what was done at the corresponding layer at the source. Eventually, the data is in the form in which it was when it started out at the source. The data is now ready to be dealt with by the receiving application. The set of layers and protocols is the *network architecture*.

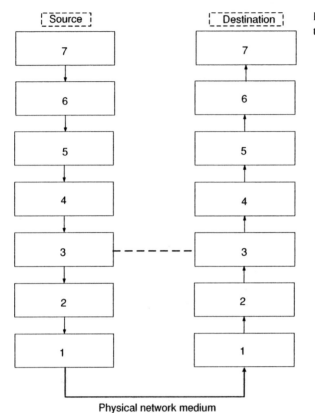

FIGURE 3.1. Communication between layers

Physical network medium

3.1.1 Advantages of Layering

Organising a network architecture in layers as described above has a number of advantages. It makes design less complex because any problem is broken down into separate components. It is a more flexible way of working than having one big monolithic program that performs all functions needed by the network. If it is necessary to enhance or modify the system, only one module needs to be changed, and this should have no knock-on effects on the rest of the system. The application programming interfaces (APIs) between the layers are tightly defined and programmers write network software to these APIs.

3.2 OSI 7-Layer Reference Model

The OSI 7-layer reference model was devised by the International Organisation for Standardisation (ISO). During the 1980s, different computer manufacturers had their own network architectures and protocols. This situation often made it

FIGURE 3.2. OSI 7-layer model

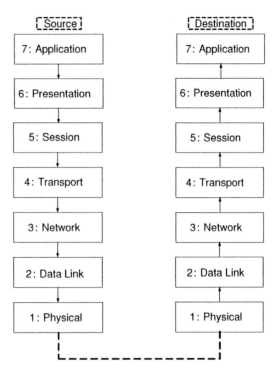

difficult to network together computers made by different manufacturers. The aim of OSI was to devise an architecture containing standard protocol layers that all vendors would use, resulting in complete *interoperability* between all network devices and network software. The OSI model had seven layers (see Fig. 3.2). Some new protocols were devised and some existing protocols were incorporated into the model. Although a few protocols that were designed for OSI are still in use, for example, the Intermediate System to Intermediate System (IS–IS) routing protocol, overall OSI was a failure as a practical network architecture. However, the OSI model is still important as a means of describing and teaching about network protocols. Each of the seven layers performs a particular network function. Summaries of these functions are given below.

3.2.1 Physical Layer

The Physical Layer is concerned with the transmission of bit patterns over a communications channel. It is responsible for how the binary 0s and 1s are represented, for example, what voltage levels are used. It is also concerned with the control signals to set up and tear down connections. Connectors and pin assignments are also specified by the Physical Layer. EIA/TIA-232 (or RS232-C) is an example of a Physical Layer protocol.

3.2.2 Data Link Layer

The Data Link Layer handles the errors that result from the physical transmission media. In this layer, the raw bit patterns from the Physical Layer are organised into *frames*. These frames are acknowledged by the destination if they are received correctly. The Data Link Layer also performs *flow control*. It can speed up or slow down the rate at which the source is sending data, according to how much buffer space is available with the receiver. HDLC (see Section 6.3) is a typical Data Link protocol.

3.2.3 Network Layer

The Network Layer is concerned with the routing of packets across a network. The message from the source is split up into packets. The packets are then sent off to the destination. The Network Layer is concerned with addressing. The source address in a packet identifies the sending computer. The destination address identifies the computer that finally receives the packet. Internet Protocol (IP) is an example of a Network Layer protocol.

3.2.4 Transport Layer

The Transport Layer is responsible for end-to-end connections between hosts (a *host* is an end user's computer that is connected to a network). This layer masks the characteristics of the underlying network, which may change with advances in technology. Transport Layer protocols are implemented on the hosts, not on each machine in the chain that links these hosts.

The commonest type of Transport-Layer connection involves the establishment, maintenance and termination of a logical connection (virtual circuit) between two hosts, where the data that is sent from the source is delivered in the order in which it was sent. Any errors are detected and corrected and flow control is carried out. Transmission Control Protocol (TCP) is the most important example of a Transport Layer protocol.

3.2.5 Session Layer

The Session Layer deals with the establishment, maintenance and termination of *sessions* between two users. This is similar to logging in and out of a time-sharing computer system, but over a network rather than from a directly connected terminal. Security precautions, such as authentication of users by password, belong in this layer. The UNIX X Window system, a client-server system that offers a windowing environment over a network, is an example of a Session Layer protocol.

3.2.6 Presentation Layer

The Presentation Layer deals with data formatting, data compression and data encryption. Examples of data formatting are the need to convert between different character codes such as ASCII and EBCDIC and between different ways of representing integers such as big-endian and little-endian. The presentation of graphical images, sound and moving images is also dealt with in the Presentation Layer. For example, the portable network graphics (PNG) binary file format, used for displaying images on the Internet, is part of the Presentation Layer.

The Presentation Layer also looks after data compression. Compression is carried out using algorithms that make files smaller than they originally were. Any repeating bit patterns are replaced by shorter bit patterns (*tokens*). If the files are made smaller in this way, they can be transmitted in a shorter time.

Encryption is another function carried out in the Presentation Layer. Using a mathematical key, the outgoing file is scrambled to make it unintelligible to anyone who intercepts it. At the other end, the same key or a mathematically related key can be used to unscramble (decrypt) the data and turn it back into its original form.

3.2.7 Application Layer

The Application Layer contains a number of protocols that users need to be able to communicate over a network. HyperText Transfer Protocol (HTTP), which is used to transfer pages on the World Wide Web, is but one example out of many Application Layer protocols.

3.3 Encapsulation

Data is sent over a network from a source to a destination. The data cannot be sent until it has been encapsulated, that is, packaged up into a suitable form to be transmitted over the network. During the encapsulation process, the data has protocol information added to it as it is passed down through the OSI layers. This protocol information consists of headers (address information), trailers (for error control) and other items.

The data encapsulation process is illustrated in Fig. 3.3. Having been sent from the source, the data travels through the Application Layer and on down through the other layers. As the various layers carry out their services, the packaging of the data changes. A number of steps must be performed in order to encapsulate the data.

1. First of all, the data has to be built. If, for example, an e-mail is being sent, the alphanumeric characters of which it is composed will have to be converted into a form that can travel across the network. If compression and/or encryption are necessary, these functions will be performed.
2. Next, the data will have to be packaged up for transport from one end to the other. The data is divided up into *segments*. This will ensure that the sending and receiving hosts are able to communicate reliably.
3. The data must now be put into a *packet* or *datagram*. The datagram will include a header containing the addresses of the source and destination. Devices in the network will use these addresses to route the packet.

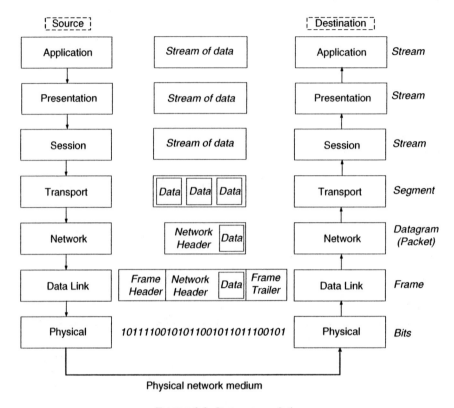

FIGURE 3.3. Data encapsulation

4. The packet must be put into a *frame* so that the data can be sent to the network device at the other end of the link. Every network device in the chain of links leading from source to destination needs framing so that it can connect to the next device.
5. Finally, the frame needs to be converted into a bit pattern (1s and 0s) so that it can actually be transmitted over the medium. The medium does not need to be the same along the complete path from source to destination. For example, an e-mail might start out from a portable machine connected wirelessly to a LAN, then pass onto a network wired with copper cable, then onto a WAN link wired with fibre-optic cable, then onto a satellite (microwave radio) link and so on.

3.4 TCP/IP Model

The OSI 7-layer model was devised before the OSI protocols. As we saw, relatively few OSI protocols are in use, but the model is widely used as a means of classifying protocols. In the case of TCP/IP, on the other hand, the protocols came first and

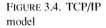

FIGURE 3.4. TCP/IP
model

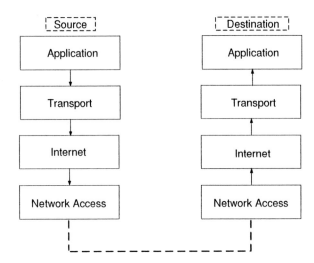

the model was devised later. The instigator of TCP/IP was the US Department of Defense (DOD). The aim of TCP/IP was a robust communication system that would still function even if it were partially destroyed in a war.

The model has four layers: Application, Transport, Internet and Network Access. Beware! Although the TCP/IP Application Layer has the same name as the OSI Application Layer, the functions that it performs are not quite the same. The layers of the TCP/IP model are shown in Fig. 3.4.

Figure 3.5 shows how the protocols fit together into the TCP/IP suite. Many more TCP/IP protocols exist than are shown in the diagram, but those shown are some of the commonest. HyperText Transport Protocol (HTTP), File Transfer Protocol (FTP), Simple Mail Transfer Protocol (SMTP) and Domain Name System (DNS) are all explained in Chapter 7. Simple Network Management Protocol (SNMP) is explained in Chapter 9. At the Transport Layer, the two main protocols are TCP and User Datagram Protocol (UDP). These are explained in Chapter 6. IP, also explained in Chapter 6, is the sole protocol at the Internet Layer and allows

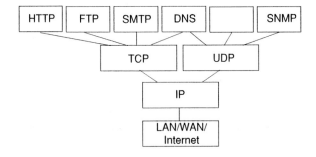

FIGURE 3.5. TCP/IP

universal communication between computers. The network technology that is being used by protocols in the top three layers resides in the Network Access Layer.

3.5 The OSI and TCP/IP Models Compared

Figure 3.6 shows the OSI and TCP/IP models side by side. An obvious similarity between the two models is that the TCP/IP transport and Internet layers have very similar counterparts in the OSI transport and network layers. Both models have an Application Layer, but the TCP/IP Application Layer performs the functions of the OSI application, presentation and session layers combined. Another difference is that the TCP/IP Network Access Layer carries out the functions of the OSI data link and physical layers. The OSI model is of more use for classifying protocols but few of its protocols are used to any great extent. TCP/IP protocols on the other hand, are very heavily used, but the model itself is less useful than the 7-layer model. The upshot is that networking students need to know about both the models.

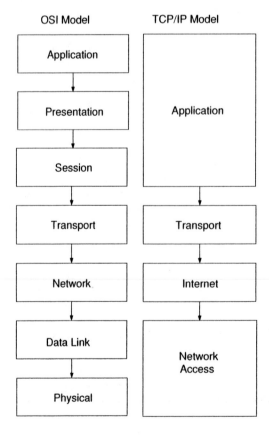

FIGURE 3.6. The OSI and TCP/IP models compared

3.6 Networking Standards

It is important to have networking standards. The main reason for these standards is to make sure that hardware and software from different vendors can work together. We can classify standards into three categories: formal standards, proprietary standards and de facto standards. Formal standards are those developed by an official body, for example, the OSI 7-layer model and TCP/IP. Proprietary standards are those devised by one vendor for use with the company's products. An example of a proprietary standard is the now defunct Digital Equipment Corporation's DECnet, which worked only with DEC's products. De facto standards are those supported by more than one vendor but which have no official standing. An example of such a standard is the AT command set for modems. This was devised by the Hayes modem company (a proprietary standard initially) but was then taken up by every other modem manufacturer.

3.6.1 Networking Standards Bodies

There are many standards bodies that issue formal standards relevant to computer networking and telecommunications. Below are brief descriptions of just a few of these.

The Institute of Electrical and Electronics Engineers (IEEE) produces standards for electrical engineering, computers and control technology. It is responsible for the 802.3/Ethernet standards, among others (http://www.ieee.org). 802.3/Ethernet is discussed in Chapter 4.

The Internet Engineering Task Force (IETF) is concerned with the Internet architecture and the operation of the Internet (http://www.ietf.org). Among other standards, it is responsible for the TCP/IP protocols. It maintains a repository of Requests for Comments (RFC) documents, a set of technical and organisational notes about the Internet. Some RFCs contain definitions of Internet standards, such as protocols.

The American National Standards Institute (ANSI) is an independent, non-profit organisation that administers and coordinates the US standardisation and conformity assessment system (http://www.ansi.org). The fibre-distributed data interface (FDDI) is an example of an ANSI networking standard. FDDI is briefly discussed in Chapter 4.

As we saw in Section 3.2, ISO is the International Organisation for Standardisation (http://www.iso.org), which devised the OSI 7-layer model. ISO is a network of many national standards institutes, including the British Standards Institution (BSI) and ANSI.

The International Telecommunication Union Telecommunication Standardisation Sector (ITU-T) produces telecommunications standards such as the V.92 modem standard (http://www.itu.int/ITU-T). The ITU-T was formerly called the Consultative Committee on International Telegraph and Telephone (CCITT).

The Electronic Industries Alliance (EIA) and the Telecommunications Industry Association (TIA) are US organisations, which issue such standards as

TIA/EIA-232 (formerly known as RS232). TIA/EIA-232 defines an interface between data terminal equipment (for example, a computer) and data circuit terminating equipment (for example, a modem). The EIA and TIA Web sites can be found at http://www.tiaonline.org and http://www.eia.org.

The European Telecommunications Standards Institute (ETSI) is an independent, non-profit organisation which produces telecommunications standards (http://www.etsi.org).

The World Wide Web Consortium (W3C) develops specifications and software for the World Wide Web (http://www.w3.org). HTML (see Section 7.3.1) and Extensible Markup Language (XML) are specified by W3C.

3.7 Summary

This chapter has looked at networking models and standards. The chapter started with an explanation of network layering. The OSI 7-layer model, an important way of describing networks, was examined. The principles of data encapsulation were then explained. Another important networking model, TCP/IP, was then described. The OSI and TCP/IP models were then briefly compared. The importance of networking standards was highlighted. Finally, several important networking standards bodies were mentioned.

3.8 Questions

1. What are the advantages of organising network architectures in layers?
2. Which of the following does a Physical Layer protocol deal with?
   - control signalling
   - plugs and sockets
   - checking for errors
3. Match the layer of the ISO/OSI 7-layer model to the facts about it:

Layer

   (a) Physical Layer
   (b) Data Link Layer
   (c) Network Layer
   (d) Transport Layer
   (e) Session Layer
   (f) Presentation Layer
   (g) Application Layer

Facts

   (i) Uses the raw transmission facility provided by the Physical Layer and makes the communication channel appear free of errors.
   (ii) The environment in which users' programs operate and communicate.

    (iii) Concerned with establishing and maintaining a communication path between two users.

    (iv) Concerned with the format of the data being exchanged by the communicating parties.

    (v) Concerned with routing 'packets' across a network.

    (vi) Concerned with the mechanism for transmitting bit patterns over a communication channel.

    (vii) Hides all the network-dependent characteristics from the layers above it.

4. What are the layers in the TCP/IP model?
5. What is the TCP/IP suite?
6. What is an RFC?
7. Match the organisation to the facts about it:

Organisations

    (a) IEEE
    (b) ISO
    (c) ITU-T
    (d) W3C
    (e) IETF

Facts

    (i) Responsible for specifications and software for the World Wide Web.
    (ii) Produces LAN standards, among others.
    (iii) Concerned with the operation and evolution of the Internet.
    (iv) Responsible for the OSI 7-layer reference model.
    (v) Responsible for world telecommunications standards.

4
Local Area Networks

In this chapter we look at various aspects of LANs. The chapter starts with an account of some of the factors that need to be considered when planning a LAN. Decisions about whether to choose a peer-to-peer or client-server LAN and whether to select a wired or wireless network are considered. Various components and devices for both wired LANs and wireless LANs (WLANs) are described. Several wired LAN technologies are briefly described, but the chapter concentrates on Ethernet, which is the commonest technology by far.

4.1 Building LANs

Several decisions need to be taken when planning a LAN. Should it be peer-to-peer or client-server? Should it be a wireless network? What kind of network technology should be used?

4.1.1 Peer-to-Peer and Client-Server LANs

Whether the network is organised on a peer-to-peer or a client-server basis, the same fundamental client-server technology and Request-Response Protocol are used. (Client-server technology is explained in Chapter 7.)

Peer-to-Peer LANs

In a peer-to-peer network, the computers are equals (peers). None of the computers has control over the LAN, and the computers act as client or server computers as necessary. In a peer-to-peer LAN, a given computer can be acting as client or server at different times. Peer-to-peer LANs usually exist principally to share files and are normally based around a hub or switch. A peer-to-peer LAN is illustrated in Fig. 4.1.

Peer-to-peer LANs are easy to install and require little maintenance. There is no need for a network administrator. Users are in control of their own resources and they can choose whether to share their files with other users. This can cause

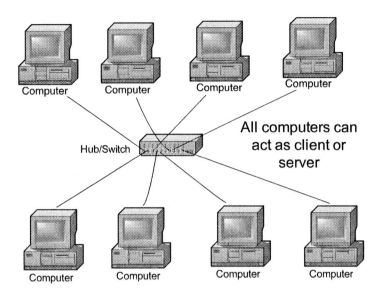

FIGURE 4.1. Peer-to-peer LAN

security problems. It is advisable to limit a peer-to-peer network to about 10 nodes (a *node* is a computer that is attached to a network), or it may not work efficiently.

Client-Server LANs

Client-server technology is described in Section 7.1. In a client-server network, not all the computers are equal. There is a special server computer, which is dedicated to the server role. It responds to requests from all the other computers (the client computers). Typically, it provides file and print services and perhaps some other applications. The client computers are usually ordinary desktop computers and the server computer is rather more powerful. The server computer may have extra memory and a more powerful processor or multiple processors. It will always have special software. Its operating system (OS), known as a *network operating system* (NOS), is likely to be either a different version from that running on the client computers or else a completely different OS. The NOS controls the interaction of the client computers with the server computer and with each other. The most popular NOS for PC LANs is Microsoft® Windows®. Novell NetWare® is an alternative choice. There may be more than one server computer in the network. A client-server LAN is illustrated in Fig. 4.2.

User accounts and security are centralised on the server computer, which makes administering a large network much easier than if it were organised on a peer-to-peer basis. It is also easier to back up the files because they are all kept in one place.

There are a few disadvantages to client-server LANs. The server computer is a single point of failure: the network cannot function without it. The network needs

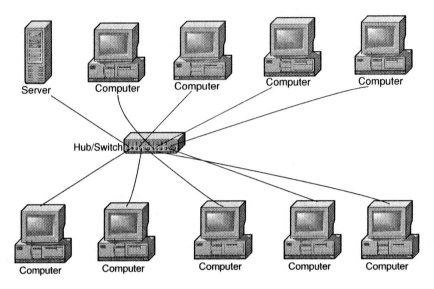

FIGURE 4.2. Client-server LAN

a trained, dedicated administrator, which increases the cost. The special software needed also makes the client-server LAN more expensive than a peer-to-peer LAN.

4.1.2 Transmission Medium

When planning a LAN, one must decide whether to use cabling or wireless communications. The options for cabling were set out in Section 2.10. The default choice for a wired LAN would be UTP cable laid out in a star topology.

Wireless networks are described in Chapter 10. The chief disadvantages of WLANs are poor security and relatively low data rate. However, WLANs are easy to set up compared with wired LANs and make it very easy to move the computers about. A typical WLAN is illustrated in Fig. 4.3. As shown in Fig. 4.3, a WLAN is usually connected to a wired network, which facilitates long distance communications.

4.1.3 Components and Devices

Components and Devices for Wired LANs

Each PC on the network will contain a network interface card (NIC). This is a circuit board that fits into a slot on the motherboard of the PC. Alternatively, the NIC circuitry might already be built into the PC's motherboard. The NIC lets the PC connect into a network. It encodes the data that is to be sent out, following the rules for the physical medium that is in use (a cable system or some other medium). Also, if the medium is shared, the NIC ensures that only one

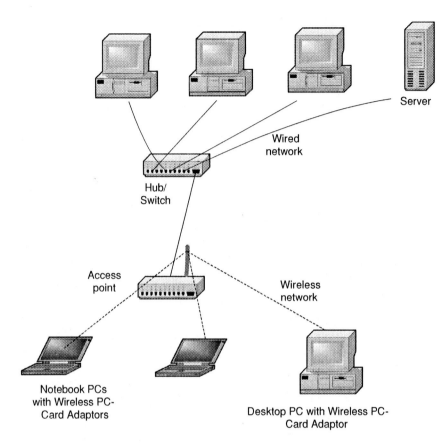

Server

Wired
network

Hub/
Switch

Access
point

Wireless
network

Notebook PCs
with Wireless PC-
Card Adaptors

Desktop PC with Wireless PC-
Card Adaptor

FIGURE 4.3. WLAN

computer sends data at a time. In addition, it detects errors in transmission. Each
network technology needs a particular kind of NIC. For example, an Ethernet NIC
is necessary to connect to an Ethernet network. There are different kinds of NIC
for the various types of PC bus (for example, peripheral component interconnect
(PCI)). The connector that NIC has will vary according to the cabling used. With
Ethernet, for example, there is a choice of twisted pair cable or fibre-optic cable.
Most NICs come with drivers for the most popular OSs. They are usually software
configurable. A typical Ethernet NIC (for the PCI bus and fitted with an RJ-45
port) is illustrated in Fig. 4.4. A laptop PC will probably use a PC-card (Personal
Computer Memory Card International Association (PCMCIA)) NIC. NICs are
usually built into PCs, whether server, desktop or portable, and do not normally
need to be added.

Ethernet NICs usually support such standards as IEEE 802.1p and IEEE 802.1q.
IEEE 802.1p is an important prioritisation standard for IP telephony (IP telephony
is described in Section 7.7.2). 802.1p gives IP-based voice transmissions priority

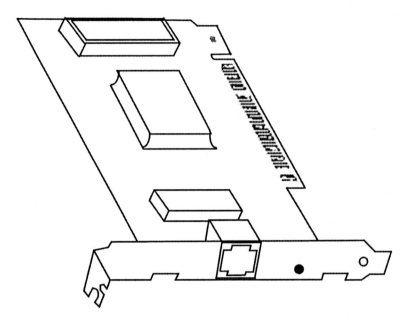

FIGURE 4.4. NIC

over data so as to reduce the latency (delay) and jitter (variation in delay) to which IP networks are prone and that voice cannot tolerate. IEEE 802.1q is a standard that supports *virtual LANs* (VLANs). (IEEE 802.1q and VLANs are discussed later in this section.). NICs can often process TCP/IP checksums too. If a NIC supports *wake on LAN*, its host PC can be switched on by sending it a special packet over the network.

Unless the LAN is very small, the network equipment apart from the workstations themselves is safely locked away inside one or more *wiring closets*. A wiring closet is simply a walk-in cupboard that contains racks of network hardware. The cable from each PC normally feeds into a *patch panel*. A patch panel is illustrated in Fig. 4.5. The patch panel acts like a small switchboard and is a convenient means of connecting various pieces of networking equipment together. Fixed into the patch panel from the back are many individual jacks (or sockets). The plugs on

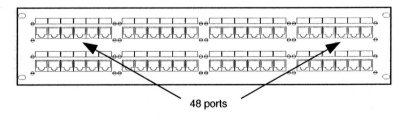

48 ports

FIGURE 4.5. Patch panel

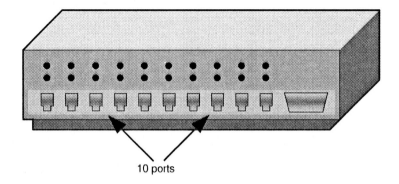

10 ports

FIGURE 4.6. Hub

the end of the data cables plug into the jacks. If Category 5e UTP cable is in use, Registered Jack-45 (RJ-45) plugs and jacks are used. Other kinds of cable may need different plugs and jacks.

Other Internetworking components which may be needed are hubs, switches and routers. To connect together more than two computers, either a hub or a switch is necessary. (A crossover cable, described in Section 2.10.1, can be used if we are just connecting one computer to one other.) A *hub* is an OSI layer 1 device which merely repeats (boosts) any signal sent from one of the computers on the network to which it is attached to all the other computers. An alternative name for a hub is a multi-port repeater (a repeater with several ports). A hub is a very simple device, which does not understand network addresses of any kind. A typical hub is illustrated in Fig. 4.6.

Instead of a hub, it is more common to use a layer-2 switch. The switch is a computer in its own right, which understands layer-2 addresses such as Ethernet addresses. A switch can be used like its forerunner, the *bridge*, to connect LAN segments. A bridge is shown in Fig. 4.7 and an Ethernet switch in Fig. 4.8.

The switch builds up tables of media access control (MAC) addresses (Ethernet addresses in the case of an Ethernet network), and can thus work out on which segment a frame should be transmitted. (Please see Sections 4.2.1 and 4.2.2 for a discussion of MAC addresses.) Bridges have only two or three ports but a switch has many. The high number of ports that a switch has means that it can be used in place of a hub. If a switch is used in an Ethernet network instead of a hub, it

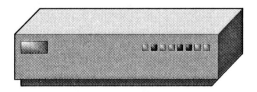

FIGURE 4.7. Bridge

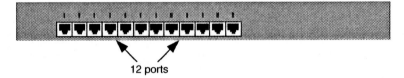

12 ports

FIGURE 4.8. Ethernet switch

will effectively increase the available bandwidth in the network. This is because, unlike a hub, a switch permits several PCs on an Ethernet network to communicate at the same time and in full duplex mode. In this case, there are no collisions and Ethernet's CSMA/CD access protocol (see Section 4.2.2) is not used.

Layer-2 switches have so much intelligence that they are able to provide *VLANs*. A VLAN is a LAN that does not exist physically. It consists of a logical group of devices or users, selected from the devices or users on an actual, physical LAN. For example, users in a company's Accounts department can be grouped together into their own VLAN, while people in the Human Resources (HR) department might belong to another VLAN. The various members of these two departments might be dispersed over several floors of a building, as is the case in Fig. 4.9. The devices within a VLAN can communicate only with each other. Communication

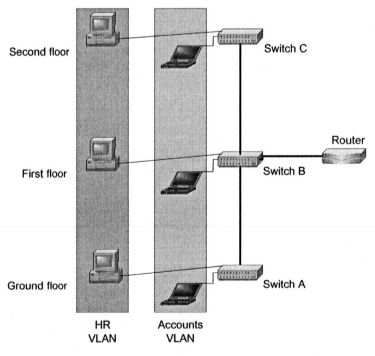

FIGURE 4.9. VLANs

Preamble	Destination address	Source address	Tag	Length/ Type	Data	Frame check sequence

FIGURE 4.10. VLAN tag

between VLANs needs a router. (Brief details of routers are given later on in this section and fuller details in Chapter 5).

When the 802.1q VLAN standard is in use, every Ethernet frame contains a 4-byte *tag* that can be used to define the membership of the VLAN groups. The Ethernet switch inserts the tag into the Ethernet frame and recalculates the frame check sequence (CRC). The position of the tag is shown in Fig. 4.10. Please refer to Section 4.2.2 for an explanation of the other fields in the Ethernet frame.

VLANs are configured with software and when establishing them there is no need to move equipment about or reconnect cables. VLANs make it easy to add new stations or change the LAN in any way. VLANs also contribute to the security of the network. The traffic on the Accounts VLAN in Fig. 4.9 stays within that VLAN and nobody else can pry into the accounting files. Frames are switched only between switch ports that have been defined to belong to the same VLAN. VLANs also help networks to work more efficiently because those objects on the network (users and devices) that communicate with each other most often can be grouped together.

One disadvantage of network devices such as switches is that they add *latency* to the network. Latency is the delay between the time when a frame leaves the sending device and the time when the front of the frame reaches the receiving device. Layer-2 switches can operate in three different modes: Cut Through, Store and Forward, and Fragment Free. In Cut-Through operation, the switch starts to transfer a frame that it has received as soon as it knows the MAC address of the destination. The advantage of doing switching in this manner is that the latency is very low. On the other hand, since the CRC is not checked, faulty frames as well as error-free ones are switched.

In contrast, in Store-and-Forward mode, the whole frame is read into the switch, stored briefly and then forwarded to the destination. This process takes longer than Cut-Through switching but has the advantage that invalid frames are thrown away by the switch rather than being passed on. Another advantage is that the frame can be sent out at a different data rate from that at which it was received.

Fragment-Free mode is a compromise between Cut Through and Store and Forward. Here, the first 64 bytes of the frame are read. This is because any errors are likely to fall within the first 64 bytes. The Fragment-Free mode of operation is not as fast as Cut-Through switching, but it does give a greater chance that the frame being switched is worth sending on.

If we need to connect two or more networks or VLANs together, a router is necessary. Routers, as the name would suggest, can do routing. In other words, they can understand the addresses used by layer-3 protocols such as IP and make decisions about where an incoming network packet should be sent next. The kind of

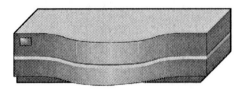

FIGURE 4.11. Router

router that is usually used is a special computer, specifically designed to do routing and carry out a few other related network functions. Such a router is illustrated in Fig. 4.11. However, alternatively it is possible to use an ordinary PC, running under an ordinary OS, such as Microsoft Windows or Linux. This PC will have special routing software running on it to allow it to act as a router. Routers are mainly used for connecting WANs together, so more details of routers are given in Chapter 5.

A rack containing networking equipment is shown in Fig. 4.12. Normally, such a rack would be safely locked up inside a wiring closet because security is very important. Racks are made in standard widths (for example, 19") and can accommodate equipment of standard thicknesses.

Components and Devices for WLANs

The *access point* (AP) shown in Fig. 4.3 is a hardware device, although alternatively the AP might consist of a software running on a standard computer. It is the AP that lets the wireless devices connect to the wired LAN. The AP also helps to increase security. The wireless counterpart of the NIC that is used on a wired computer (see Section 2.1) is the *radio*—a wireless transmitter/receiver. For laptop computers, this is usually a PC-card. PC-cards are built to PCMCIA standards. For desktop computers, universal serial bus (USB) and PCI radios are often used; compact flash radios are designed for small personal digital assistants (PDAs) and other mobile computing devices. Sometimes the radio is built into the computer. It is not essential to use an AP in a WLAN. Peer-to-peer (or *ad hoc*) WLANs can be constructed using only client radios. This is fine for a small or temporary network.

4.2 Types of Wired LAN

This section concentrates on Ethernet because of its near ubiquity in the LAN. A few other types of LAN are briefly described at the end of the section, however.

4.2.1 Logical Link Control and MAC Sub-Layers

In Section 3.2.2, we encountered the OSI Data Link Layer (layer 2) and its functions. For LAN protocols, layer 2 is divided into two sub-layers: the logical link control (LLC) sub-layer and the MAC sub-layer. LLC is the upper sub-layer. It

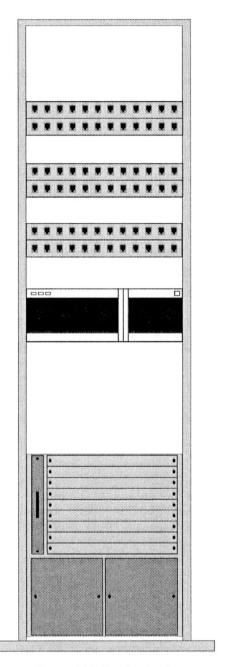

FIGURE 4.12. Populated rack

Logical Link Control Sub-layer							
Media Access Control							
Physical Layer	Ethernet 802.3	Token Ring 802.5	Wireless LAN 802.11x	Other LAN standard	Other LAN standard	Other LAN standard	Other LAN standard

FIGURE 4.13. LLC and MAC sub-layers

offers a common interface between the Network Layer (OSI layer 3) and the MAC sub-layer. It also offers reliability and flow control. LLC is a subset of High-level Data Link Control (HDLC), a wide-area Data Link Layer protocol, which is described in Section 6.3. When a computer wants to transmit, it is the MAC sub-layer that is responsible for putting the physical address of the destination computer into the data frame. The physical address is the address of the destination computer's NIC. Figure 4.13 shows the LLC and some of the more important MAC protocols.

4.2.2 Ethernet

Ethernet is far and away the most important standard for LANs. It has a fairly long history, during which it has evolved considerably. Its success is due to several factors. It is fairly simple, very reliable and above all cheap compared with rival technologies.

DIX was the first Ethernet standard. It got its name from the three companies that published it: Digital Equipment Corporation, Intel and Xerox. A few years later, the IEEE brought out the 802.3 standard. This is slightly different from the DIX Ethernet standard. It covers both OSI layer 1 and the lower part of layer 2, which can be seen in Fig. 4.13. At this stage in its history, Ethernet ran at 10 Mbps. Gradually, the maximum data rate of Ethernet has got faster and faster, moving from 10 Mbps to 100 Mbps to 1 Gbps (1000 million bps), then to 10 Gbps, 40 Gbps and so on. At all of these data rates, the format of the Ethernet frame is almost identical, while the Physical Layer can vary considerably.

The IEEE uses the following naming scheme for its family of Ethernet standards. First of all, there is a number that indicates the data rate in megabits per second. This number is followed by the word 'BASE', to indicate the use of baseband transmission (that is, using just one unmultiplexed channel). After this, there are one or two letters that show what type of medium is being used. For example, 100BASE-T means that the data rate is 100 Mbps and that baseband transmission and twisted-pair copper cabling are being used.

Carrier Sense Multiple Access/Collision Detection

The MAC protocol that non-switched variants of Ethernet use is carrier sense multiple access/collision detection (CSMA/CD). In the original form of Ethernet, all the computers were attached to a bus (a piece of coaxial cable which acted as a common highway for data transmission). Only one conversation between two network stations at a time was possible and a protocol such as CSMA/CD was needed to allow a computer access to the bus. When CSMA/CD is in use, a station that wishes to transmit listens to the bus. If there seems to be no activity, the station transmits (carrier sense). Multiple access means that all stations have access to the network medium (the cable). Once a station starts transmitting, all other stations will almost immediately detect the transmission and will wait until it has finished before trying to send anything themselves. However, it is still possible that two stations will both detect that the bus is idle, and that both start to transmit at about the same time. Then there will be a collision of data. The reason why this can happen is that any signal takes some time to propagate along the bus. Collision detection is needed to deal with this problem.

If a station detects a collision while it is transmitting, it sends a brief jamming signal. This signal lets the other stations know that there has been a collision. After sending the jamming signal, the station ceases transmission and then waits for a random time period. When this period is up, the station attempts to transmit again. If there are repeated collisions, this indicates a busy medium. To adjust for this, the time delay between repeated retransmission attempts is progressively increased. This is called the binary exponential backoff algorithm. If there are sixteen unsuccessful attempts to transmit (a very rare occurrence), the frame transmission is abandoned and the upper layer is informed of this.

Ethernet Frame Format

The Ethernet II (DIX) frame format is slightly different from the IEEE 802.3 version. The Ethernet II frame is shown in Fig. 4.14 and the IEEE 802.3 frame in Fig. 4.15. The first field of the Ethernet II frame is the 8-byte Preamble. The purpose of this field is to warn the other stations on the network that a frame is coming. In IEEE 802.3, this field is split into two parts but there is no difference in the bit patterns. The first seven bytes carry timing information, while the eighth is

8	6	6	2	46-1500	4
Preamble	Destination address	Source address	Type	Data+Pad	Frame Check Sequence

FIGURE 4.14. Ethernet II frame format

7	1	6	6	2	46 - 1500	4
Preamble	Start Frame Delimiter	Destination address	Source address	Length/ Type	LLC Header + Data + Pad	Frame Check Sequence

FIGURE 4.15. IEEE 802.3 frame format

the Start Frame Delimiter, which indicates the end of the timing bits. The timing information was necessary for the operation of 10-Mbps Ethernet. Though it has not been needed for any higher-speed versions, it has been kept for reasons of compatibility.

In both types of frame, the next two fields are for the destination (receiving station) and source (sending station) addresses. Both these addresses are 48 bits long and are usually shown as 12 hexadecimal digits. Every Ethernet card in the world has a unique MAC address. The first six hex digits indicate the manufacturer of the card; the second six are a unique identifier. For example, a certain Ethernet NIC has the following MAC address: 00-02-44-37-60-FA. The 00-02-44 part of the number identifies the manufacturer; 37-60-FA is the unique identifier.

The purpose of the next (two-byte) field differs in the two types of frame. In Ethernet II, the receiving station has to find out which higher-layer protocol is being carried in an incoming frame. It needs to know this in order to know to which upper-layer protocol it must give the data. It finds this out by looking inside the Type field. In IEEE 802.3, this field can be used as a Type field, but alternatively can be used to carry the length of the data in bytes. There is no need to use this field to identify the protocol if the LLC field (missing from Ethernet II) is being used to do this. If the number is equal to or greater than 600 hexadecimal (1536 decimal), then it is taken to indicate the length.

The whole point of sending an Ethernet frame is to carry some data. The Data field is the place where the data is put. The greatest size of a frame that is allowed in low-speed versions of Ethernet is 1518 bytes; the minimum size is 46 bytes. If the frame would otherwise be below the minimum size, it is padded out with extra bytes to make it legal. The IEEE 802.3 frame also carries the LLC information within the Data field. The 1000Base-T Gigabit Ethernet standard permits frames larger than 1518 bytes. Up to 9 kbytes can be carried in one frame—a so-called *jumbo* frame.

Finally, in the Frame Check Sequence (FCS) field, there is a 32 bits CRC code to check for errors. This checks the integrity of the whole frame except the Preamble/Start Frame Delimiter and of course the CRC field itself. (CRCs were explained in Section 2.6.1.) Any frame with an invalid CRC is simply thrown away without being processed any further because it is useless.

Ethernet Developments

Originally, Ethernet LANs always used coaxial cable. The cable formed a physical bus to which the stations were attached. To this day, the standard graphical

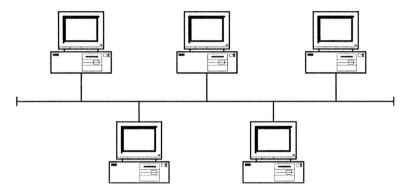

FIGURE 4.16. Ethernet bus

representation of an Ethernet is normally a diagram such as that in Fig. 4.16, which shows the cabling as a bus. However, when the 10BASE-T standard was devised, the cabling became twisted pair, with the stations connected together via a hub. Gradually, Ethernet switches have supplanted hubs and the fastest kinds of Ethernet are purely switch based. With high-speed forms of Ethernet, the pattern has been to bring out optical-fibre-based standards first and then to introduce twisted-pair copper standards as soon as technology permitted. For example, the 1000BASE-T (twisted-pair) standard came out some time after the other Gigabit Ethernet standards. In Table 4.1 details of some of the more important Ethernet Physical-Layer standards are given. Another recent trend has been to use Ethernet for WAN connectivity. 10-Gigabit Ethernet (10 GbE) permitted this.

4.2.3 Other Types of Wired LAN

Token Ring and Fibre Distributed Data Interface

Ethernet is not the only type of wired LAN. At one time, Token Ring (IEEE 802.5) was also very popular. It works in a rather different way from Ethernet. As the name suggests, the stations are wired in a (logical) ring. Access to the LAN is controlled by a *token*—a pattern of bits which constantly circulates around the ring. When a station wishes to transmit, it needs to get hold of the token, change one of the bits in the token to show that it is no longer free and append its message to the token. The frame format includes the address of the destination station. As the frame travels around the ring, each station looks at the destination address to

TABLE 4.1. Some Ethernet physical-layer standards.

Name	100BASE-TX	1000BASE-T	1000BASE-SX	1000BASE-LX	10-Gb E (several)	40-Gb E
Data rate	100 Mbps	1000 Mbps	1000 Mbps	1000 Mbps	10,000 Mbps	40,000 Mbps
Cabling	UTP Cat 5	UTP Cat 5e	Fibre	Fibre	Fibre + copper	Fibre

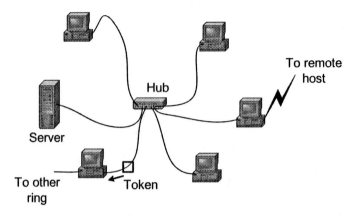

FIGURE 4.17. Token Ring LAN

see which station the frame is for. If it sees its own address it will read the message; otherwise it will ignore it. When the frame gets back to the sending station, the sender frees up the token and puts it back onto the ring.

The topology is a physical star, with all the stations connected to a hub as shown in Fig. 4.17. However, the logical topology is a ring, in which the flow of information is controlled in a ring. (Modern Ethernet networks are 'physical star, logical bus': the network works on a bus principle but is wired as a star.) The data rate of Token Ring networks was originally 4 Mbps. It then increased to 16 Mbps and ultimately reached 100 Mbps. Token Ring can guarantee that the maximum waiting time before gaining access to the network will not be above a certain figure. Such a network is termed *deterministic*. By contrast, Ethernet is regarded as *non-deterministic*. Token Ring was a good technology but Ethernet was cheaper and has largely displaced it.

FDDI is a large-scale, ring-based token passing system, with built-in fault tolerance, that was designed to take advantage of fibre-optic cabling. Again, Ethernet has largely supplanted it.

Asynchronous Transfer Mode LANs

A point-to-point network (see Section 5.6 for further information) that has been successfully used in LANs is asynchronous transfer mode (ATM). ATM is really a WAN technology but it has also been used in LANs, where it is especially suitable for carrying multimedia information. ATM is more expensive than Ethernet and this is the main reason why it has never been used in LANs to any great extent. It is a cell-based technology that uses switches. (Switches are described in Section 4.1.3.) Data is sent out in 53-byte *cells*, rather than in variable-length frames as in an Ethernet or Token Ring. These fixed-length cells are what is switched through the ATM network.

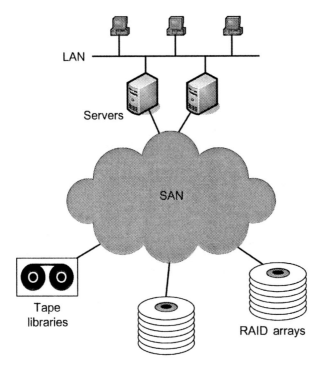

FIGURE 4.18. SAN

4.3 Storage Area Network

A *storage area network* (SAN) is a special network that is dedicated to storage. It links together one or more server computers with storage devices such as Redundant Array of Independent Disks (RAID) systems and tape libraries. The server(s) can access any device in the SAN's storage pool. A SAN usually offers a high data transfer rate. The networking technology that is used is often Internet Small Computer System Interface (iSCSI). This carries Small Computer System Interface (SCSI) commands to control the storage devices over an IP-based Ethernet network. Fibre channel, a high-speed fibre-optic network technology, is sometimes used instead of iSCSI. As well as hardware, a SAN usually includes special software to manage, monitor and configure it. A SAN is illustrated in Fig. 4.18. Note that it is a separate network from the LAN.

4.4 Summary

This chapter has looked at various aspects of LANs. The chapter started with an account of some of the factors that need to be considered when planning a LAN. Factors affecting the choices between peer-to-peer and client-server LANs and between wired and wireless networks were then considered. Various components and devices for both wired LANs and WLANs were also described. Ethernet, being by far the most important LAN technology, was covered at some length. Then, some other wired LAN technologies were described. The chapter finished with a brief sketch of SANs.

4.5 Questions

1. What are the advantages and disadvantages of client-server LANs?
2. What is a NIC and what does it do?
3. What advantages do Ethernet switches possess over Ethernet hubs?
4. What are virtual LANs (VLANs) and why are they useful?
5. Explain the three different modes of operation of layer-2 switches.
6. Describe the two sub-layers at the Data Link Layer of LAN protocols.
7. Describe how shared Ethernet controls access to the medium.
8. Why is it necessary to have a maximum and a minimum frame length when using Ethernet?
9. Describe the Token-Ring access method.
10. (a) What is the purpose of SANs and what network technologies do they use?
    (b) How do SANs differ from network attached storage (NAS)? (Answering (b) will involve some research outside this text.)

5
Wide Area Networks

Wide area networks (WANs) were briefly introduced in Section 1.2. We now look at WANs in a little more detail. The chapter starts with a look at the general characteristics of WANs. After a brief mention of the use of the public switched telephone network (PSTN) for computer networks, two packet-switching technologies, X.25 and Frame Relay, are described. Integrated Services Digital Network (ISDN), an all-digital, circuit-switched service, comes next. Digital leased lines are then described. This is followed by coverage of digital subscriber line and cable modem, which offer alternative 'always-on' broadband services. Then, some ways of accessing LANs remotely are described. Next is a section on routers, which are devices that are used to connect networks together. Finally, the use in WANs of two technologies that were described in Chapter 4, ATM and Ethernet, is covered.

5.1 General Characteristics of WANs

WANs are used to carry data over long distances. This could be within a region of a country, across a whole country or even from one side of the world to another. The transmission facilities that are used nearly always belong to *carriers*—telecommunications companies that provide long distance links for other companies or individuals to use. For example, if a company has more than one site it can use a WAN to link up the LANs at those sites. This lets the sites share information. Such a situation can be seen in Fig. 1.2. WANs can carry several kinds of traffic, for example, voice, data and video, of which voice and data are the commonest. In terms of the OSI 7-layer model, WANs are located at the Physical Layer and Data Link Layer. WAN data rates are generally lower than those of LANs.

5.2 Public Switched Telephone Network

The PSTN is the ordinary, fixed-line (landline) network that has been in use for a century or so. When computer communications first started, the PSTN was a convenient network to use. Since the telephone network was designed to carry

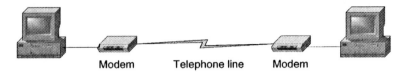

FIGURE 5.1. Use of modems

voice traffic rather than data, conversion of the digital signals from the computer into the kind of signals that can be carried over the PSTN is necessary. Most of the PSTN (the trunk lines) has been digital for several years, but the *local loop*, the line between the customer premises and the local exchange, is normally analogue.

In Section 2.4.4, the differences between analogue and digital signalling were explained. Amplitude, frequency and phase modulation and how these can be made use of in the modem were also explained (please see Section 2.5). Figure 5.1 shows modems being used to connect two PCs over a phone line.

5.3 X.25 Networks

The X.25 protocol was devised in the 1970s to connect devices with Data Terminal Equipment (DTE) interfaces and devices with Data Circuit Terminating Equipment (DCE) interfaces to packet-switched data networks. A DTE is a device such as a computer or router. A DCE is the device that connects to the service provider's network. A modem is an example of a DCE. Figure 5.2 illustrates connection to an X.25 'cloud'. The term *network cloud* is often used to refer to a WAN when we are not interested in its internal details.

When X.25 is in use, the data is divided into packets and transmitted over virtual circuits. (Virtual circuits were explained in Section 2.7.3.) X.25 can be used with either switched or permanent virtual circuits. It is unsuitable for high-speed applications or those that do not tolerate latency or jitter, such as voice or video. It is fine for low-speed terminal access, however. For example, in the United Kingdom, when the national lottery was set up, the networks used to connect terminals in shops to the central computer centre were largely based on X.25. Such a system needed reliability above all, rather than good figures for latency and jitter. X.25 networks are reliable because error checking is carried out on a link-by-link basis. The reason for all this error checking is that X.25 was designed to run over analogue networks, where transmission errors were fairly common.

FIGURE 5.2. X.25 connections

5.4 Frame Relay

In the previous section, we learnt that X.25 was designed for analogue networks. With the advent of digital networks X.25 was found to be too slow, so a more modern approach to packet-switching networks, Frame Relay, had to be devised. Since digital networks were more reliable than analogue networks, there was no need for Frame Relay to include link-by-link error checking. Any error checks could be done by a higher layer protocol at the end stations. Frame Relay functions only at OSI layers 1 and 2, while X.25 provides layer 3 services as well.

As the name would suggest, data is broken up into frames before being sent out over the Frame-Relay network. Just as in the case of X.25, the data is sent over virtual circuits (either SVCs or PVCs). PVCs are commonly used to construct *virtual private networks* (VPNs), which provide the equivalent of a private network but run over a public network. Before Frame Relay, if an organisation needed a WAN, private lines or circuit switching over a leased line were necessary. Single, dedicated lines are not needed for WAN-to-WAN connections with Frame Relay. This reduces costs.

Frame Relay is so much faster than X.25 that it can be used to connect LANs together. Frame Relay is ideally suited to carrying a high volume of traffic, which occurs unpredictably in bursts. Such traffic is typical of LANs. Even voice traffic can be sent using Frame Relay.

An important feature of Frame Relay is that frame-relay service providers are able to offer their customers tightly defined service agreements. If the frame-relay service fails to perform to the level that has been agreed, then the user can be compensated. There is a committed information rate (CIR) at which data is transmitted. But if the traffic and the service agreement allow this, data can burst above the committed rate for short periods.

The Frame-Relay data frame, Link Access Procedure for Frame Mode Services (LAPF), is based on HDLC (HDLC is described in Section 6.3). The frame includes a field for the data-link connection identifier (DLCI). The DLCI, a number, represents the virtual circuit to which the frame belongs. In other words, it is the destination address of the frame.

To gain access to a Frame-Relay network, a Frame Relay Access Device (FRAD) can be used. The sending FRAD breaks up the stream of data into frames for transmission over the network. The receiving FRAD carries out the complementary process, turning frames back into the original data stream. The use of FRADs is illustrated in Fig. 5.3. Inside the Frame-Relay cloud are Frame-Relay switches, wherein virtual circuits are set up. An alternative choice of device to a FRAD is a router equipped with an interface suitable for Frame Relay.

5.5 Integrated Services Digital Network

In Section 5.2 we saw that trunk telephone lines are usually digital but the local loop is often analogue. ISDN is an all-digital telephone network, in which both

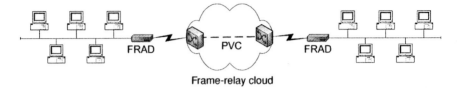

Frame-relay cloud

FIGURE 5.3. Use of FRADs

the trunk lines and the local loop are digital. Such an arrangement means that all sorts of data can be sent using the same system, since everything travelling over the network is a stream of bits. In other words, the network can offer *integrated services* of several different kinds.

There are two different kinds of ISDN: Basic Rate Interface (BRI) and Primary Rate Interface (PRI). Both are circuit-switched services. BRI is for small businesses or home users. BRI has two 64-kbps channels that can carry voice or data traffic. These are known as bearer channels (B channels). In addition, there is a 16-kbps delta channel (D channel) that is primarily used for signalling. However, since this channel does not have to carry much signalling traffic, it is often used to provide a slow X.25-type packet switching service.

For larger businesses ISDN PRI exists. This has 30 (23 in North America) 64-kbps B channels and a 64-kbps D channel. The total bit rate of ISDN primary rate (except in North America) is 2.048 Mbps. Many B channels can be simultaneously connected, making PRI ISDN suitable for such applications as videoconferencing. This can be rather expensive, however.

BRI has been very convenient for small businesses. Compared with the analogue PSTN (see Section 5.2 above), ISDN has a very short call setup time of just a few milliseconds. Just one of its D channels offers a higher data rate than an analogue modem link. Using *bonding*, the two 64-kbps channels can be combined to give an effective throughput of 128 kbps. (Bonding has also been used with analogue modems).

ISDN can be used to top up the capacity of a leased line connection (see Section 5.6 for information about leased lines). A router can be configured to open an ISDN link whenever the leased line is being used above a certain threshold. The leased line alone is normally in use. The ISDN line is used only when demand reaches a peak.

ISDN can also be used to back up a leased line. For example, a certain company might have a site in London and a site in Manchester connected by a leased line. If the leased line goes down, a backup ISDN line can replace it for as long as necessary. A router can be configured to bring the ISDN connection into play automatically.

Charges for ISDN lines are similar to those for ordinary fixed-line telephone lines. There is normally an installation charge and a quarterly line rental charge, but most of the money that the customer pays is for how long the line is used. Such a charging structure makes ISDN economical for fairly light usage.

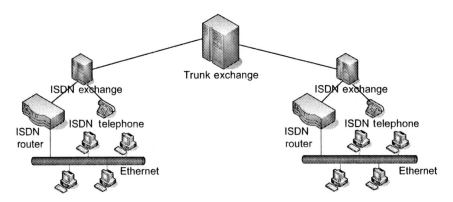

FIGURE 5.4. ISDN BRI configurations

Examples of ISDN BRI configurations are illustrated in Fig. 5.4. Connection to the network can be direct, as is the case for the ISDN telephone shown in Fig. 5.4, or indirect, using a router with an ISDN interface. An individual computer might be fitted with an ISDN card (very similar in appearance to the Ethernet card shown in Fig. 4.4). Alternatively, the computer might be connected via an ISDN *terminal adaptor* (essentially the same thing as the card but contained in a box that is separate from the computer) or a router.

5.6 Leased Lines

A leased line is used when an organisation needs a permanent, dedicated, *point-to-point* link. (A point-to-point link is a link from one place to another place.) The leased line provides a communications path that has been set up in advance from one site to another using the facilities of a telecommunications carrier company.

This system allows tight budget control because the cost does not depend on the amount of usage. For a monthly fee, the organisation is free to send as much data as it likes down the line, up to its maximum capacity. Usually, the cost of the rental depends on the data rate and the distance between the two sites that are being connected. Leased lines are usually more expensive than Frame Relay, particularly when many sites are connected. Two advantages of leased lines are that there is negligible latency and jitter and that the line is always available. Such features may be essential for certain kinds of application. The disadvantages include the cost compared with most of the alternative ways of setting up a WAN. Leased lines are not very flexible either. The data rate offered by a leased line seldom corresponds to the exact traffic requirements. (We have already seen in the previous section how it is often necessary to top up the carrying capacity of a leased line using ISDN.) If the capacity of the leased line needs to be changed, this usually entails an employee of the carrier visiting the site.

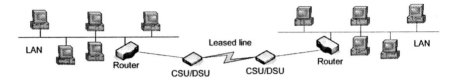

FIGURE 5.5. Typical leased line configuration

At one time, leased lines always used to be analogue but digital leased lines have now taken over almost completely. To connect to an analogue leased line, a special, synchronous modem is needed at each end of the line. The equipment that organisations usually use with a digital leased line consists of a router and a device called a Channel Service Unit/Data Service Unit (CSU/DSU) at each end of the link. The CSU/DSU may take the form of a card that is fitted to a router or computer, or may be contained in a separate box, as is shown in Fig. 5.5. The CSU/DSU is the DCE device that connects to the digital line. It performs conversion between the kind of data frames used on the LAN and those used on the WAN link. The CSU/DSU also protects the carrier's network from damage that could be caused by the customer's network. The link between the router and the CSU/DSU in Fig. 5.5 is a serial cable using a protocol such as EIA/TIA-232 or a near equivalent at the Physical Layer.

Leased lines can be shared using multiplexers (see Fig. 5.6). This helps to keep costs down because both voice traffic and data traffic can share the line. Some CSU/DSUs have multiple ports and have a built-in multiplexing capability.

The digital leased line services available in Europe and much of the rest of the world are the E-carrier series. The T-carrier series of digital leased line services is used in North America and a few other places. There are a few differences between the E-carriers and T-carriers, such as the data rates offered. For example, the E3 standard offers a data rate of 34.368 Mbps, whereas the equivalent T-carrier standard, T3, offers a data rate of 44.736 Mbps.

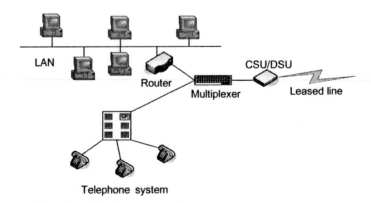

FIGURE 5.6. Use of a multiplexer with a leased line

5.7 Digital Subscriber Line

5.7.1 Advantages and Disadvantages

Digital subscriber line (DSL) technology uses advanced modems to achieve high data rates over standard twisted-pair copper cable in the local loop. It is referred to as a *broadband* technology. Essentially, the term 'broadband' means using a wide band of frequencies to transmit signals over more than one channel at the same time. This contrasts with the *baseband* technology typically used in LANs, where there is only one channel.

The term *xDSL* can be used to refer to all kinds of DSL technology. The two main variants are Symmetric DSL (SDSL) and Asymmetric DSL (ADSL). SDSL uses all of the bandwidth of the line for data transmission. The data rate is the same in both directions. SDSL was intended for use by businesses as a cheap alternative to leased lines. ADSL was intended for home users. ADSL splits the bandwidth up, using most of it for digital data transmission but reserving a small amount for analogue voice transmission. The ADSL data rate is much faster in one direction than in the other, which is why it is termed 'asymmetric'. ADSL was designed like this because home users were assumed to be downloading a large amount of data from the Internet, but sending out only a little data. It was also assumed that home users want to keep their standard, fixed-line analogue telephone.

To be able to provide DSL, the service provider needs to place a *DSL Access Multiplexer* (DSLAM) inside the local telephone exchange. This device allows multiple subscriber lines to be multiplexed together for long-distance transmission over a high-speed leased line. If ADSL is in use, the subscriber needs, in addition to the ADSL modem itself, either a device called a *splitter* or individual *line filters*. These separate the DSL signal from the analogue telephone service. Sometimes the splitter is built into the modem. ADSL devices are illustrated in Fig. 5.7.

Data rates offered by ADSL vary greatly, depending on the type of service. Very High Speed Digital Subscriber Line 2 (VDSL2) is claimed to deliver up to 100 Mbps in both directions. Other variants of DSL are much slower. Although DSL technology can potentially give very high data rates over the existing local loop, there are limiting factors. The greater the distance from the local telephone exchange, the slower the data rate. The quality of the copper cable in the local loop also affects the data rate. Although DSL services are much cheaper than leased lines, the service is unreliable in comparison.

5.8 Cable Modems

Cable modems provide broadband connectivity to domestic users. The cable modem service depends on cable television being installed in the neighbourhood. Although the technology used is totally different from that used in ADSL, the experience that cable modems offer the consumer is rather similar. Like ADSL, a cable modem service is an 'always-on' service, which is always connected to the

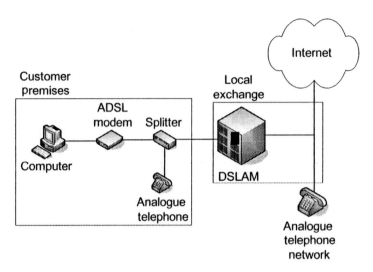

FIGURE 5.7. ADSL equipment

Internet. The data rates that can be obtained are similar to those offered by DSL. Cable modems are rarely used by businesses, as they are considered too unreliable and insecure.

Figure 5.8 shows a part of a typical cable modem network. The cable modem modulates and demodulates computer data for transmission and reception via the cable TV system. The *head-end* is the place where the cable company is connected to the Internet and where it receives television channels. Fibre-optic cable carries the signals most of the way from the head-end to the customer's house, but coaxial cable is used for the last part of the journey. Data over Cable Service Interface Specification (DOCSIS) defines the standards for transferring data using a cable modem system.

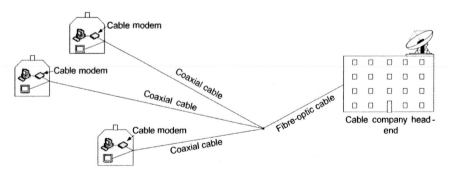

FIGURE 5.8. Cable modem network

5.9 Remote Access to LANs

If a user needs to access a LAN remotely, for example, from a hotel or from home, he or she has the choice of a remote node connection, a remote control connection or connecting via a Web browser.

5.9.1 Remote Node

In remote node working, the remote computer acts as a node or workstation on the LAN. It can access all the resources of the LAN, for example, any attached printers. Remote node is useful if the remote user wants to look inside a file on the LAN's server computer or wants to copy a file from the server to the remote PC. All the data from the LAN travels to the remote computer as if it were a local PC. If the remote user has a high-speed connection, remote node is fine.

5.9.2 Remote Control

On the other hand, if either the connection or the remote PC is slow, then Remote Control is a better method. Here, all the data from the LAN is not transferred to the remote user's PC. Instead the user's PC on the LAN does the processing, but it is under the control of the remote PC. The remote user does not get the data files from the LAN PC, but just sees the results of the processing on the screen of his or her computer. The remote user can capture and save these screens. For the remote user, it is just as if he or she were sitting at the keyboard of the PC on the LAN. The remote user's mouse clicks and keystrokes can control what is happening on the LAN PC. It is only the keystrokes and mouse movement that are sent from the remote user's PC and only screen changes that are sent back to the remote user's PC.

5.9.3 Remote Working via the Web

Alternatively, the remote user—perhaps working from home or perhaps on the road—may use the Internet to connect to the LAN. In this case, the LAN files are made available via the Web using Web server software. The remote PC acts as though it is part of the LAN. For security reasons, the remote user normally connects via a VPN. The VPN gives the remote user a secure tunnel through the Internet from the remote machine to the local machine. While in transit, the files are encrypted and cannot be interfered with by a third party. There are several techniques that can be used to provide a VPN over the Internet, but Secure Sockets Layer/Transport Layer Security (SSL/TLS) is very commonly used. These protocols are described in Chapter 8.

5.10 Routers

As we learnt in Section 4.1.3, when we need to connect two or more networks together, a router is usually necessary. With suitable software, any PC can act as a router. But usually the term *router* refers to a special machine that does not function as a general-purpose computer. The basic components of a specialised router are the same as those of a normal PC. There is a processor, some memory, a system bus and input/output interfaces. But in a dedicated router, unlike in an ordinary PC, there will also be a specialised operating system, which can run the router's configuration files. The configuration files contain rules and instructions to control the way in which data packets flow through the router. The router uses a *routing protocol* to decide on the optimal path for packets. Routing protocols are discussed in more detail in Chapter 6, but here let it suffice to say that the routing protocol is completely different from the protocol that is being routed, such as IP.

Here is a very simple example of a router configuration file. Configuration files can be much more complex than this.

interface Ethernet0/0
ip address 192.7.6.1/24
no shutdown

interface Serial0/0/0
ip address 201.26.12.1/24
no shutdown

router rip
network 192.7.6.0
network 201.26.12.0

This router has two interfaces—one Ethernet interface (Ethernet0/0) and one serial interface (Serial0/0/0). Figure 5.9 shows a simplified rear view of such a router.

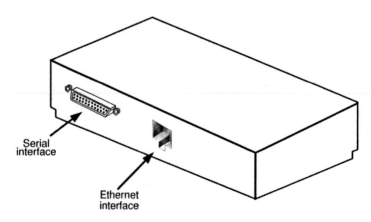

FIGURE 5.9. Simplified rear view of a router

The Ethernet interface is used to connect to a LAN and the serial interface is used to connect to a WAN, perhaps via another device such as a CSU/DSU or a modem. In each of the first two sections of the configuration file, the first line states which interface is being configured. The second line gives the interface an IP address and subnet mask (subnet masks are explained in Section 6.1.6). The third line ('no shutdown') makes the interface active.

The last section of the file indicates that the router is to use the Routing Information Protocol (RIP), which is a routing protocol. The command 'router rip' makes the router exchange *routing tables* with neighbouring routers automatically every few seconds. A router's routing table contains its knowledge about open paths through networks. It is possible for a network administrator to configure static routes, but it is usually more convenient to allow a routing protocol to maintain the routing tables dynamically.

The networks to which the router is attached are listed in the last two lines of the configuration file. These two lines tell the router that these are the networks about which it must inform its neighbouring routers. This configuration file is for a Cisco® router and uses commands from the Cisco Internetwork Operating System® (IOS), but configuration files for other makes of router are fairly similar. The interconnected networks are known as an *internetwork*. The internetwork that is referred to in the sample configuration file given above is illustrated in Fig. 5.10. The other router shown in Fig. 5.10 would also have its own configuration file.

Routers can be used to segment LANs but their main use is in WANs. They work at OSI layer 3, the Network Layer. They examine layer-3 packets such as IP

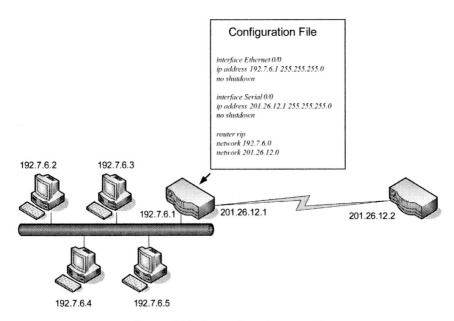

FIGURE 5.10. Routers in an internetwork

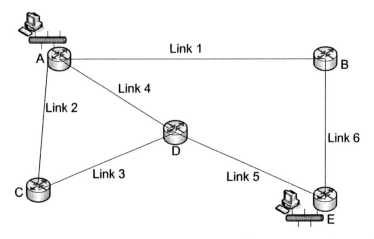

FIGURE 5.11. Internetwork for Table 5.1

datagrams. Since they are able to understand layer-3 addressing, they can make decisions about where to send packets based on network addresses. The central capabilities of a router are an ability to select the best path for a packet and an ability to switch it to the correct interface. The router finds out the best path by consulting its routing table.

A router's routing table contains an entry for at least some of the routers in the system of which it is a part. The entry shows on which link a packet should be transmitted when the final destination is that node. Table 5.1 shows the routing table for Router A in Fig. 5.11. This is a simplified example. The exact format of the routing table would depend on the type of the router and the routing protocol in use. The symbol used in Fig. 5.11 that looks like a drum with arrows on top of it is the standard symbol for a router. This symbol is shown more clearly in Fig. 5.12.

In Table 5.1, there are multiple entries for all nodes (except A) in case of a failure. If either a router or a link goes down, it is important that there are alternative possibilities for routes. For example, imagine that a packet needs to be sent from a PC on the LAN attached to router A to a PC on the LAN attached to router E. The routing table suggests that the packet should be sent out of the router on link 4. However, if this is not possible because either link 4 or router D is down, there

TABLE 5.1. Routing table for router A in Fig. 5.11.

Destination	Link	Alternative link	Alternative link
A	—	—	—
B	1	4	2
C	2	4	1
D	4	2	1
E	4	1	2

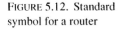
FIGURE 5.12. Standard symbol for a router

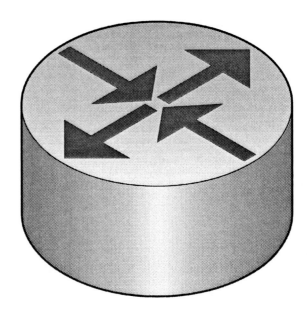

is an alternative route via link 1 (or even link 2, though this would appear to be a more roundabout route to router E).

We cannot tell which routes are really the best ones merely by inspecting Table 5.1. Some routes use more links than others but some of those links may be longer. It is quite possible that a route using four links may turn out to be shorter than one that uses only two links. Some links may have higher data rates than others, which might result in a route consisting of four links being better than one with only two links. As we shall see in Chapter 6, some routing protocols use more sophisticated *metrics* (ways of measuring how good routes are) than others.

5.11 ATM in the WAN

ATM was mentioned in Section 4.2.3 as a LAN technology. We learnt there that ATM is a point-to-point, switch-based and cell-based technology which was designed to be suitable for multimedia traffic. Though ATM never fulfilled its promise as a LAN technology, WAN carriers have used it heavily.

Figure 5.13 shows how ATM can be used for various kinds of traffic. It also shows the three layers of ATM (which roughly cover OSI layers 1 and 2) and the functions that they perform. We can see from the diagram that each ATM cell carries a payload of only 48 bytes. This is rather short for data, but for voice and video the advantage is that an ATM switch causes minimal latency. The switching takes place over virtual circuits.

ATM offers several guaranteed classes of service. Constant bit rate (CBR) provides a virtual, fixed-bandwidth transmission circuit for applications that need a

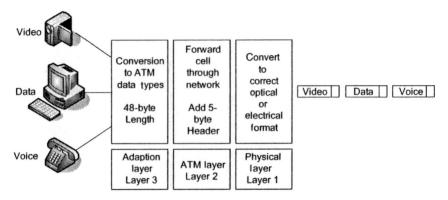

FIGURE 5.13. ATM layers

steady supply of bandwidth. Examples of such applications include voice and full-motion video, where it is important that latency and jitter are kept to a minimum. Variable bit rate (VBR) is for LAN-type traffic, which happens in bursts. VBR includes real-time and non-real-time service classes (VBR-RT & VBR-NRT). Unspecified bit rate (UBR) gives no guarantees as to if or when transmitted data will arrive at the destination. Available bit rate (ABR) gives minimal bandwidth guarantees.

5.12 Ethernet in the WAN

As we saw in Section 4.2.2, Ethernet has been the main type of network for LANs for many years. However, it is also used to provide WAN links. One variant of 10-Gigabit Ethernet, 10GBASE-ER, supports a link length of up to 40 km using single-mode fibre-optic cabling. It can do this because it has some compatibility with the WAN Physical-Layer standard Synchronous Optical NETwork/Synchronous Digital Hierarchy (SONET/SDH) OC-192, which has a data rate of 9.958464 Gbps. (SONET and SDH are very similar standards for synchronous data transmission over fibre-optic networks. SONET is the United States (ANSI) version of the standard and SDH is the international (ITU) version. OC-192 is a standard data rate.)

Carrier Ethernet uses Ethernet technology to provide long-haul links that offer the same performance and availability as standard WAN services (such as the E- and T-series digital leased line services). It supports both data and voice. Carrier Ethernet can scale up and down flexibly through the range of Ethernet data rates according to the need. Its principal attraction is its low cost compared with other communications carrier technologies. With Carrier Ethernet, an organisation's various sites can be connected by Ethernet from end to end, as shown in Fig. 5.14.

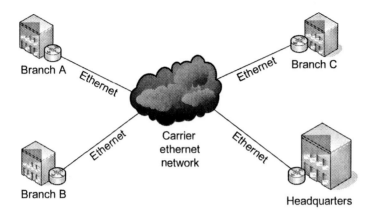

FIGURE 5.14. Carrier Ethernet

5.13 Summary

This chapter has looked at various aspects of WANs. The analogue PSTN can be used for computer communications if nothing better is available. However, businesses usually use other WAN technologies. The packet-switching technology X.25 was the forerunner of the much faster Frame Relay. ISDN is an all-digital, circuit-switched service, which can be used for voice and data of various kinds. Digital leased lines can be used for point-to-point connections. The various forms of DSL offer an 'always-on' broadband service, using the copper lines that were installed for the 'last mile' of the PSTN. Cable modem offers a similar service over a cable TV infrastructure. Three different ways of accessing LANs remotely were described. Routers are important devices that are used to connect networks. ATM, although it has been used in LANs to a limited extent, was expressly designed to carry multimedia information over long distances. Ethernet, though fundamentally a LAN technology, is also used for WANs.

5.14 Questions

1. Explain the difference between DTE and DCE.
2. What does 'CIR' stand for and what is its purpose in Frame-Relay service agreements?
3. What do 'BRI' and 'PRI' stand for? Explain the differences between these two kinds of ISDN.
4. How long would it take to transfer a 250-MB file over an ISDN link of 64 kbps? Is the answer realistic?
5. What does a CSU/DSU do?
6. What is the difference between ADSL and SDSL?
7. Distinguish between the Remote Control and Remote Node methods for remote access to LANs.

8. Using Table 5.1 as a model, construct the routing table for router D in Fig. 5.11.
9. Explain the ATM classes of service.
10. Which WAN service would you recommend for the following applications?
    (a) videoconferencing (i.e., transmitting video and audio back and forth be-
        tween two or more different sites)
    (b) low-speed connection to the Internet
    (c) high-speed connection to the Internet

6
Network Protocols

This chapter deals with network protocols of various kinds, especially transmission control protocol/Internet protocol (TCP/IP) and related protocols. It concentrates heavily on IP and TCP themselves. While some attention is given to version 6 of IP, material on IP version 4 occupies most space in the section about IP. A section on Internet Control Message Protocol (ICMP), which is used on TCP/IP networks to send error messages and informational messages of various kinds, precedes the material on TCP. High-Level Data Link Control (HDLC), a layer-2 protocol that is used in WANs, features next. Multiprotocol label switching, which permits highly efficient routing, is briefly covered. Finally, two different classes of routing protocols, which allow routers to inform each other about networks that they know about without human intervention, are described.

6.1 Internet Protocol

IP was described very briefly in Chapter 3. In this chapter more details of IP will be given. We shall be concentrating on version 4 of IP (IPv4), although some attention is paid to version 6 (IPv6) in Section 6.1.7. A diagram showing the format of the IPv4 datagram header can be found in Appendix A.

6.1.1 IPv4 Addresses

If two computers need to communicate with each other, then there must be some kind of addressing system that allows them to identify and find each other. In Section 4.2.2, we saw that Ethernet addresses are 48 bits long, equally split between bits indicating the manufacturer and a unique identifier. Whereas the MAC addresses used by a layer-2 protocol such as Ethernet are 'flat', IP addresses (layer 3) are hierarchical, consisting of a network part and a host part. The network part of the address is used to identify and locate the network to which a host is connected; the host part identifies and locates the host on that network. Every computer on a TCP/IP network must have an IP address.

An IPv4 address is a 32-bit binary number. For the benefit of humans, it is usually written down as four decimal (denary) numbers separated by full stops (dots), for example 192.168.1.33. This way of expressing IP addresses is called *dotted decimal*. Each of the four parts of the address is called an *octet* because it is eight bits long. As an explanation of why we do not usually write down IP addresses in binary, consider the binary version of 192.168.1.33: 11000000101010000000000100100001. A sequence of bits such as this is difficult for even highly numerate human beings to deal with, though it presents no problems at all to a computer.

When routers forward IP packets from the sending network to the destination network, the packets must include the addresses of both networks. The address of the destination network is needed so that the routers can deliver the packet to the right network. The router that is directly connected to the destination network can use the host part of the IP address to find the host. This hierarchical system somewhat resembles the postal system. For a letter to be delivered, first of all it has to reach the right post office using the name of the town. After that, the post office uses the house number and the name of the street to deliver the letter to its final destination.

Address Classes

Three classes of IP address cater for large, medium-sized and small networks. Class A addresses are for large networks, Class B for medium-sized networks and Class C for small networks. (In addition to these three classes, Class D exists for multicasting, sending the same message to a group of hosts, and Class E exists for research use.) Classes A, B and C are illustrated in Fig. 6.1.

With three octets given over to host addresses, each Class A address makes available over 16 million host addresses. Only the leftmost octet is used for the network portion of the address and the other three octets are for the host portion. The leftmost bit of a Class A address is always 0. The address 127.0.0.1 (*loopback* address or *localhost*) is used for testing IP software. Any address whose leftmost octet is a decimal value between 1 and 126 inclusive is a Class A address.

Class B addresses were intended for medium-sized networks. The first two octets are used for the network part of the address and the last two are for the host part

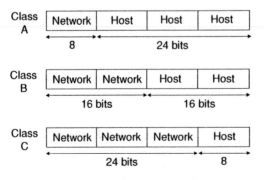

FIGURE 6.1. IP address classes

TABLE 6.1. IP address ranges

Class	Address range (decimal)	Address range (binary)
A	1–126	00000001–01111110
B	128–191	10000000–10111111
C	192–223	11000000–11011111

of the address. The leftmost two bits of the first octet are always 10 in a Class B address. An address whose leftmost octet is a decimal value between 128 and 191 inclusive is a Class B address.

Class C addresses were designed for small networks with no more than 254 hosts. All Class C addresses begin with the three bits 110. An address whose leftmost octet is a decimal value between 192 and 223 inclusive is a Class C address. The first three octets are used for the network part of the address and the last octet is the host part of the address. Table 6.1 shows the ranges of the leftmost octet in address classes A to C.

6.1.2 Reserved Addresses

There are some possible IP host addresses that we cannot use. First of all, we cannot use the network address, which identifies the network itself, as a host address. Please refer to Fig. 6.2. If a computer anywhere outside Network A sends data to a host on Network A, that host will be seen as 194.216.4.0. The individual addresses of the hosts on Network A are used only when the data has reached Network A. Only the router that is directly attached to Network A will know about

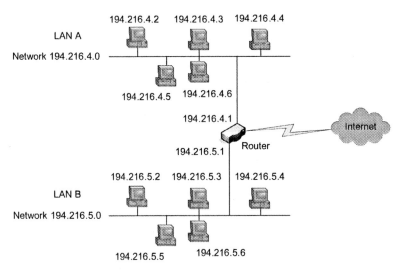

FIGURE 6.2. Network address

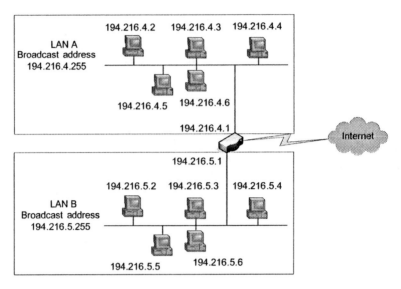

FIGURE 6.3. Broadcast address

these; other routers will not. The situation in LAN B is just the same in this respect. As we can see in Fig. 6.2, LAN B's network address is 194.216.5.0.

Note that the router interface in Network A has an IP Address that belongs to Network A; the interface in Network B has an IP address from Network B. Not shown in Fig. 6.2 is the address of the router's WAN interface, which will be completely different from the addresses on its two Ethernet interfaces.

An example of a Class A network address is 117.0.0.0. 117.0.0.13, for example, is a host on that network. In a Class A address, the first octet is the network portion and the last three octets are the host portion. A Class B example is 183.22.0.0. 183.22.0.254 is an example of a host on that network. In a Class B address, the first and second octets are the network portion and the remaining two octets are the host portion.

Another IP address that we cannot use as a host address is the *broadcast address*. The broadcast address is illustrated in Fig. 6.3. The address 194.216.4.255 will reach all network interfaces belonging to LAN A. The address 194.216.5.255 will reach all network interfaces belonging to LAN B. If data is sent to the broadcast address, it will go to all the hosts on the LAN. When a host sends data to all hosts on a network at once, this is called a *broadcast*. In binary, the host part of a broadcast address is all 1s. For example, the broadcast address for LAN A is 11000010.11011000.00000100.11111111 in binary.

6.1.3 Address Resolution Protocol

For a TCP/IP packet to be able to reach its destination, it needs *both* an IP address and a MAC address. It follows that a network device that wants to send a

TABLE 6.2. ARP table

Internet address	Physical address
192.168.0.1	00-02-4a-8c-6c-00
192.168.0.6	00-06-5b-f1-c6-7e
192.168.0.7	00-02-44-37-60-fa

packet needs both the IP and the MAC address of the destination. Network devices maintain Address Resolution Protocol (ARP) tables, which contain the correspondences between the IP addresses and the MAC addresses of other devices on their LAN. ARP tables are kept in random access memory (RAM). Whenever a network device needs to transmit data, it consults its ARP table. A typical ARP table is shown in Table 6.2.

Once the sending device knows the IP address of the destination, it needs to know the MAC address too. It looks in its ARP table for this. If it finds an entry in the table for the destination IP address, it can look up the destination MAC address from there.

A network device builds its ARP table in two ways. First of all, it has to analyse the traffic on its Ethernet segment to find out whether data that has been sent out is for it. During this process, it writes the IP addresses of datagrams that it sees and their associated MAC addresses to the ARP table. But sometimes a computer wants to send a message to a station whose MAC address is not in its ARP table. In this case, it has to send out an *ARP request*.

The ARP request is a broadcast to all devices in the network. The ARP request packet contains the sender's hardware Ethernet address and its IP address. It also includes the target machine's IP address. All the network devices examine the ARP request packet that has been broadcast to them. If one of these finds that its own IP address is the target address, it will respond directly to the enquiring device with its Ethernet address. The sender now has the target's Ethernet address and can encapsulate its IP datagram inside an Ethernet frame and send it off. The ARP request and response is illustrated in Fig. 6.4.

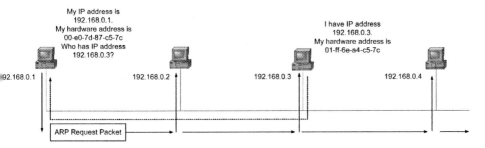

FIGURE 6.4. ARP request and response

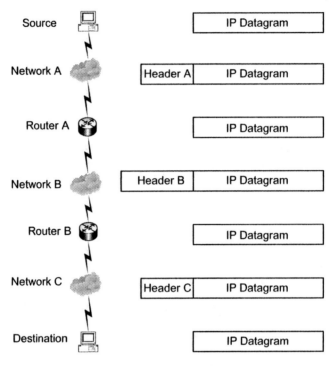

FIGURE 6.5. Stages in the journey of a datagram

6.1.4 Fragmentation

When an IP datagram arrives at a network device in a data link frame, the receiver extracts the datagram and discards the frame header. Each network in an Internet (two or more interconnected networks) may be different at the Data Link Layer. Fig. 6.5 shows what happens to an IP datagram at each stage of its journey across an Internet. Whenever it goes across a particular network, the datagram is encapsulated in the correct type of frame for this network.

Every network has a *maximum transmission unit* (MTU). For example, the standard Ethernet MTU is 1500 bytes and that of 16-Mbps token ring is 17,914 bytes, but the standard MTU for the Internet is only 576 bytes. Therefore, it is quite possible that an IP datagram may be too large for a particular network across which it has to travel. In this case the datagram has to be *fragmented* (divided up into smaller pieces). When a router receives an IP datagram bigger than the MTU of the network that it is going to be sent over, it divides the datagram into fragments. When the datagram reaches the destination, it must be *reassembled* (put back together again). Fragmentation and reassembly are illustrated in Fig. 6.6.

An IP datagram starts its journey on the left-hand side of Fig. 6.6, where it is in a token ring LAN with a large MTU size. Since the next network is an

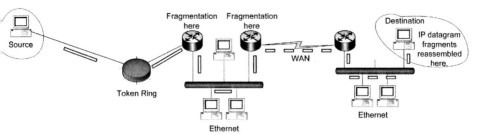

FIGURE 6.6. Fragmentation and reassembly

Ethernet LAN, the router that connects the two LANs together has to fragment the original datagram into smaller pieces. The next router along knows that the data must now be put onto a WAN with an even smaller MTU size than the Ethernet LAN had, so it has to fragment again. The final router does not need to do any fragmentation, as the datagram is now moving to another Ethernet LAN, which has a larger MTU than the WAN network. Finally, the target computer reassembles the fragments using information that was put into their headers when the fragmentation happened.

Path MTU Discovery

Path MTU discovery is an alternative to expecting routers to fragment IP datagrams. The transmitting host finds out the largest datagram that it can send to the destination. It first sends a datagram of the MTU size of the first link in the chain of links that stretches to the destination. There is a flag in an IP header that instructs a router that receives it not to fragment the datagram under any circumstances. This is called the Don't Fragment (DF) flag (please see a figure showing the IPv4 datagram header format in Appendix A). The transmitting host sets the DF flag so that the receiving router does not fragment the large datagram that it has received, even it is necessary to do so for the datagram to be able to travel over the next link in the chain. If the datagram is too large, the router will throw it away and send an ICMP message back to the host that transmitted the datagram (see Section 6.1.8 for further details of ICMP). This message tells the host that fragmentation was needed and what the MTU is for the next link. When the host receives this ICMP message, it can adjust the size of the datagrams that it is sending out accordingly. This procedure may need to be carried out several times before the host finally knows the path MTU. The host can now use the path MTU as the maximum size for the datagrams that it is sending out. This will guarantee that the routers along the path will not need to do any fragmentation. The system is efficient because it cuts down the amount of work that routers have to do. Every now and then the host will send out a large datagram to see if a new route has been found. Path MTU discovery is illustrated in Fig. 6.7.

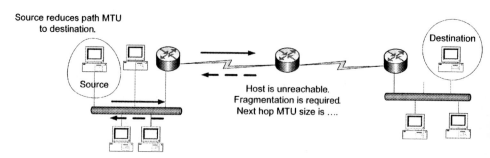

FIGURE 6.7. Path MTU discovery

6.1.5 Ways of Assigning IP Addresses

In addition to its MAC address, any host on an IP network needs an IP address. The ways of giving a host an IP address divide into static and dynamic assignment. In static assignment, the administrator of the network has to enter the host's IP address manually. If the network is small and does not very change very often, static assignment is fine. Some kinds of network device demand static address assignment. For example, server computers need an unchanging address. This is so that other devices know where to find the services that they offer. Routers also need static addresses. A screen for static address assignment in Microsoft® Windows® is shown in Fig. 6.8. In operating systems where no graphical user interface (GUI) is available, commands will be used to assign a static IP address. For example, the command 'ip address 192.168.0.1/24' gives an interface on a router that accepts Cisco-style commands an IP address and subnet mask (see Section 6.1.6 for an explanation of subnet masks).

Alternatively, dynamic assignment can be used. There are three different mechanisms for dynamic address assignment. All of these involve a server that will dole out IP addresses on request. The first two mechanisms, Reverse Address Resolution Protocol (RARP) and the Bootstrap Protocol (BOOTP), are much less commonly used than the Dynamic Host Configuration Protocol (DHCP). Accordingly, we are going to concentrate on DHCP here. When setting up a Windows client PC to use DHCP to get an address, one will use the 'Obtain an address automatically' option instead of the 'Use the following IP address' option shown in Fig. 6.8. When the DHCP server receives a request from an unknown hardware address, it can assign an IP address from a pool of available addresses. These addresses can be recycled when they are released. The DHCP server can also configure other items automatically. For example, it can configure the subnet mask, the default gateway address (the address of the router that the computer will use to access another network by default) and the DNS address (see Section 7.2).

The DHCP system is illustrated in Fig. 6.9. The DHCP server 'leases' IP addresses to a client for a certain time, for example one day. The sequence of events is as follows. The client computer broadcasts a request for the location of a DHCP server. All the local DHCP servers reply to the request by offering an IP address.

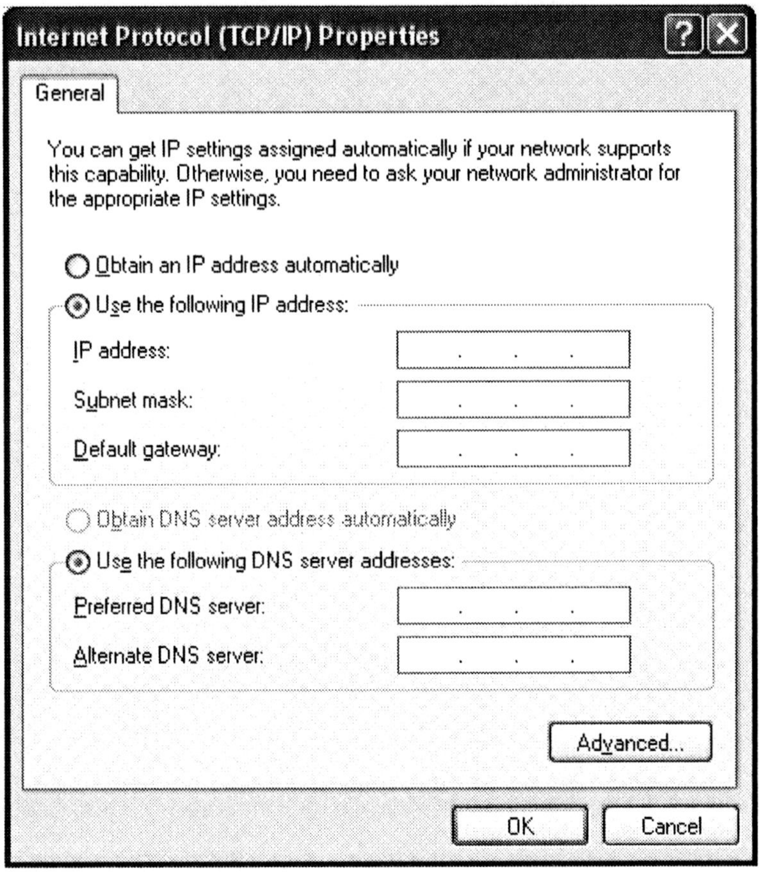

FIGURE 6.8. Assigning a static address

If the client gets more than one offer, it selects the best, for example the one with the longest lease. It sends out a broadcast asking to lease this IP address. The DHCP server that made the best offer responds and all the other servers rescind their offers.

Using an auto-configuration protocol such as DHCP is advantageous in large networks. This avoids having to configure a large number of machines by hand. New machines can be added to the network more easily. There is less chance of making errors (for example, duplicate IP addresses being configured).

6.1.6 Shortage of IP Addresses

It is essential that all devices connected to public networks should have unique IP addresses. As the Internet rapidly grew bigger and bigger, a danger arose that there would be insufficient IP addresses available. The system of address classes

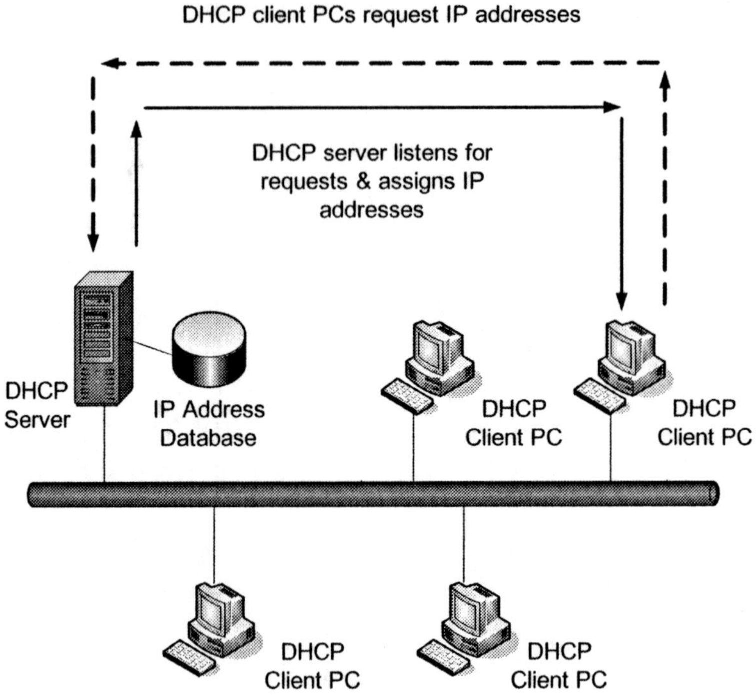
DHCP client PCs request IP addresses
DHCP server listens for requests & assigns IP addresses
DHCP Server
IP Address Database
DHCP Client PC
DHCP Client PC
DHCP Client PC
DHCP Client PC

FIGURE 6.9. DHCP

(see Section 6.1.1) appears to be rather wasteful. For example, certain large organisations took all the Class A addresses long ago, even though they could not actually use all the 16 million plus host addresses that belong to each Class A network. There have been several partial solutions to the shortage of addresses. These include private IP addresses, network address translation (NAT), subnetting, variable-length subnet masks (VLSM) and classless inter-domain routing. The ultimate solution, IPv6, is covered in Section 6.1.7.

Private IP Addresses

Certain ranges of IP addresses are reserved for use as private addresses. These can be used only within a private network and cannot be used on public networks. The ranges are shown in Table 6.3. The same private addresses can be used simultaneously in many different networks all over the world.

Network Address Translation

NAT can be used in conjunction with private IP addresses. The idea behind NAT is that internally a network can use different addresses from its external address, the address seen by devices on the Internet. NAT is usually performed by routers. NAT takes traffic from the internal network and presents it to the Internet as if it were

TABLE 6.3. Private IP address ranges

Class	First address	Last address
A	10.0.0.0	10. 255. 255. 255
B	172.16.0.0	172.31. 255. 255
C	192.168.0.0	192.168.255. 255

coming from only one computer, which has only one IP address. An example of NAT is shown in Fig. 6.10. It can be seen in the figure that one of the interfaces of the router and all the other devices on the internal network have private addresses ranging from 192.168.0.1 to 192.168.0.5. The interface that is connected to the Internet has a completely different (public) address. The NAT router uses a *port mapping table*, so that it knows which device on the internal network is sending or receiving data via the external address at any one time. (Port numbers are explained in Section 6.2.6.)

Another advantage of NAT is that it hides the internal structure of the network from any potential attacker. The attacker is not given an idea of how many hosts there are on the internal network or how these are organised.

Subnetting

Subnetting is another technique that is used to make the most efficient use of IPv4 addresses. As part of the discussion, we will first investigate standard subnet masks. Any Internet device that is using IP needs to find out what IP network a given network device belongs to (including its own network interface). It does this by performing a logical AND operation on its address and subnet mask. Table 6.4

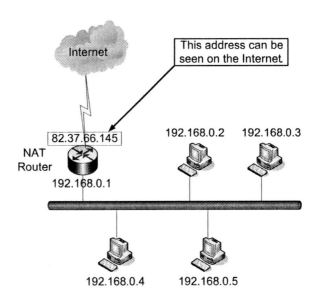

FIGURE 6.10. Network
address translation

TABLE 6.4. Standard subnet masks

Class	Subnet mask	
A	255. 0. 0. 0	(/8)
B	255. 255. 0. 0	(/16)
C	255. 255. 255. 0	(/24)

shows the standard subnet masks for the three address classes with two alternative ways of expressing the masks.

According to Table 6.4, the standard subnet mask for a Class C address is 255.255.255.0 or /8. Such a subnet mask indicates that the first three octets of the address are network bits and the last octet is host bits. The reader can try for himself or herself to relate the masks for Classes A and B to the information on these address classes that is given in Section 6.1.1. In binary, the standard Class C subnet mask is 11111111.11111111.11111111.00000000. Let us now see what happens when a network device needs to know to which network a given Class C address, say 192.168.0.2, belongs. It performs a bitwise logical AND operation between 192.168.0.2 and 255.255.255.0, the standard Class C subnet mask. In binary, this is as follows:

Address:	11000000.	10101000.	00000000.	00000010
Subnet Mask:	11111111.	11111111.	11111111.	00000000
Result:	11000000.	10101000.	00000000.	00000000

The result of the AND-ing operation is that the network device now knows that the device with address 192.168.0.2 belongs to the 192.168.0.0 network. Although a human being can see this at a glance, a machine, having no intuition, has to work it out using a logical operation. Although this may seem to be a clumsy process, a computer can carry out logical operations of this sort extremely fast. When a router receives an IP datagram, it has to find out which network it belongs to by applying the appropriate subnet mask. It can then consult its routing table to find out which network to forward it to.

So far, the reader will probably have received the impression that the system of address classes is inflexible. However, there is an alternative to using the standard subnet masks. It is possible to use custom subnet masks and ultimately to move the boundary between the network and host parts of the address almost at will. Part of the host field of the address can be used as part of the network field. This allows a network to be divided into interior networks (subnets). Externally, only one network address is sufficient to access the site. A great advantage of this system is that it keeps the size of external routing tables to a minimum. An example of a custom subnet mask is given in Fig. 6.11.

In Fig. 6.11, we see that the first host bit of the last octet has been 'borrowed' to become part of the network field. Whereas the standard Class C subnet mask (255.255.255.0) would give no subnets and 254 hosts, a subnet mask

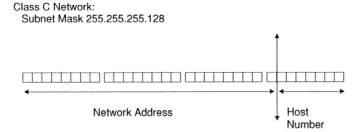

Class C Network:
Subnet Mask 255.255.255.128

Network Address

Host
Number

FIGURE 6.11. Subnetting

of 255.255.255.128 gives two subnets with 126 hosts on each subnet. Fig. 6.12 shows the effect of various custom Class C subnet masks on the number of subnets and hosts that are available. We can see from the figure that as the number of subnets increases, the number of hosts that are possible on each subnet decreases. The node number of a host on a given subnet is added to the subnet address to give the complete IP address for the node. For example, with a subnet mask of 255.255.255.128 and a network address of 193.78.142.128, host 1 on this network would have the IP address 193.78.142.129.

Variable-Length Subnet Masks

Some routing protocols (see Section 6.5 for a discussion of routing protocols) allow VLSM. With VLSM an organisation can use more than one subnet mask inside the same network address space. In effect, VLSM allows the subnetting of a subnet.

Classless Interdomain Routing

Classless interdomain routing (CIDR, pronounced 'cider') gets round the problem of waste of addresses that is posed by the IP address classes. The 'classful' addressing system meant that any organisation that required more than 254 host addresses had to have a class B address, which gave over 65,000 addresses, the majority of which would be completely wasted. The owners of Class A addresses,

	255.255.255.0	0 subnets	254 hosts
	255.255.255.128	2 subnets	126 hosts
	255.255.255.192	4 subnets	62 hosts
	255.255.255.224	8 subnets	30 hosts
	255.255.255.240	16 subnets	14 hosts
	255.255.255.248	32 subnets	6 hosts
	255.255.255.252	64 subnets	2 hosts

FIGURE 6.12. Effect of the subnet mask

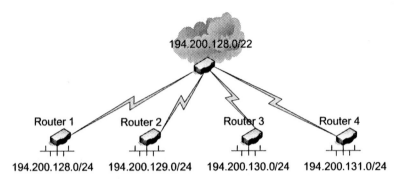

FIGURE 6.13. Route aggregation

with 16 million available host addresses, were even more profligate. CIDR was designed for Internet service providers (ISPs) so that they could put together contiguous blocks of addresses to give efficient addressing schemes. Using CIDR a block of addresses can be represented by just one summary address. This is termed *route summarisation* or *aggregation* or *supernetting*.

For example, if an organisation needed about 1000 addresses, four Class C networks of 250+ hosts each could be supernetted to represent approximately 1000 hosts with a single summarised address. Fig. 6.13 illustrates route aggregation. Four Class C routers with a 24-bit mask are summarised at the ISP router with a 22-bit mask. The Class C addresses are as follows.

Router 1: 194.200.128.0 (binary: 11000010.11001000.10000000.00000000)
Subnet mask: 255.255.255.0 (binary: 11111111.11111111.11111111.00000000)
Router 2: 194.200.129.0 (binary: 11000010.11001000.10000001.00000000)
Subnet mask: 255.255.255.0 (binary: 11111111.11111111.11111111.00000000)
Router 3: 194.200.130.0 (binary: 11000010.11001000.10000010.00000000)
Subnet mask: 255.255.255.0 (binary: 11111111.11111111.11111111.00000000)
Router 4: 194.200.131.0 (binary: 11000010.11001000.10000011.00000000)
Subnet mask: 255.255.255.0 (binary:
11111111.11111111.11111111.00000000)

These are summarised as 194.200.128.0/22, which substantially reduces the size of the ISP router's routing table.

Those routing protocols that support VLSM also support CIDR. Note that the subnet masks in the diagrams (for example, /24) are expressed using the CIDR format rather than the older (255.255.255.0) format.

6.1.7 IP Version 6

IPv6 is the next generation of IP. It is designed to improve upon IPv4 in various ways. It is easier to configure and more secure than IPv4. It is also designed to support large-scale applications, peer-to-peer applications and mobile applications.

Diagrams showing the formats of the IPv6 datagram and the IPv6 base header can be found in Appendix A.

The most obvious advantage of IPv6 is its addressing capacity. IPv6 uses 128-bit network addressing instead of IPv4's 32-bit addressing. 128-bit addressing provides enough addresses to give every person alive today over a million addresses each. There are no address classes in IPv6: the boundary between the network prefix and host suffix can fall anywhere. Dotted decimal notation would be unwieldy, and so 'colon hexadecimal' (colon hex) is used instead to represent the underlying binary. Colon hex consists of groups of 16-bit numbers in hexadecimal separated by colons, for example 6ADC:8564:FFFF:FFFF:0:1380:8E01:FFFF.

The format of the IPv6 header is very different from that of IPv4. The basic IPv6 header (*base header*) is simpler, with fewer fields. Any additional information is stored in optional *extension headers*. This header system is extensible, allowing new features to be added more easily than with IPv4. The header is only as large as it needs to be, which gives greater efficiency. A *flow label* is included in the base header. The flow label is used to forward datagrams along a prearranged path so that demanding applications such as audio and video can get the quality of service that they need.

Address auto-configuration is built into IPv6. It allows a large number of IP hosts to discover the network easily and to get new, globally unique addresses. This means that devices such as mobile phones, small handheld computers and various domestic appliances can be deployed on a 'plug-and-play' basis. There is no need for manual configuration or DHCP servers as with IPv4. Duplicate address detection (DAD) is built in.

Security in IPv6 is better than in IPv4 in that the IP security protocol (IPSec) is mandatory in IPv6 but only optional in IPv4. (IPSec is explained in Section 8.2.1.) IPv6 makes encryption (scrambling data to keep it secure), authentication (finding out if someone or something is who or what he/she/it claims to be) and VPNs easier to implement. It offers access control, confidentiality and data integrity without needing extra firewalls (firewalls are described in Section 8.3).

IPv6 uses multicasts instead of broadcasts for such purposes as router discovery and router solicitation requests. This saves network bandwidth and improves network efficiency. Mobile IP is part of IPv6. It allows mobile computers to keep their network connections while roaming about.

IPv4 and IPv6 need to be able to coexist. The Internet is such that there cannot be a 'big bang', in which all IP-based communications suddenly switch from IPv4 to IPv6. Some parts of the world, for example Far Eastern countries such as China, were much more receptive to IPv6 early on than countries such as the USA. The fact that the USA had the lion's share of IPv4 addresses goes some way towards explaining this.

6.1.8 Internet Control Message Protocol

IP provides so-called 'best-effort delivery'. In other words, if there is a problem in delivering a datagram to the destination, it can be discarded. It is important that the source host knows about such problems, and so ICMP exists to provide an error-reporting mechanism. Various errors can be detected. One problem that might occur is that a packet's Time to Live (TTL) has expired. The TTL limits the number of routers that a datagram is allowed to pass through before it is discarded (see Fig. A.1 in Appendix A). The TTL is set when the source host sends the datagram. It is decremented by every router that it passes through on its journey. If the TTL ever gets down to zero, the datagram is thrown away. Another potential problem is that, for some reason, there is no route to the destination network. It may be impossible to deliver a datagram to the destination host because there was no reply to an ARP request. Errors of these kinds can be reported to the source host using ICMP. The router sends a message encapsulated in an IP datagram back to the source. This message carries information about the problem that has arisen.

As well as error messages, ICMP is also used to transmit informational messages. For example, it is used to discover a replacement router when a router has failed. *Ping*, a very useful utility program for testing reachability, makes use of ICMP echo request and echo reply. We shall now devote some space to an exploration of Ping.

If datagrams can be delivered from IP host A to host B, we can say that A is *reachable* from B. Ping tests reachability in the following way. Ping sends a datagram from B to A (ICMP echo request). Host A echoes this datagram back to B (ICMP echo reply). Here is an example in which a host is pinged from a Microsoft Windows computer. By default there are four pings (and, it is to be hoped, four replies) when using Windows.

ping bs47c
Pinging bs47c.staffs.ac.uk [193.60.1.15] with 32 bytes of data:
Reply from 193.60.1.15: bytes = 32 time < 10 ms TTL = 63
Reply from 193.60.1.15: bytes = 32 time = 1 ms TTL = 63
Reply from 193.60.1.15: bytes = 32 time < 10 ms TTL = 63
Reply from 193.60.1.15: bytes = 32 time < 10 ms TTL = 63
Ping statistics for 193.60.1.15:

 Packets: Sent = 4, Received = 4, Lost = 0 (0% loss)

 Approximate round trip times in milli-seconds:

 Minimum = 0 ms, Maximum = 1 ms, Average = 0 ms

ICMP echo messages are also used by another very useful utility program called *traceroute* (*tracert* in Windows). This can be employed to trace the complete route from host X to host Y. The route is the list of all the routers along the path from X to Y. Host X sends out ICMP echo messages with an increasing TTL. Whenever a router decrements the TTL to 0, it sends back an ICMP message, including its own address as the source address. When the TTL is 1, the echo message only gets as far as the first router. The first router discards the echo message and sends back an ICMP message saying that the TTL was exceeded. When the TTL is 2, the message gets as far as the second router. The TTL is increased by 1 each time host X has another attempt at sending the echo message until a message is received back from the destination host. Here is an example in which a route is traced from a Windows host.

tracert www.google.com
Tracing route to www.google.com [216.239.39.100] over a maximum of 30 hops:

1	8 ms	8 ms	8 ms	10.33.0.1
2	12 ms	6 ms	9 ms	gsr01-du.blueyonder.co.uk [62.31.176.129]
3	10 ms	10 ms	7 ms	172.18.4.37
4	24 ms	33 ms	29 ms	atm7-0-wol-hsd-gsr-linx.cableinet.net [194.117.158.130]
5	27 ms	25 ms	24 ms	e41-isp1-gw1-uk.cableinet.net [194.117.140.9]
6	25 ms	25 ms	27 ms	ibr01-g2-0.linx01.exodus.net [195.66.224.69]
7	26 ms	25 ms	27 ms	212.62.2.209
8	111 ms	10 ms	112 ms	bbr02-p1-2.whkn01.exodus.net [209.185.249.133]
9	104 ms	105 ms	112 ms	bbr01-p3-0.stng02.exodus.net [209.185.9.102]
10	105 ms	104 ms	106 ms	dcr01-g2-0.stng02.exodus.net [216.109.66.1]
11	106 ms	105 ms	111 ms	csr11-ve241.stng02.exodus.net [216.109.66.90]
12	103 ms	105 ms	106 ms	216.109.88.218
13	108 ms	105 ms	105 ms	dcbi1-gige-1-1.google.com [216.239.47.46]
14	106 ms	103 ms	113 ms	www.google.com [216.239.39.100]

6.2 The Transport Layer of TCP/IP

Transport Layer protocols (OSI Layer 4) work on top of IP to transport data from an application running on a source host to the same application running on a destination host. The most important of these protocols is TCP, which will be discussed in some detail. User Datagram Protocol (UDP), the second most important Transport-Layer protocol, will get less attention.

6.2.1 Introduction to Transmission Control Protocol

TCP has to transport data between the source and the destination accurately and reliably. It also has to regulate the flow of data. One of the most important services that it provides is data segmentation, in which the data is chopped up into segments. *Segment* is the special name that is used to refer to a packet of data at the Transport Layer. Other important functions performed by TCP are establishing and maintaining connections between two machines, as well as getting rid of these connections once they are no longer needed. TCP provides flow control using sliding windows. It ensures that the transfer of data is reliable by using sequence numbers and acknowledgements (ACKs). A diagram showing the TCP segment format can be found in Appendix A.

6.2.2 Connection-Oriented and Connectionless Working

The terms connection oriented and connectionless describe different kinds of communication. In connection-oriented working, when devices communicate with each other, they first do *handshaking* to set up a connection from one end to the other. Handshaking is not done only at the Transport Layer. For example, modems also carry out quite a complex handshaking process to negotiate their communications parameters. Duplex communications are essential for connection-oriented working. TCP is a good example of a connection-oriented protocol.

In connectionless working a dedicated end-to-end connection is not set up. Instead, the data is simply sent out in the hope that it will arrive at the destination. There is no checking whether the destination is ready to receive the data, or even whether it still exists. A walkie-talkie radio is an example of connectionless communication. IP and UDP are examples of connectionless network protocols.

6.2.3 Flow Control

If the sending host were allowed to send data segments as quickly as it could, irrespective of all other considerations, the receiving host might not be able to cope with the flood of segments. Data could be lost if the receiver could not deal with the incoming bytes of information quickly enough. It might be forced to discard some of the data because there was not enough room in its buffers. TCP lets the sender and receiver negotiate with each other to find a data rate that is mutually acceptable.

6.2.4 Three-Way Handshake

Before TCP data transfer can start, a connection-oriented session has to be established. The sender initiates a connection and the receiver must accept this. Once the connection has been set up, the two sides keep checking that the data is being received with no errors. TCP uses a three-way handshake to open and close a connection and to synchronise both ends of the connection. During the open connection handshake sequence, beginning sequence numbers are exchanged. If any data subsequently gets lost, the sequence numbers make it possible to recover it. The open connection handshake sequence for two hosts, X and Y, is illustrated in Fig. 6.14. Note how the sequence numbers are incremented after each message is sent.

In Fig. 6.14, we can see that host X first requests synchronisation (SYN). In the second handshake, Y acknowledges the SYN request of X. The final handshake acknowledges that both ends have reached agreement that a connection has been established. Data transfer can now commence.

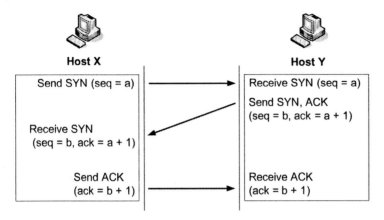

FIGURE 6.14. Three-way handshake

6.2.5 *Windowing*

The receiver needs to get all the data segments in the same order as they were transmitted, undamaged and with no duplicate segments. One way to guarantee this is to let the receiver acknowledge every data byte before the next one is transmitted. This scheme is illustrated in Fig. 6.15.

However, making the sender wait for an ACK before sending every byte is rather inefficient. Therefore, TCP, like most reliable connection-oriented protocols, lets there be more than one unacknowledged data byte in transit at a time. The number of outstanding, unacknowledged bytes is called the *window size*. (The reader is invited to relate this discussion to the discussion of ARQ mechanisms that was presented in Section 2.6.1.)

The ACKs that TCP uses are called 'expectational'. This means that the ACK number refers to the segment that is expected next. (The ACKs that are shown in

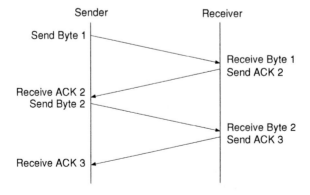

FIGURE 6.15. Simple windowing system

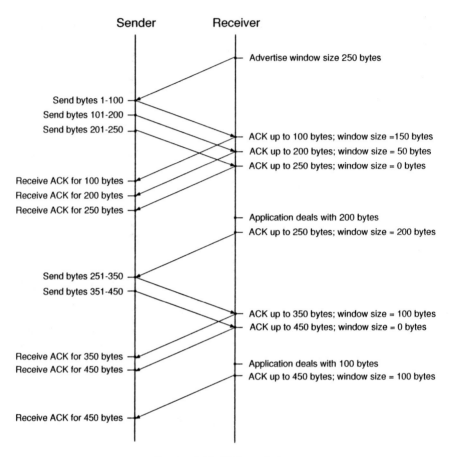

FIGURE 6.16. Sliding window

Fig. 6.15 are of this kind.) If the receiver finds that a segment is missing from a sequence (that is, there is a missing sequence number) the segment is sent again.

The TCP window size is not fixed, but is negotiated dynamically during a session. This windowing system is used for flow control. The sender and receiver may be working at different speeds, so the receiver needs to be able to tell the sender to stop sending any more data if its buffer is full. The receiver sends a *window advertisement*. The advertisement shows how much buffer space it has available in terms of a number of bytes. The sender is allowed to send only as much data as the receiver has space for. As the data is received, the ACKs show a smaller and smaller window. When the window advertisement is 0, the sender must stop sending any more data. When the receiving application deals with some data, it sends an ACK with a new window size. The sender and the receiver have separate window sizes because they are communicating on a full-duplex basis. Fig. 6.16 shows how the TCP sliding window operates. (In practice, the window sizes are likely to be somewhat larger than those shown in the figure.) There is also a congestion-control window, which is of the same size as the receiver's flow-control window most of the time.

6.2.6 Port Numbers

TCP uses *port numbers* to pass data to the upper protocol layers. The port numbers identify different conversations that are on the network simultaneously. For example, the client PC in Fig. 6.17 has two different Web browsers running. Each of the browsers is connected to a different Web server. The TCP software running on the PC is able to sort out which data is for which application by using the port numbers. It can do this because the two applications have set up their connections with different port numbers. Each of the conversations shown in Fig. 6.17 has its own full-duplex TCP connection. The complete address consists of an IP number plus port number. For example, in numerical form the address for the connection to the Web server in the top right-hand corner of Fig. 6.17 is 64.86.203.2:1727. The portion before the colon is the IP address; the portion after the colon is the port number.

Well-known Port Numbers are low port numbers (below 1024) that are always used for standard TCP/IP applications. For example, Telnet (see Section 7.4) uses Port 23, while HTTP uses Port 80, as can be seen in Fig. 6.17. If a well-known port number is not involved, a random port number above 1023 is used. The client PC in Fig. 6.17 is using the originating source port numbers of 1727 and 1743.

6.2.7 User Datagram Protocol

UDP is a connectionless alternative to TCP in the TCP/IP protocol stack. Unlike TCP, it does not give ACKs, does not guarantee delivery and does not do windowing. It is an *unreliable* protocol, whereas TCP is *reliable*. When UDP is in use, any errors that occur or retransmissions that are needed must be dealt with by

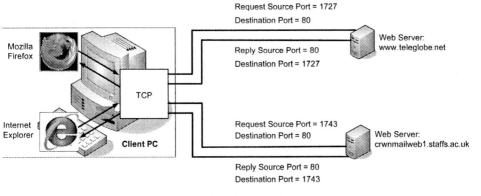

FIGURE 6.17. Port numbers

higher-layer protocols. All UDP does is sends and receives datagrams. The main difference between UDP and IP is that UDP adds port numbers, to indicate to which application the data belongs.

UDP is used wherever there is no need for sequences of segments that must be put together. Among the Application-Layer protocols that use UDP are DHCP, DNS, Trivial File Transfer Protocol (TFTP) and Simple Network Management Protocol (SNMP). UDP is faster than TCP. Whenever communications are time sensitive, UDP is often used. For example, it is used for Internet telephony (see Section 7.7.2), where speed is of the essence.

6.3 High-Level Data Link Control

When data needs to be sent out over a WAN link, it is passed from the Network Layer for delivery. The Data Link Layer *encapsulates* (builds up a frame round) the Network Layer data. Every time that a data frame reaches a router, the router strips off the frame information so that it can read the layer-3 address inside. When the router has found out, after consulting its routing table, where the data packet should be sent next, the data packet is re-encapsulated in the appropriate data link frame for transmission on the next leg of the journey.

As its name would suggest, HDLC is a Data Link Layer protocol. It is used in WANs. HDLC and several other closely related layer-2 protocols use the frame that is shown in Fig. 6.18. The figures above the fields indicate the number of bits that each field occupies.

Every HDLC frame begins and ends with a Flag field. The distinctive bit pattern of this field is always 01111110. There is a possibility that this pattern might appear somewhere in the data field, which would confuse the receiving device. So, the sender always inserts an extra 0 bit after every five 1s in the data field. This is called *bit stuffing* and it ensures that the flag sequence only ever occurs at the beginning and end of a frame. The receiver automatically removes the stuffed bits from the data.

The address field is normally superfluous, as most WAN links are point to point. The control field shows the type of the frame. There are three types of frame. *Unnumbered* frames are for line setup information. *Information* frames carry data. *Supervisory* frames deal with flow control and error control. A sophisticated windowing system, similar to that used by TCP, may be used for flow control. The checksum field (FCS field) actually contains a CRC. The reader might wish to compare the above description of the HDLC frame with those of the Ethernet frames given in Section 4.2.2.

8	8	8	>= 0	16	8
Flag	Address	Control	Data	Checksum	Flag

FIGURE 6.18. HDLC frame

As mentioned above, HDLC is one of a family of closely related Data Link Layer protocols. Link access procedure balanced (LAPB) is used for X.25. Link access procedure for frame mode services (LAPF) is used in Frame Relay. Link access procedure D-channel (LAPD) is used in the ISDN D-channel.

6.4 Multiprotocol Label Switching

IP forwarding, described in the first paragraph of Section 6.3, is a laborious process. It can often work too slowly when routers try to deal with large traffic loads. The idea behind multiprotocol label switching (MPLS) is to supplement standard IP forwarding by adding a *label* to packets. This four-byte label is added to the packets as they enter the MPLS network. The label is inserted into the layer-2 frame between the layer-2 header (Ethernet, for example) and the IP header. Wherever possible, the routers then base their forwarding decisions on the value in the label. This is much simpler and more efficient for routers than having to look through large routing tables. The label acts as an index to the routing table and only needs one lookup (a lookup of the MPLS label) rather than the many more lookups that might be needed when using classical IP forwarding. MPLS can work only with routers that are capable of understanding it, but it has many advantages. It increases speed and reduces delay and jitter. It offers guaranteed quality of service for voice and video. Virtual private LAN service (VPLS) securely connects two or more Ethernet LANs over an MPLS network. To the user it is as if he or she is on a very large Ethernet segment. The details of MPLS are beyond the scope of this book but suffice it to say that it has become very widely used.

6.5 Routing Protocols

An administrator can configure a router by entering routes manually. In a large network where many changes are happening, maintaining the routing tables in this way could be very costly in terms of both time and money. Fortunately, routing protocols exist which can maintain routing tables automatically. Routing protocols let routers share information with each other about open paths through networks of which they have knowledge. It is important not to confuse routing protocols with the protocols that are routed. IP is a good example of a routed protocol. A packet belonging to a routed protocol contains an address that lets it be sent from one network device to another. Examples of routing protocols are Routing Information Protocol (RIP) and Open Shortest Path First (OSPF). Both of these are examples of open-standard protocols but proprietary protocols also exist.

There was a description of routing tables in Section 5.10 and a sample routing table was given in Table 5.1. A routing protocol learns about routes. It finds out what the best routes are and puts these in the routing table. We say that an internetwork has *converged* when all the routers that belong to it possess the same knowledge

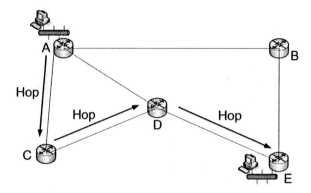

FIGURE 6.19. Router hops

of routes through it. The routers get to a state of convergence as a result of talking to each other and sharing their knowledge.

There are two types of routing protocols: distance vector and link state. A router that is using a *distance-vector* protocol regularly sends copies of its routing table to its neighbours. The name distance vector refers to the method that is used to measure the distance (or *metric*) from one network device to another. A common metric is *hop count*—a measure of the number of hops (links) between one router and another. Hops are illustrated in Fig. 6.19.

The route from router A to E going via routers C and D in Fig. 6.19 is three hops long. (The links from A to B, from B to E and from A to D are also hops, though not labelled as such in the diagram.) The RIP distance-vector protocol uses hop count as its metric. In Fig. 6.20, we see the exchange of routing tables. Router Y sends copies of its routing table to its neighbours, Routers X and Z. Routers X and Z send copies of their routing Tables to their neighbours, which include router Y. The other routers in the internetwork also send their routing tables to

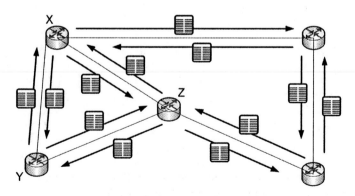

FIGURE 6.20. Distance-vector routing

their neighbours. This happens automatically every few seconds (every 30 s by default in the case of RIP).

Link-state routing protocols work in a manner rather different from distance-vector routing protocols. Each router in an internetwork keeps a map of the topology of the whole internetwork. The router is able to build this map because it broadcasts small packets called link-state advertisements (LSAs) to all the other routers in the internetwork whenever there is a change in the state of a link. It also receives broadcasts of LSAs from the other routers. The LSAs contain information on the status of a link between two routers (for example, the link between router M and router N is up). The router uses the information from the LSAs to build its map of the topology of the internetwork. The router applies an algorithm called shortest path first (SPF) to its database of topological information. This produces a routing table in which the router doing the calculation is the source host.

Link-state routing protocols possess certain advantages over distance-vector protocols. Firstly, routing updates are sent only when there is a change in the topology. Distance-vector protocols send updates on a regular basis, whether or not any changes have happened. Convergence happens faster than with distance-vector routing. On the other hand, link-state protocols work the router's CPU harder and need more memory than distance-vector protocols.

6.6 Summary

This chapter has looked at various network protocols. The IP protocol, which carries all the traffic on the Internet, was described in some detail, particularly Version 4. Version 6 was also mentioned. IP is responsible for moving packets from source to destination across networks. It supplies a connectionless, unreliable service. ICMP, which is used on TCP/IP networks to send error messages and informational messages of various kinds, was covered next. TCP received a lot of attention. It works on top of IP to give a reliable, connection-oriented service. It guarantees end-to-end delivery of packets. It corrects lost, corrupted, out-of-order and delayed packets. HDLC, a layer-2 protocol that is used in WANs, was described. Multiprotocol label switching, which permits highly efficient routing, was briefly covered. Finally, two different classes of routing protocols, distance vector and link state were described. Routing protocols allow routers to inform each other about open paths through internetworks automatically.

6.7 Questions

1. What is 'dotted decimal'?
2. To which IPv4 address class does the address 193.60.1.15 belong?
3. What is the purpose of a 'broadcast address'?
4. What service does IP provide?

5. (a) What are the differences between IP addresses and Data Link Layer addresses?
   (b) Give an example of each kind of address.
   (c) When a message is sent from one computer to another, how is the destination IP address translated to a Data Link Layer address?
6. Describe the structure of IPv4 address classes.
7. Why might an IP datagram need to be *fragmented*?
8. Where are IP fragments reassembled?
9. Explain *path MTU discovery*.
10. What is a *default gateway*?
11. (a) How many subnets does the Class C subnet mask of 255.255.255.224 give?
    (b) How many hosts can there be on each subnet?
12. What is the purpose of the TTL field in the IP datagram structure?
13. What is the *ping* utility program used for?
14. What is the purpose of the *traceroute* (tracert) utility program?
15. What functions does TCP perform?
16. Explain the differences between connection-oriented and connectionless working.
17. Explain the steps in the TCP three-way handshake.
18. What is the purpose of *port numbers*?
19. What is the smallest number of bits that there can be in an HDLC frame?
20. The following sequence of bits is to be sent out over a link in the user data field of the HDLC protocol. Write down what the sequence will be after *bit stuffing* has taken place.
    0111111101010101111101110000001111110101
21. Explain the differences between *distance-vector* and *link-state* routing protocols.

7
Internet Application Layer Protocols

In the previous chapter, we saw how IP packets carry TCP segments or UDP datagrams across networks. Now it is time to look at what happens in the top layer of a TCP/IP-based network, the Application Layer. This chapter starts with an explanation of client-server technology, which underlies most Internet activities. The following applications are examined in turn: the Domain Name System (DNS), the World Wide Web, Remote Access, File Transfer, E-mail, the delivery of streamed content over the Internet and Voice over IP (VoIP). The main protocols for each of these applications are discussed. The chapter ends with brief descriptions of peer-to-peer (P2P) file sharing and instant messaging (IMI).

Note that all the applications described below depend on TCP/IP and the underlying network to deliver the data. If necessary please refer back to Chapter 3 or forward to Section 7.4.1 for a reminder of the encapsulation process.

7.1 Client-Server Applications

Client-server technology is commonly used on networks. Examples of client-server applications are Web browsers, File Transfer Protocol (FTP) and e-mail. Such applications have two components: client and server. Typically, the local machine runs a client application and the remote system supports the corresponding server application. The client requests services and the server provides services in response to the client's requests (Fig. 7.1).

In a client-server application, the following sequence is constantly repeated: client-request, server-response. For example, if a user wishes to access a certain Web page, the Web browser requests a special kind of address called a Uniform Resource Locator (URL) from a remote Web server on behalf of the user (see Section 7.3.2 for further details of URLs). Once the Web server has found the address, it responds to the request. The client can then either request more information from the same Web server or can access another Web page from a different Web server (Fig. 7.2). More details of this process are given in Section 7.3.

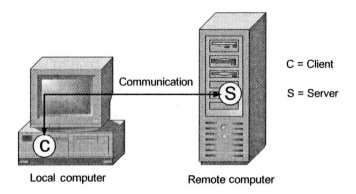

FIGURE 7.1. A client-server application

7.2 Domain Name System

7.2.1 Difficulties with Using Numerical IP Addresses

In the previous chapter, we saw that the Internet depends on IP, which uses a 32-bit numerical address (or 128 bit in the case of IPv6), usually expressed in dotted decimal format. It is possible to download a page from the Internet by specifying a numerical address, as shown in Fig. 7.3 (compare with Fig. 7.2).

FIGURE 7.2. Client-server request–response

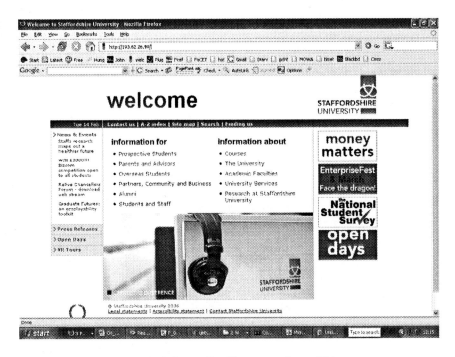

FIGURE 7.3. Using an IP address to retrieve a Web page

However, it is not easy for human beings to remember numerical addresses for Web sites. The *DNS* allows us to use textual names instead of numeric addresses, which is a much more attractive idea.

A *domain* is a group of computers that belong together for some reason. For example, they may be located in the same place or belong to the same type of business. A *domain name* is a string of characters, usually a name or an abbreviation. This string of characters represents the numeric address of an Internet site. In Table 7.1, there is a list (not exhaustive) of generic top-level domains.

Many two-letter country code top-level domains also exist. Examples include the following:

.uk – United Kingdom
.de – Germany (Deutschland)

7.2.2 Domain Name Server

A DNS server is a network device that responds to requests from client machines to translate domain names into numerical IP addresses. The DNS consists of a hierarchy of different levels of DNS servers. The complete system forms a worldwide distributed database of names and their corresponding IP addresses. Any application that uses domain names to represent IP addresses uses the DNS to translate names into numerical IP address. Microsoft® Windows® Active Directory (a

TABLE 7.1. Top-level domains

Domain	For use by
.aero	Air-transport industry
.biz	Businesses
.com	Companies
.coop	Cooperative associations
.edu	US educational institutions
.gov	US government
.info	For anyone
.int	International organisations
.mil	US military
.museum	Museums
.name	For registration by individuals
.net	Networks
.pro	Accountants, lawyers and doctors
.org	Non-commercial organisations

directory service that offers a way of managing the objects that make up network environments) also depends on DNS.

If the local DNS server is able to translate a domain name into its IP address, it does so and returns the result directly to the client. This is illustrated in Fig. 7.4.

If the local DNS server is not able to carry out the translation, it passes the request on to the next higher level DNS server. This server tries to translate the address. If it is able to translate the domain name, it returns the result to the client. If it cannot manage the translation, it sends the request to the next higher level DNS server. This carries on until either the domain name has been translated or the top-level DNS server has been reached. If the top level DNS server cannot find out the answer, then an error is returned.

7.3 World Wide Web and HyperText Transfer Protocol

The World Wide Web is perhaps the best known service offered over the Internet. The Web has grown extremely fast, mainly because it allows very easy access to information.

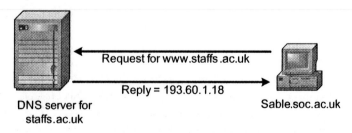

FIGURE 7.4. Direct DNS query

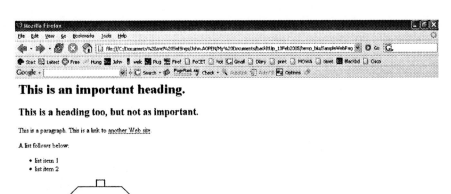

FIGURE 7.5. A typical Web page

7.3.1 HyperText Markup Language

Web pages are usually composed with a markup language called HyperText Markup Language (HTML). HTML causes a Web page to appear on screen in a particular way. It uses *tags* such as <p> and </p> to structure the text into paragraphs, lists, hypertext links and so on. An example of a Web page and the HTML that specifies its content is shown in Figs. 7.5 and 7.6. By comparing Figs. 7.5 and 7.6, note the effects of the various tags. The HTML source text has been kept as simple as possible. Normally, more HTML would be included. Many people compose Web pages using a specialised HTML editor, but others just use a simple text editor.

There are several other varieties of markup language, such as Extensible HTML (XHTML) and Extensible Markup Language (XML), but these will not be discussed here.

7.3.2 Hyperlinks

In the Web page illustrated in Figs. 7.5 and 7.6, there is a hyperlink (http://www.staffs.ac.uk) to another Web site. This kind of address is called a URL. By clicking on such links, users can navigate around the Web very easily; this, indeed, is one of the Web's main attractions. In the URL http://www.staffs.ac.uk, the 'http://' part instructs the browser to use the HyperText Transfer Protocol (HTTP).

```
<h1>This is an important heading.</h1>
<h2>This is a heading too, but not as important.</h2>
<p>This is a paragraph. This is a link to <a
href="http://www.staffs.ac.uk">another Web site</a>.</p>
A list follows below:
<ul>
<li>list item 1</li>

<li>list item 2</li>
</ul>
Here is a picture:
<img src="book2003APicture.gif" width="180" height="162">
```

FIGURE 7.6. HTML source for Web page in Fig. 7.5

The 'www' part is the name of the server that the browser must contact (the name 'www' is often used for the name of a Web server). The 'staffs.ac.uk' part identifies the domain entry of the Web site.

7.3.3 Web Browser

Commonly used Web browsers are Microsoft Internet Explorer, Mozilla Firefox and Opera. Though these differ in their details, quite radically in some respects, they are all based on the same principles. A Web browser (just like the other applications covered in this chapter) is a client-server application and has a client and a server component. A Web browser presents data in the form of Web pages. The pages are multimedia: not just text but also sound, still pictures and moving pictures. The page shown in Fig. 7.5 typifies this.

When the user starts a Web browser, the first thing that usually appears is the 'home' page. The URL of the home page was previously stored in the browser's configuration. To move away from the home page, there is the choice of clicking on a hyperlink or typing a URL in the browser's location bar. The Web browser then examines the protocol that is specified in the URL to find out if it needs to start another program and discovers the target Web server's IP address.

After that, the Transport Layer, Network Layer, Data Link Layer and Physical Layer start off a session with the Web server. The browser (client) sends the HTTP server data containing the directory name of the Web page location (and possibly also a specific file name for a particular page). If the browser does not supply such a name, then the server will use a default location.

The server's response to the browser's request will be to send all of the files specified in the HTML instructions. In the case of the page shown in Figs. 7.5 and 7.6, both a text file and a graphics file will be sent. The browser puts all the files together and displays the page. If the user then clicks on another page that is located on a different server, the whole sequence starts off again.

7.3.4 HyperText Transfer Protocol

Each type of Application Layer program has its own application protocol or protocols. In the case of the World Wide Web, HTTP is the most important protocol, for it is the one that is used to transfer pages of information. In an HTTP transfer, a TCP/IP connection is established between the client and the server. The HTTP GET command is then used to retrieve a file from the server. In HTTP version 1.0, the original version, as soon as the server sents back its response, the TCP/IP connection was broken. This meant that a new TCP/IP connection had to be established for every file sent. However HTTP 1.1, the current version, allows the TCP/IP connection to persist through multiple request–response sequences. This arrangement reduces the overhead of TCP/IP. The HTTP POST command can be used to transfer data from browser to server but this is much less frequently used than GET. (There are also other HTTP commands that will not be mentioned in this text.)

Caching in Web Browsers

The above explanation of Web browsers ignores the fact that caching (pronounced like 'cashing') is usually used. Web browsers tend to reference pages frequently and a cache (temporary disk storage) is used to improve performance. A copy of items can be kept on the local disk for a certain time.

7.4 Remote Access and the Telnet Protocol

Being able to access a computer remotely is a very useful facility. Telnet (terminal emulation) permits logging into an Internet host and then executing commands. The Telnet client is called the local host and the server is called the remote host. The Telnet server software is called a *daemon* (pronounced like 'demon'). The relationship between a client and a server is illustrated in Fig. 7.7.

To connect to a remote machine via Telnet, you must select a connection option. You are prompted for a hostname, a terminal type and possibly a port (see Fig. 7.8).

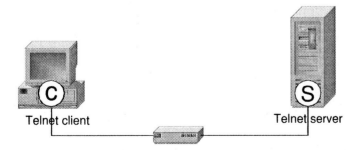

Telnet client

Telnet server

FIGURE 7.7. Telnet client and server

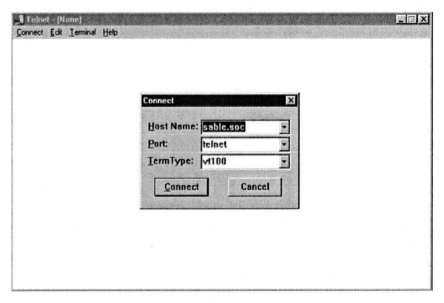

FIGURE 7.8. Telnet options

The hostname is the IP address or DNS name of the remote computer. The terminal type is the type of terminal emulation that your computer is going to use. The port selected will be the telnet port. Fig. 7.9 shows a typical login prompt.

FIGURE 7.9. The Telnet login prompt

When you use Telnet, your computer acts as a dumb terminal with no processing power of its own. The keystrokes that you make are sent to the remote host and all the processing is done on the remote computer.

7.4.1 Encapsulation of Telnet Commands

Telnet is a TCP/IP Application Layer protocol and it depends on TCP/IP to set up a session. (In terms of the OSI 7-layer model, the Telnet commands work at the Application Layer, the formatting is done at the Presentation Layer and transmission is done at the Session Layer.) From the TCP/IP Application Layer, the data is passed to the Transport Layer. At the Transport Layer, it is divided up into segments, a port address is added and a checksum to detect errors is calculated. Next, at the Network Layer, the IP header is added, including the IP addresses of the source and destination. The data is then passed to the Data Link Layer. The packet is encapsulated in a frame that includes the MAC addresses of the source and destination and a frame trailer. (An ARP request may be needed to find out the MAC address of the destination.) The frame now travels over the physical medium (for example, a copper cable) to the next device (for example, a router). The encapsulation process is illustrated in Fig. 7.10.

At the final destination (the remote host computer), the Data Link Layer, Network Layer and Transport Layer put back together the original Telnet commands. The remote host computer carries out the commands and sends the results back to the local client computer. To do this, just the same process of encapsulation as was used to deliver the commands from the Telnet client is employed. The sequence of sending commands and receiving results is repeated until the local client has done whatever work it needed to. At that point, the client terminates the session.

It is important to note that Telnet is not regarded as a secure protocol. Since the user sends his or her password in unencrypted form over the network, it is not hard for an intruder to find out the password. The same is true of FTP (please see the next section for details). Secure Shell (SSH) is a protocol and program that includes all the functionality of Telnet, but is secure.

7.5 File Transfer and the File Transfer Protocol

FTP can be used to transfer files from or to an FTP server (*downloading* or *uploading*). Downloading means transferring files from a remote host (server) to the local host (client). Uploading means moving files from the local client to a remote server. An example of downloading is copying freeware programs from the Internet to install them on a home computer. An example of uploading is moving Web pages that one has prepared on one's home computer to a Web site so as to publish them on the Internet. Being able to move files around easily like this is one of the Internet's main advantages.

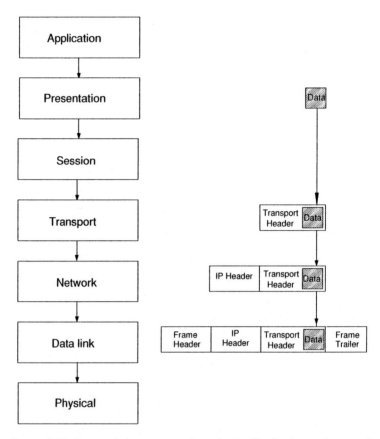

FIGURE 7.10. Encapsulation sequence from the Application Layer downwards

Like Telnet, FTP is a client-server application, which needs server software running on the remote computer that can be accessed by client software running on the local computer (Fig. 7.11).

FTP can be used in various ways. The user has the following choices of interface: command-line, GUI based or Web browser based. The command-line version is

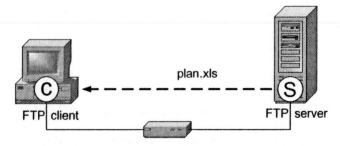

FIGURE 7.11. File transfer between FTP server and client

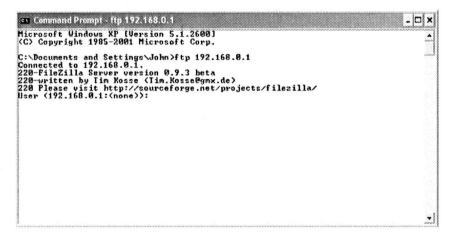

FIGURE 7.12. Invoking FTP from the command prompt

the hardest to use of the three but is very flexible (see Fig. 7.12 for a screenshot of FTP being invoked from the command line). A sample of FTP commands is given in Table 7.2 (the list is not exhaustive).

A typical GUI-based FTP client program is illustrated in Fig. 7.13. The FTP client shown in the figure is FileZilla, a free program, but many others are available.

The third form of interface is a Web browser. Instead of entering 'http:' into the location bar as normally, the user enters 'ftp:' followed by a location (see Fig. 7.14). This instructs the browser to use FTP to download the file, rather than HTTP.

Anonymous FTP

Anonymous FTP services, where the user does not need an account on the remote host, are common on the Internet. The username that is used when logging in anonymously is 'anonymous' and the password is one's e-mail address. When using command-line FTP or a GUI-based client such as FileZilla, it is possible to log into an FTP server on which one has an account using one's own username and password. The user may then both download and upload files if the directory permissions are set to allow this.

TABLE 7.2. Some FTP commands

FTP Command	What it does
open *remote machine*	Opens connection to remote machine
Quit	Ends the FTP session
get *file*	Transfers (i.e., copies) a file from server to client
put *file*	Transfers (i.e., copies) a file from client to server

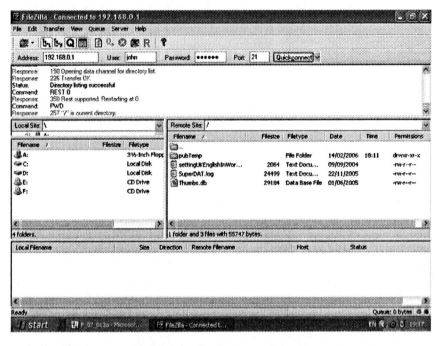

FIGURE 7.13. File transfer with FileZilla

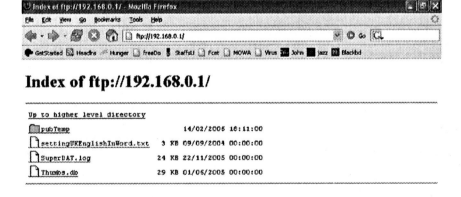

Index of ftp://192.168.0.1/

FIGURE 7.14. Using FTP from a browser

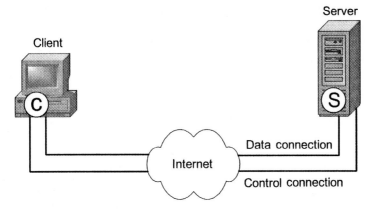

FIGURE 7.15. FTP control and data connections

TCP Control and Data Connections

An FTP session is established in the same way as a Telnet session. Just as with Telnet, the FTP session is maintained until the client terminates it or there is an error.

FTP uses a control connection, a TCP connection to a remote machine, to send commands. A second TCP connection is used for the data. The two connections are illustrated in Fig. 7.15. To avoid confusion between these two connections, different TCP port numbers are used for each.

Using the control connection, it is possible to manipulate directories and files on the server if one has sufficient privilege to do so.

FTP Transfer Modes

Data transfer can be done in ASCII or binary mode. Binary transfer produces an exact copy of the bits, whereas ASCII transfer preserves the formatting of text files. It is important to choose the correct mode, though Web browsers and GUI-based FTP clients are able to choose the appropriate mode automatically.

After file transfer is completed, the data connection terminates automatically. At the end of the session the user logs out. This action closes the command link and ends the session.

7.6 Electronic Mail

Electronic mail (E-mail) allows messages to be sent between computers that are connected together over a network. E-mail has existed in some form for about 30 years. The first e-mail systems simply consisted of using file transfer protocols and there were several disadvantages to such an arrangement. There was no feedback to let the sender know that a message had arrived. It was not possible to send multimedia messages. In modern e-mail systems, these problems have been resolved, as we shall see.

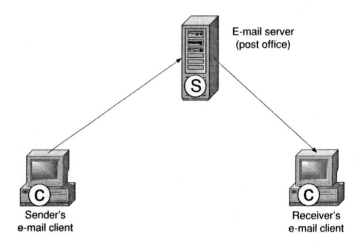

FIGURE 7.16. Sending an e-mail

7.6.1 Transmitting a Message to an E-mail Server

When an e-mail message is sent, two separate processes have to be carried out. First, the e-mail is sent to the receiver's 'post office' (the technical name for the post office is *message transfer agent* (MTA)). Then the e-mail has to be delivered from the post office to the receiver's e-mail client (the technical term for the e-mail client is *user agent* (UA)). These processes are illustrated in Fig. 7.16.

If an e-mail facility is available to you, try doing the following:

1. Start your e-mail client (e.g., Outlook, Eudora).
2. Type in the e-mail address of the person to whom you want to send a message.
3. Enter the subject of the message.
4. Compose the message.

The recipient's e-mail address will look something like this: a_person@ yahoo.co.uk. The address comprises two parts: the name of the recipient and the address of the recipient's post office, separated by an @ sign. The post office address is a DNS name, which stands for the IP address of the recipient's post office server (Fig. 7.17). This part of the address is what will be used to get the message as far as the post office. The recipient's name does not matter to the e-mail system at this stage.

7.6.2 E-mail Standards

The standard protocol for sending electronic mail over the Internet is the Simple Mail Transfer Protocol (SMTP). A different protocol, as we shall see later, is used to retrieve mail from a mailbox.

The format of e-mail messages is structured according to the standard RFC822. The key idea is the distinction between the envelope of the message and what

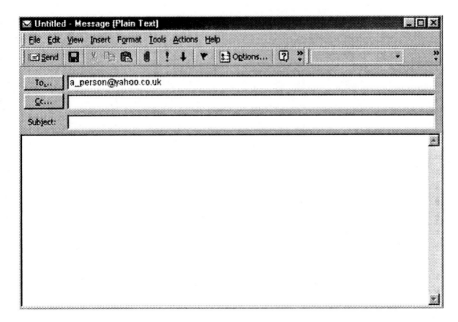

FIGURE 7.17. E-mail address

the envelope contains. The envelope encapsulates the message and contains the necessary information for transporting the message, such as the destination address, the priority of the message and so on. The MTAs use the envelope for routing, just as a postal service does with physical mail. The message content inside the envelope has two parts: the header, which contains control information for the user agents and the envelope where the actual, meaningful message is placed.

A full e-mail message is shown in Fig. 7.18. The user does not normally see as many details as this. The forward path, which follows the SMTP command TO, is used to route the message to the destination. Note that a return path is also specified. This can be used to let the sender know that the message has arrived at the destination, to send any error messages to the sender and for the recipient to send a reply. The maximum message size for SMTP is only 64K. In the example quoted below, ESMTP (Extended SMTP, which allows much longer messages than normal SMTP) is used.

Multipurpose Internet Mail Extensions

E-mail messages are normally ASCII plain text, but sometimes we wish to send an attachment. There is a large variety of potential types of attachment, for example a spreadsheet, a piece of music, a picture or a video. We need a standard way of encoding and decoding attachments that will be used at both ends of the communication. The commonest standard for e-mail attachments is the Multipurpose Internet Mail Extensions (MIME). MIME also allows messages in languages

```
Return-Path: <ssdesk@bighotel.com>
Received: from camcord2-smrly1.igtei.net (camcord2-smrly1.igtei.net
[128.23.173.4]) by mail.staffs.ac.uk (8.9.1/8.9.1) with ESMTP id
VAB18434 for <J.Cowley@staffs.ac.uk>; Sun, 13 May 2004 21:25:08 +0100
BST)
From: ssdesk@bighotel.com
Received: from ae1.travelweb.com (ae1.travel.com [207.248.14.24])by
camcord2-smrly1.gtei.net (Postfix) with ESMTP id 33E18481A for
<J.Cowley@staffs.ac.uk>; Sun, 13 May 2004 20:25:01 +0000 (GMT)
Received: from ae1 (localhost [127.0.0.1]) by ae1.travel.com
(8.9.3+Sun/8.9.3) with SMTP id NAB08430 for <J.Cowley@staffs.ac.uk>;
Sun, 13 May 2004 13:25:04 -0700 (MST)
Date: Sun, 13 May 2004 13:25:04 -0700 (MST)
To: J.Cowley@staffs.ac.uk
Subject: Confirmed Reservation Notification
Content-Type: text/plain
Content-Transfer-Encoding: 7bit
Mime-Version: 1.0
Message-ID: <23137631.989785505049.JavaMail.abc@af1>
```

THANK YOU FOR CHOOSING BIG HOTELS. WE LOOK FORWARD TO YOUR STAY WITH
US.

FIGURE 7.18. Full e-mail message

that have different character sets from English, for example, Arabic and Chinese. The commonest standard method for encoding binary messages is Base64. In the Base64 scheme, groups of 24 bits (3 bytes) are broken up into four 6-bit units. Each of these units is sent over the network as an ASCII character.

Use of DNS for E-mail

The DNS was explained in Section 7.2. It is crucial to the operation of an e-mail system, as a DNS server is needed to translate domain names to IP addresses. When the e-mail client sends a message, it has to ask a DNS server to find out what is the IP address that corresponds to the domain name part of the recipient's address. First, the local DNS server is queried (see Fig. 7.19). If it knows the answer then it will give the e-mail client the IP address of the recipient's post office. The message can then be segmented at the Transport Layer, passed on to the Internet Layer (OSI Network Layer) and encapsulated for transmission. If that server does not know the answer it may have to ask another DNS server. That server may in turn have to query another etc.

Up to this point, the part of the e-mail address with the recipient's name has not been used. It now becomes important. The server checks whether the recipient belongs to the post office (Fig. 7.20). If the recipient does not belong, an error message and the original e-mail message are sent back to the sender. If the recipient does belong to the post office, the server stores the message. The e-mail is now ready for the recipient to download it from the server.

7.6.3 Fetching the E-mail from the Server

Now that the e-mail message has been transferred to the recipient's mailbox, the second stage of the e-mailing process can take place. The recipient can check

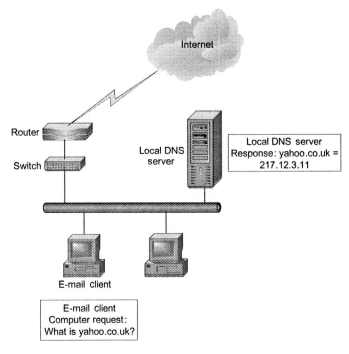

FIGURE 7.19. E-mail client DNS request

whether there is a message in the mailbox, and if so, download it. The recipient's e-mail client asks the server whether there is any mail to download. To do this, it uses the post office address that was entered when the e-mail client was configured (see Fig. 7.21 for an example of an e-mail client configuration screen).

There has to be another DNS query to find the mail server's IP address. When the IP address has been discovered, the request to the mail server is divided into

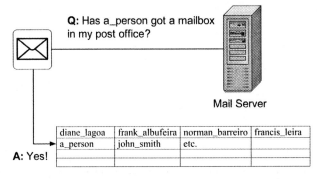

FIGURE 7.20. Mail server checks for a matching mailbox

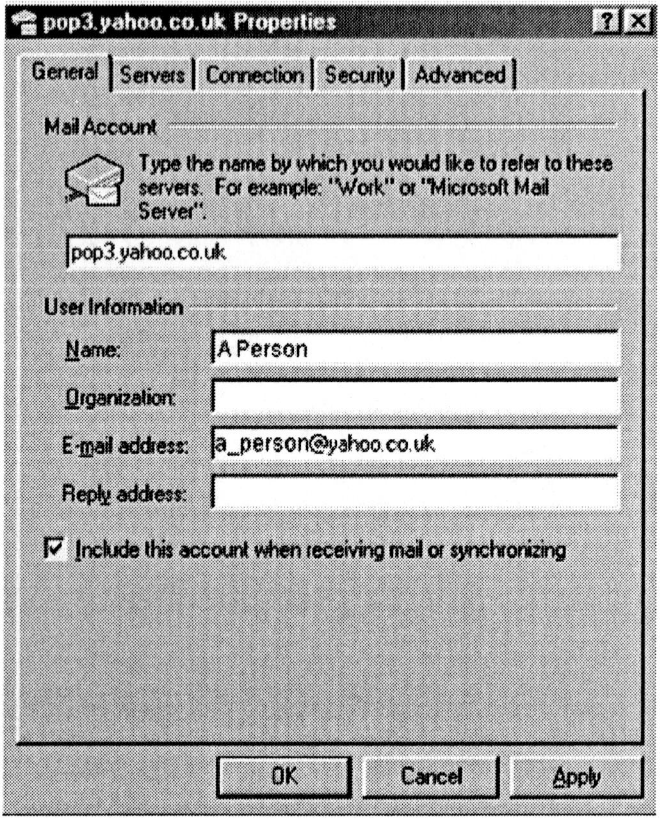

FIGURE 7.21. Configuring an e-mail client

segments at the Transport Layer, put into IP packets at the Internet Layer and finally encapsulated and sent over the Internet to the mail server. At the mail server, the packets comprising the request are put back together again in the correct order and checks for errors are carried out. The mail server then examines the request. If everything about the request is OK, it sends all of the recipient's e-mail messages to him or her. When an e-mail message arrives at the recipient's computer, it can be read. If the recipient replies to a message or forwards it, the whole sequence described above is repeated.

Protocols for Retrieving Mail

Post Office Protocol (*POP*) has been the most frequently used protocol for retrieving mail. POP allows users to connect to a mail server and download messages. POP version 3 (POP3) is the latest version. The description of fetching e-mail from a server given above assumes the use of POP3.

The *Internet Message Access Protocol* (*IMAP*) is gaining popularity. IMAP provides the same service as POP3, but with a number of important improvements. It allows proper secure authentication mechanisms, whereas POP3 is very insecure. IMAP allows multiple mailboxes to be managed at the same time and allows multiple mail commands to be executed concurrently.

7.7 Delivery of Streamed Content Over the Internet

From a technical point of view, delivering audio or video information over the Internet in timely fashion is a challenging problem. TCP/IP was not designed to perform such a feat, yet it has been adapted to do so with remarkable success. In this section, two different kinds of streamed content are considered: streaming audio and VoIP.

7.7.1 Streaming Audio

If an entire file had to be downloaded before it could be played, this might involve a long wait. Streaming audio avoids such a delay. The streaming client is a *media player*, for example, Winamp, RealPlayer or Microsoft Windows Media Player. The server is often a specialised *media server*, which is optimised to perform such a function. Real-time Streaming Protocol (RTSP), described in RFC 2326, is often used to control the delivery of streamed data over a network. It emulates the kind of commands that are used to control a CD or DVD player, for example, Play, Fast-forward, Fast-rewind, Pause and Stop. The interaction of client and server is shown in Fig. 7.22. The user selects a song to play by clicking on its title and

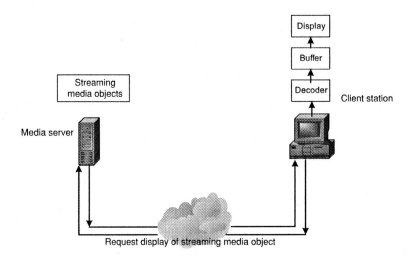

FIGURE 7.22. Interaction of streaming media client and server

a *metafile* is downloaded. The metafile carries just the name of the song and its location, for example 'http://www.luvlymusik.com/audio/trk257k.rm'. The music starts playing even though only part of the file has been downloaded.

The music is usually transmitted by means of the Real-time Transport Protocol (RTP), which is described in RFC 1889. RTP normally runs over UDP and offers neither error correction nor flow control. TCP, a connection-oriented protocol, would be unsuitable for streaming because it is too slow. RTP is designed to support multicasting of real-time data, but it can also be used for unicasting (communicating with a single receiver). RTP provides timestamping and sequence numbers, which allow samples to be played back at the destination in the right order, even if they arrive out of order. Timestamping also facilitates synchronisation of multiple streams, for example, an audio and a video stream that belong to the same Moving Picture Experts Group (MPEG) file. A payload type identifier indicates the format of the payload and the encoding algorithm, for example, MPEG-1 audio layer 3 (MP3). The receiving application can use this identifier to decide how to play the data. RTP can also be used for Internet telephony and video on demand. RTP Control Protocol (RTCP) is a special control protocol, which works together with RTP.

7.7.2 Voice over IP

The terms VoIP and IP Telephony are used to describe the employment of IP networks to carry voice traffic. The aims of VoIP are to save money and to facilitate Unified Communications (UC). Money is saved because circuits can be used more efficiently than when separate circuits are used for voice and data. Management costs are lower because users themselves can manage any moves, additions or changes that happen at a site. UC makes communications more efficient, which should lead to greater customer satisfaction. Without UC, for example, a customer contacting somebody at a company might send an e-mail and then make a call from either a mobile or a fixed-line phone. With UC, the various media are combined and the customer needs to make only one call.

RTP is used over UDP and IP to transport encoded audio information between IP phones. Unfortunately, there are several contending protocol standards for call setup and call management. There is not sufficient space here to consider all of these, so we shall concentrate on just one, Session Initiation Protocol (SIP).

SIP is a TCP/IP Application Layer protocol, which is described in RFC 3261. It is designed to work with other TCP/IP protocols, for example RTP, UDP and IP. SIP can establish, modify and end multimedia sessions, including VoIP calls. SIP is responsible for establishing the IP addresses and port numbers that end systems use for sending/receiving data. The six core SIP methods are shown in Table 7.3.

For VoIP sessions, SIP works as follows. Callers and callees are identified by SIP addresses, which are URLs such as 'sip: 3221@staffs.ac.uk'. A SIP caller first locates a server and then sends a SIP request (an invitation). A SIP request

TABLE 7.3. Core SIP methods

Method	Description
INVITE	Request that a session be created
ACK	Acknowledge that a session has been created
BYE	Request that a session be terminated
CANCEL	Cancel a request that is pending
REGISTER	Register a user's location (URL)
OPTIONS	Query a host to find out its capabilities

may reach the callee directly. Otherwise, it may be redirected or may start off a chain of new SIP requests, which are carried out by proxy servers (intermediary systems involved in call setup). Users are able to register their location with SIP location servers. Interaction between a SIP server and clients is illustrated in Fig. 7.23.

7.8 P2P File Sharing

We first encountered the term *peer-to-peer LAN* in Section 4.1.1. This term is also used to refer to a system that allows people to transfer files over the Internet without a central server. By the end of 2004, 60% of the traffic on the Internet was P2P. P2P is often used for software distribution. Users who have downloaded a file can make it available for others to download from their own computer. Files are broken up into pieces and the pieces can be downloaded from different places at the same time. If one host goes down, the file will still be able to be downloaded from other places. BitTorrent is an example of a P2P system. Unfortunately, P2P has also been used to transfer illegal copies of songs, films and so on. As a result, several P2P networks were shut down.

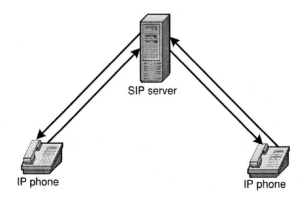

FIGURE 7.23. Interaction between a SIP server and clients

7.9 Instant Messaging

Communication by e-mail is not fast enough in all situations. One problem with e-mail is that when a message is sent out the sender cannot tell whether the addressee is on-line. Thus, the sender cannot tell how soon the message is likely to be received and replied to. IM systems allow users to maintain a list of people with whom they can exchange instant messages. There are several proprietary IM systems. Gaim (http://gaim.sourceforge.net) is free software that supports several systems.

All IM systems work in roughly the same way. IM client software allows a service user to connect to the IM server and log in. The client sends the host computer's IP address and the port number that the client is using to the server. The server creates a file that contains this information as well as a list of *contacts* (or *buddies*). Having created the contact list, the server finds out whether any of our user's contacts are logged in. If it finds any, it sends the details to the IM client. The IM client can now present to the service user a list of all the contacts who are logged in. When the user clicks on the name of any contact that is shown as being on-line, he or she can send a message directly to the contact's computer, on a P2P basis, without the server's being involved.

7.10 Summary

This chapter has looked at the Application Layer of TCP/IP-based networks. The chapter started with an explanation of client-server technology, which underlies most Internet activities. The following applications were examined in turn: the DNS, the World Wide Web, Remote Access, File Transfer, E-mail, the delivery of streamed content over the Internet and VoIP. The main protocols for each of these applications were discussed. The chapter ended with brief descriptions of P2P file sharing and instant messaging.

7.11 Questions

1. (a) Table 7.1 gives some examples of top-level domains. Find out some more examples of such domains by researching on the Internet and/or in books.
   (b) Find out some more examples of two-letter country code top-level domains, in addition to the examples given in Section 7.2.1.
2. (a) What is the difference between Internet names and Internet addresses?
   (b) Give an example of both.
   (c) How are names translated to addresses?
3. Find out what a *URI* is (not mentioned in this text). How does it differ from a *URL*?

4. The HTTP commands GET and POST were mentioned in Section 7.3.4. Find out what other HTTP commands exist and what their purpose is.

5. Look at the explanation of the encapsulation procedure for the Telnet protocol given in Section 7.4.1. Write down the encapsulation steps involved in transferring a file using FTP.

6. FileZilla, a free FTP client program, was mentioned in Section 7.5. Find out about alternative FTP client software.

7. What are the SMTP, POP3 and IMAP for?

8. Research the e-mail RFC 1939 (which describes POP3) and RFC 2060 (which describes IMAP) on the Internet and/or in books. Find out how many commands have the same name in the two standards.

9. Rashid Rasool Khan (email address = Rashid_Rasool@mymail.com) is sending an e-mail message to Yiorgos Zacharias (email address = Yiorgos_Zacharias@amblecote.com). The message has a graphics image attached (car.jpeg). Yiorgos Zacharias uses POP3 to access his email account. The following information is also known:

Rashid Rasool Khan's host address = 128.1.0.5
Rashid Rasool Khan's default gateway address = 128.1.0.254
Rashid Rasool Khan's DNS server address = 128.2.0.254
Rashid Rasool Khan's mail server = mail.mymail.com
Yiorgos Zacharias's host address = 192.4.5.6
Yiorgos Zacharias's default gateway address = 192.4.5.254
Yiorgos Zacharias's e-mail server = mail.amblecote.com
Yiorgos Zacharias's DNS server address = 192.4.6.6
Yiorgos Zacharias's POP3 username = Yiorgos_Zacharias
Yiorgos Zacharias's password = 76!p4ab

DNS table:

mail.mymail.com 128.2.0.100
mail.amblecote.com 192.4.8.100

For this transaction, answer the following:

(a) List and describe in brief all the protocol interactions (packet by packet) between Rashid Rasool Khan's computer and the network when sending the mail message.

(b) List and describe in brief all the protocol interactions (packet by packet) between Yiorgos Zacharias's computer and the network when he downloads the message.

(c) Describe the internal format of the message.

(NB: Remember to include packets from the following protocols: ARP, DNS, IP, TCP, POP3, SMTP and MIME.)

10. Why does the Real-time Transport Protocol (RTP) offer neither error correction nor flow control?

11. Find out what the Common Channel Signalling System No. 7 (SS7) protocol is for.

8
Network Security

Network security is one of the tasks of network management, other aspects of which are dealt with in the next chapter. However, network security is such an important issue that this chapter is devoted to it. The chapter starts with an explanation of several important security concepts and gives some security techniques related to these concepts. The following aspects of network security are examined in turn: Virtual private networks (VPNs); firewalls; intrusion detection and intrusion prevention systems; various kinds of attacks that may be made on networks; viruses, worms and Trojan horses; rootkits; spam e-mail; spyware and physical security. Wireless networks are covered in detail in Chapter 10 but wireless LAN security is given a section in this chapter.

8.1 Authentication, Authorisation, Confidentiality, Non-repudiation and Integrity

Unfortunately, distributed enterprise networks are much easier to attack than the centralised mainframe computers that preceded them. Five important issues in network security are authentication, authorisation, confidentiality, non-repudiation and integrity. We shall now examine these concepts one by one.

8.1.1 Authentication

Authentication (checking that someone or something is who or what he/she/it claims to be) is often done via a password. Unfortunately, passwords are not very secure. They can be guessed or stolen. Many people are unwise in their choice of password, using the word 'password' or the name of a member of their family as their password. Users even write down their passwords on Post-it® notes and stick them round the edge of their computer monitor. It is only necessary to have a single compromised password for a network to be rendered insecure. Certain TCP/IP Application Layer protocols, such as Telnet (a terminal emulation protocol) and

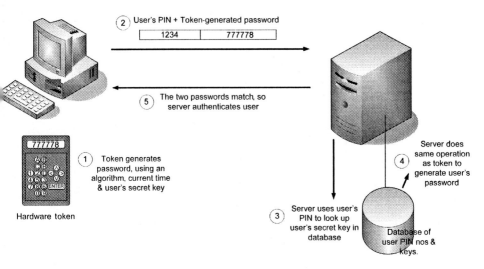

FIGURE 8.1. Time-synchronous authentication

File Transfer Protocol (FTP), send the user's password across the network in the clear. 'Sniffer' programs can be used to capture these passwords easily.

A safer form of authentication is to use an intelligent token that generates a one-time password. This password is transmitted to a secure server that verifies it and allows the user to log in. There are two forms of intelligent token: time synchronous and challenge response. In a time-synchronous system, the token and the server have to be synchronised. A random number is generated roughly once per minute by both the server and the token. To log into a server, a user has to enter a Personal Identification Number (PIN) plus the random number that the token is displaying. This is an example of *two-factor authentication*. Users have to combine something they have (the token) with something they know (their PIN number). The time-synchronous scheme is illustrated in Fig. 8.1. Encryption, referred to in Fig. 8.1, is explained in Section 8.1.3.

In a challenge–response system, users have to supply an encrypted number that is the same as the one that the server has generated. Hardware tokens are in plan view about the same size as a credit card, but are thicker. They can be either hand held or designed to plug into a computer. Software tokens are easier to crack. The challenge–response scheme is illustrated in Fig. 8.2.

Another approach to authentication uses *biometrics*. The idea here is to use something that you *are* for authentication. In other word, you use one of your physical characteristics such as your fingerprint or the pattern of the iris (the coloured part) of the eye. This can be used as one of the factors in a two-factor authentication system. One advantage of a biometric system is that users cannot forget their fingerprint or eye. The same is not true of a password, unfortunately. A disadvantage of biometric systems is that they tend to be rather expensive if deployed in large numbers.

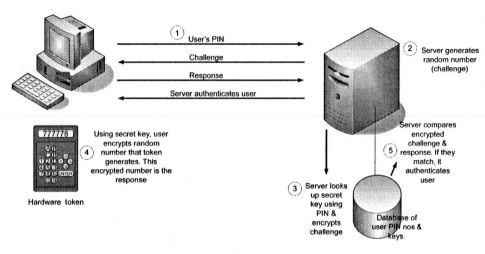

FIGURE 8.2. Challenge–response authentication

8.1.2 Authorisation

Authorisation allows network managers to control who can have access to which network resources. For example, the sales department will be prevented from accessing the payroll records. *Secure single sign-on* lets users log into the network only once and thus get access to all the resources that they are allowed to use. Inevitably, this will involve a rather complex system. Without single sign-on, however, there is a large administrative load. The network manager will have to monitor the security mechanisms used by every piece of software that is being used on the enterprise network. Single sign-on systems can be either workstation based or server based.

Kerberos is an example of a server-based system. It is named after the three-headed dog that guarded the entrance to Hades, according to Ancient Greek mythology. It is free but there are also commercial versions. It is a flexible and extensible system. A full explanation of Kerberos is beyond the scope of this book, but here is a brief sketch. Kerberos has three parts: the client software, the authentication server computer (or security server) and the application server. The authentication server computer keeps the database of encrypted user identities. It is kept in a secure location. The application server (software) usually runs on the same computer as the application to which access is being allowed. Before a user is allowed to access an application, there are exchanges between the client computer and the security server computer and between the client and the application server. The client is given an encrypted *ticket*. This authenticates the client as an authorised user and it is able to get access to authorised applications using the ticket. A very important point about Kerberos is that no passwords are sent over the network. This makes Kerberos very secure. Kerberos is illustrated in Fig. 8.3.

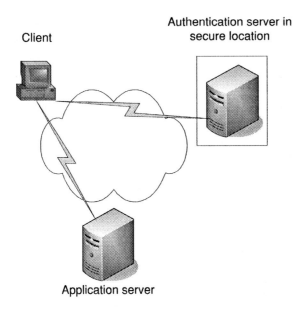

Client

Authentication server in
secure location

Application server

FIGURE 8.3. Kerberos

8.1.3 Confidentiality

Encryption is used to make sure that the information that is sent over a network can be read or altered only by authorised users. Encryption is performed by an encryption algorithm, which scrambles the data so that it cannot be read when it is travelling over the network. The encryption process turns the *plaintext* (the message in its initial form) into the *ciphertext* (the scrambled form of the message). A *key* (a value) is used to encode and decode a message. The encryption/decryption algorithm applies the key to the data.

Secret-key encryption (also known as private-key or symmetrical encryption) uses the same mathematical key for encryption and decryption. Secret-key encryption is illustrated in Fig. 8.4. The main advantage of secret-key encryption is that it is fast.

The key must be kept secret, which poses a problem. For how are we to transport the key from one place to the other, so that both ends can share it? We cannot simply pass it over the insecure network; it must be distributed 'out of band'. For example, we could hand it over face to face on a USB flash drive or send it by motorcycle courier. However, these methods will not work if we want to have secure communications from one side of the world to the other. The Advanced Encryption Standard (AES) is an example of a secret-key algorithm. This algorithm performs permutations and substitutions to transform the plaintext into the ciphertext. Permutations are rearrangements of the data; substitutions replace one piece of data with another.

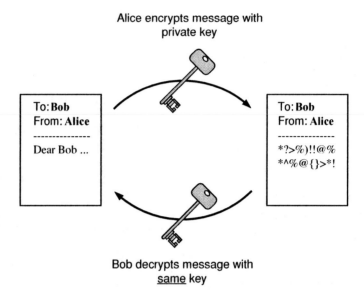

Alice encrypts message with
private key

To: **Bob**
From: **Alice**

Dear Bob ...

To: **Bob**
From: **Alice**
----
*?>%)!!@%
^%@{}>!

Bob decrypts message with
<u>same</u> key

FIGURE 8.4. Secret-key encryption

In *public-key encryption*, different keys are used for encryption and decryption. The encryption key is made available to everybody, whereas the decryption key is kept secret. Public-key encryption is illustrated in Fig. 8.5. For some reason, typical users of encryption systems are always called Alice and Bob. We shall follow that convention in this book. In Fig. 8.5, we see that Alice wants to send a message to Bob. She encrypts the message with Bob's public key, which is freely available to anybody who needs to use it. When Bob receives the message, he decrypts it with his private key, which only he possesses.

Public-key encryption is possible because the private and public keys are mathematically related. However, they are related in such a way that it is computationally infeasible to try to derive the one from the other, especially if long keys are used. It would take so long, even with a supercomputer, that it is just not worth attempting.

Public-key encryption may be supported by a public key infrastructure (PKI). The PKI is the legal, organisational and technical framework that is used to support public-key cryptography. It provides a *Digital Certificate*, which is the user's public key that has been digitally signed. This signing guarantees the identity of the owner of the certificate. Without digital certificates, somebody could compromise the security of the public-key system by making available a false public key for a certain user. A *Certificate Authority* (CA) does the digital signing. There is a hierarchy of CAs. The root CA allows the authentication of individuals, organisations or other CAs. We see an explanation of digital signatures in Fig. 8.6. Alice wants to prove to Bob that the message that she is sending him is really from her. She signs the message with her private key. Bob uses Alice's public key to decrypt Alice's signature.

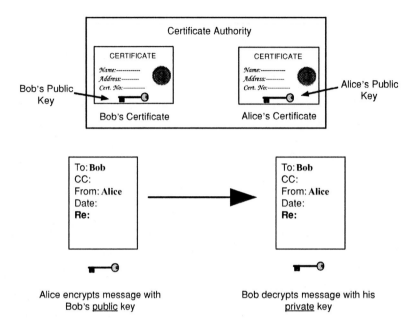

FIGURE 8.5. Public-key encryption

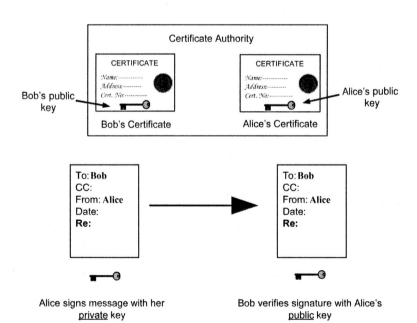

FIGURE 8.6. Digital signature

FIGURE 8.7. SSL padlock

When the Secure Sockets Layer (SSL) protocol is in use for a secure Internet connection, a yellow padlock such as the one shown in Fig. 8.7 appears in the bottom right-hand corner of the Web browser window. (SSL is covered in Section 8.2.2.) If this yellow padlock is visible, then a digital certificate that was signed by a CA somewhere on the Internet was almost certainly used to create the secure connection. The Web browser gets the digital certificate from the Web site and then checks if it is still valid by asking the CA about it. It checks whether the certificate has expired, whether the CA that issued it is genuine and so on. All that the user needs to know about this is whether he or she can see the yellow padlock. If the padlock is there, the connection can be relied on to be secure.

We saw earlier that secret-key encryption is fast. Public-key encryption is slower but more secure than secret-key encryption. A common arrangement is to use public-key encryption to get a message containing an encrypted secret key from one side to the other. Once the secret key has been received, it can be used by both parties in the communication. This is more efficient than using public-key encryption only.

8.1.4 Message Digests

Digital signatures are produced by encrypting a *message digest* with a private key. The message digest is first created by means of a *one-way hash function*. The input to the hash algorithm is a long message. The output is a short value, the hash. The hash is called 'one way' because it is supposed to be as good as impossible for somebody who possesses only the hash value to turn it back into the original message. Only the hash is used for a digital signature, not the complete message. Both the message and the digital signature are transmitted. The receiver applies the same hash function algorithm to the message as the sender used. If the result is the same as the value in the digital signature, the digital signature is considered to be valid. This is a proof that the message has not been tampered with and that the sender is authentic. The use of a message digest is illustrated in Fig. 8.8.

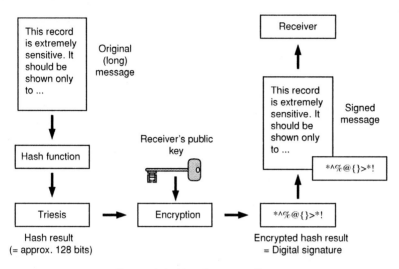

FIGURE 8.8. Use of message digest

8.1.5 Non-repudiation

Non-repudiation means preventing either the sender or the receiver of a message from denying that a message has been sent. One way of providing non-repudiation is to use a trusted third-party system usually called a *notary service*. The message is sent to the receiver via the notary service. A secure hash of the message is calculated. This secure hash is then passed to the notary service, which timestamps the message and keeps a copy of the secure hash. A notary service is illustrated in Fig. 8.9.

8.1.6 Integrity

We also need to be able to prove that the message has not been altered in transit. A digital signature can provide such proof.

8.1.7 Security Policy

A *security policy* is a document that gives rules for access, states how policies are enforced and explains the basic architecture of a security environment. It is usually several pages long and written by a committee. The policy will give guidelines on such items as passwords, encryption, e-mail attachments, firewalls and so on. Templates for writing security policies are available. The IETF has even devised a special language, Security Policy Specification Language (SPSL), for writing security policies. A list of the items that all security policies should cover is given in Table 8.1.

TABLE 8.1. Items that all security policies should cover

Item	Explanation
Identification & Authentication	Employ passwords or other methods to ensure that users are authorised.
Access control	Stop users reaching what they are not permitted to access, unless this is expressly allowed.
Accountability	Make all activity on the network linked to a user identity.
Audit trails	Keep an audit trail to help find out where and when there has been a breach of security.
Object reuse	Make secure any resource that can be accessed by more than one user.
Accuracy	Prevent security breaches happening by accident.
Reliability	Prevent users monopolising resources.
Data exchange	Ensure that all communications are secure.

8.2 Virtual Private Networks

Frame-relay-based VPNs were mentioned in Section 5.4. However, other technologies are also used to provide VPNs. A VPN is a private, secure data network which runs over a public network, for example, the Internet. Only the communicating parties can read the data. The privacy results from security procedures of various kinds. VPNs can be classified into three types. A remote-access VPN lets home workers gain secure access to their company's network. A site-to-site VPN connects remote offices over the Internet. An Extranet VPN allows a business to share some of its data with its partners, its suppliers, its customers and other businesses.

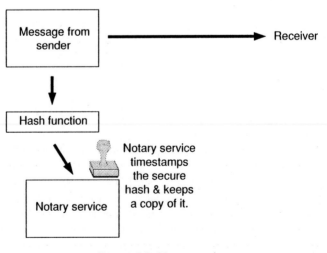

FIGURE 8.9. Notary service

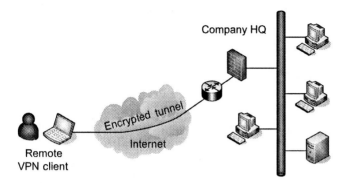

FIGURE 8.10. VPN

Figure 8.10 shows a VPN consisting of a secure, encrypted *tunnel* through the Internet. The tunnelling protocol encapsulates the data inside an additional header. This additional header contains sufficient routing information for the encapsulated packet to get through the Internet. When these packets reach the final point on the Internet, they are then decapsulated and sent on to their ultimate destination.

Non-IP-based VPNs, which use such technologies as leased lines, Frame Relay or ATM, can offer very high levels of Quality of Service (QoS). Obtaining the same levels of QoS is rather difficult over the Internet, but IP-based VPNs can be just as secure and tend to be cheaper. The protocols in use for IP-based VPNs include IP Security (IPSec), MPLS and Secure Sockets Layer (SSL)/Transport Layer Security (TLS). Since MPLS has already been covered in Section 6.4, we shall concentrate here on IPSec and SSL.

8.2.1 IP Security Protocol

IPSec (first mentioned in Section 6.1.7) is a framework of open security standards that was developed by the IETF. It allows data to be transmitted securely over public IP-based networks such as the Internet. IPSec protects IP datagrams that are being sent between network devices such as PCs, routers and firewalls. It provides confidentiality through the use of a standard encryption algorithm such as AES. IPSec provides integrity by means of a standard one-way secure hash algorithm. It also provides authentication via digital certificates.

IPSec can run on a router, a firewall or a VPN client machine depending on the particular situation. It uses two optional IP packet headers. The authentication header (AH) supports authentication and data integrity. The Encapsulating Security Payload (ESP) offers privacy via encryption. ESP can also encapsulate the IP packet, if desired. These two headers can be used either together or separately, depending on the functionality that the application needs. Internet Key Exchange (IKE) looks after transferring encryption keys. IPSec can work in transport mode or tunnel mode. In transport mode, routers use the original IP header and so only layers higher than IP are protected, for example, TCP and UDP. In tunnel mode, the

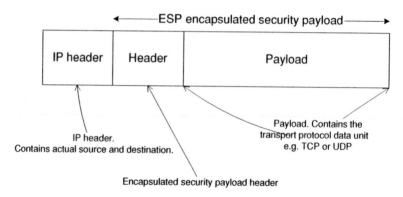

FIGURE 8.11. IPSec transport mode

whole source packet, including the original header, is authenticated and encrypted and is given a new IP header. While the packet is traversing the Internet, both the source and the destination are kept secret. Transport mode is illustrated in Fig. 8.11. Tunnel mode is illustrated in Fig. 8.12.

8.2.2 SSL/TLS-Based VPNs

SSL/TLS-based VPNs are much simpler than IPSec. No special client software is necessary because all standard Web browsers and Web servers support this way of providing a VPN. SSL is a set of Netscape proprietary protocols that run on top of TCP. These provide encryption, authentication and integrity. The application runs above SSL. In OSI terms, SSL is at the Session Layer. Unlike IPSec, SSL encrypts only the Application Layer data. TLS, an IETF open standard, is based on SSL and closely resembles it.

Normally, we access a Web page by specifying the HyperText Transport Protocol (HTTP). So if, for example, we want to reach the IETF, we type into the browser's location bar 'http://www.ietf.org/'. If, on the other hand, we want to use SSL,

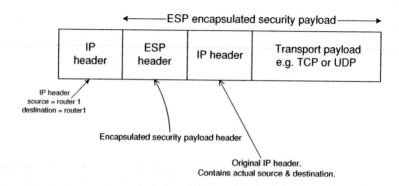

FIGURE 8.12. IPSec tunnel mode

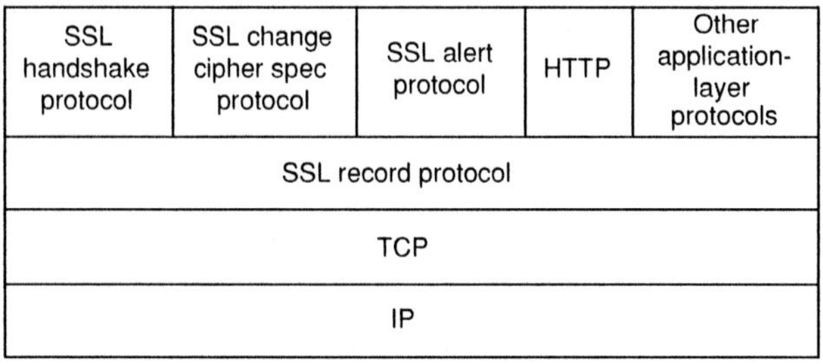

SSL handshake protocol	SSL change cipher spec protocol	SSL alert protocol	HTTP	Other application-layer protocols
SSL record protocol				
TCP				
IP				

FIGURE 8.13. SSL architecture

instead of 'http' we type 'https'. This indicates that the data is going to have to be transferred using SSL (or TLS) via TCP Port 443 (rather than the standard HTTP Port 80).

SSL consists of two layers of protocols. The SSL Record Protocol provides security services for HTTP, among other TCP/IP Application Layer protocols. It divides the application data into blocks of up to 16,384 bytes and encrypts it. Three SSL protocols work at the same level as HTTP: the Handshake Protocol, the Change Cipher Spec Protocol and the Alert Protocol. The SSL architecture is illustrated in Fig. 8.13. The Handshake Protocol negotiates various parameters to be used in the session and authenticates the remote machine. The Change Cipher Spec Protocol and the Alert Protocol are used during the session.

The sequence of events when SSL is in use is as follows. First of all, a TCP connection is set up between the client and the server on Port 443 using the normal three-way handshake. The client then sends a Hello message, which contains information about cipher suites that it knows about. The server responds to this with its own Hello message, which says which cipher suite will be used. The server next gives the client a copy of its certificate, which includes its public encryption key. It then sends a Hello Done message to the client. All exchanges up to this point are in clear text.

Now the client generates a secret session key, which it encrypts with the server's public key, and sends it to the server. This process is called the client key exchange. From this point on everything that is sent is encrypted. The client sends a change cipher spec message to reconfirm which cipher suite (set of ciphers and keys) is going to be used. Each side next sends a Finished message showing that the SSL handshake is complete. A secure, encrypted tunnel has now been set up. This uses the secret key that has been negotiated. TLS works in a similar fashion.

8.3 Firewalls

In cars there is a barrier that stops fire spreading from the engine to the passenger compartment. This barrier is known as a *firewall*. In computer networks, firewalls protect vulnerable devices. They can be positioned between the internal

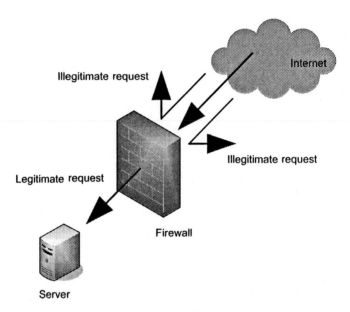

FIGURE 8.14. Firewall

network and the Web server computer or between the Web server computer and the Internet. Firewalls can be set up to control what traffic is permitted to leave the internal network, as well as what comes into it. They can be software only or a software/hardware combination. The capabilities of firewalls vary but all types protect a private network from intruders by controlling access to it. Many firewalls can hide the network addresses of individual users so that nobody from outside can find out what these are (that is, they have a NAT capability). They can log all traffic and can report suspicious events. Many firewalls can perform authentication on users. They may encrypt transmissions. Figure 8.14 shows how a firewall protects a server by refusing unwanted requests but letting through wanted requests.

A port on a firewall is sometimes used to provide a *demilitarised zone* (DMZ). The DMZ contains a device that must be accessible from the Internet. This device is usually a server computer of some kind, for example, a Web, FTP, mail or DNS server. The firewall offers the device or devices in the DMZ limited protection from attack but completely closes off the organisation's internal network from the Internet. A DMZ is illustrated in Fig. 8.15. An attacker could break into the Web server but not into the trusted internal network. The use of the term 'DMZ' in this context derives from its use to describe a military buffer zone such as the one that was established between North and South Korea in 1948.

8.3.1 Packet-Filtering Firewall

The most basic kind of firewall is a packet-filtering firewall. Packet filtering is a task that routers can perform. Certain IP addresses, subnets or Transport Layer

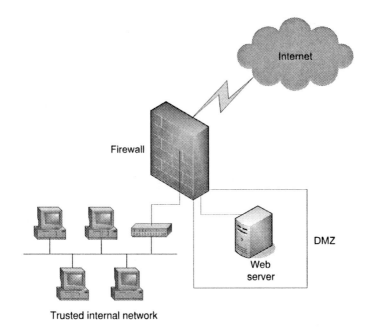

FIGURE 8.15. Demilitarised zone

(TCP or UDP) port numbers can be blocked. This is done with an *access control list*. An access control list disallows all traffic that is not explicitly permitted. Here is an example of a router access control list.

access-list 1 permit 192.168.4.0 0.0.0.255
access-list 1 deny any

The router interface to which this access list is applied will allow all incoming traffic from the 192.168.4.0 network but no other traffic. The group of dotted decimal numbers that follows the IP address looks something like a subnet mask but it actually works in a different way. Called a *wildcard mask*, its bits indicate how the router should check the corresponding address bits. A zero means check; a one means ignore. In binary, the wildcard in the above access list is 00000000.00000000.00000000.11111111. This means that the router will ignore the host part of the address and will check only the bits in the first three octets.

Intruders are able to trick a packet-filtering firewall by *packet spoofing*. This involves constructing a packet with a false sender address. So other procedures in addition to packet filtering are needed. Packet spoofing is illustrated in Fig. 8.16.

8.3.2 Application Proxy Firewall

An application proxy firewall prevents network traffic from passing directly between external and internal networks. A client on one side of the firewall sets up a

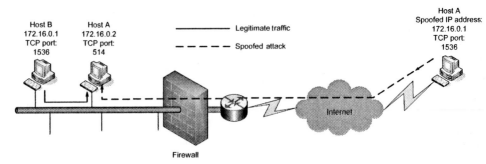

FIGURE 8.16. Packet spoofing

connection with the firewall. The firewall sets up a connection with the server on the other side. It acts on behalf of the client. The client believes that the proxy is the server; the server believes that the proxy is the client. A proxy firewall is shown in Fig. 8.17. Web server A, for example, thinks that it is communicating directly with client 1 and vice versa. In reality, as we can see, the proxy is pretending to be both the server and the client. The proxy can inspect the data and check that a packet that is being sent out to the Web server really is an HTTP packet, as it is supposed to be. It can also check that the person who is sitting at the client machine is allowed to be surfing the Web. An application proxy firewall is so called because it has to be able to understand Application Layer protocols, such as HTTP. The firewall needs a proxy for every protocol that it has to deal with.

8.3.3 Stateful Inspection Firewall

A third kind of firewall, the stateful inspection firewall, looks at the packets that come into it as a packet filtering firewall does. However, it goes further in that it can remember the port numbers that the connections use. When a connection

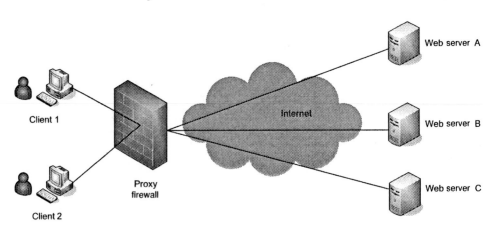

FIGURE 8.17. Proxy firewall

closes, the firewall closes the port that it was using. It can do this because it has in memory a table where it keeps information about the connections. It inspects packets at all communication layers, looking at the bit patterns and comparing these to trusted packets. A stateful inspection firewall is more complex than the other two types. However, the features that are desirable in a firewall will depend on what is required to put the company's security policy into practice.

8.4 Intrusion Detection and Prevention Systems

8.4.1 Intrusion Detection Systems

Intrusion detection systems (IDSs) monitor computer systems for suspected attempts at intrusion. They give an alarm if they detect anything untoward. IDSs can be network based or host based. In a *network-based IDS*, a sensor is placed on each network segment. This monitors all traffic on the segment. A central intrusion detection engine usually receives data from the remote sensors. This can log events and give alarms. Figure 8.18 shows a network-based IDS. As the name suggests, a *host-based IDS* is mounted on a host computer.

Some IDSs look for specific events, while others look for changing patterns. An example of a sequence of events that might trigger an alarm is several failed attempts in a row at logging in. A system such as this depends on having a recently updated database of attack patterns. If an event is not in the database, there will be no alarm. An IDS that looks for changes in patterns is able to detect previously

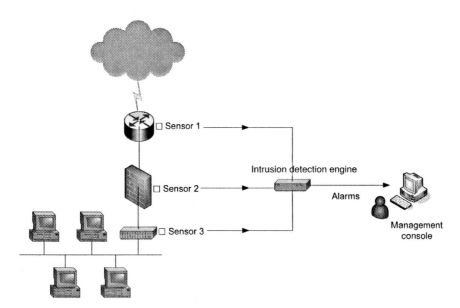

FIGURE 8.18. Network-based IDS

unknown forms of attack. It does not depend on a database of attack signatures. An example of a change of pattern is somebody logging into the network in the early hours of the morning, whereas previously this person has only ever logged in during standard working hours.

8.4.2 Intrusion Prevention Systems

An intrusion prevention system (IPS) is shown in Fig. 8.19. Unlike an intrusion detection system, an intrusion prevention system can respond so fast to an intrusion attempt that it can automatically block it. Rather than simply alert an administrator while the attempt at intrusion continues, the IPS responds automatically to attacks.

IPSs possess several advantages over IDSs. Because IPSs can block intrusion attempts in real time, any network downtime that is due to such attacks is reduced to a minimum. An IPS's active prevention system means that security costs and loss of data are reduced. Unfortunately, IPSs have the disadvantage that they can cause network performance to drop because of the amount of processing that they have to do before network traffic is allowed to pass through them. This is particularly true when an IPS has to deal with encrypted traffic, for example, in a VPN. IPSs alone cannot be relied upon to stop every kind of attack, so they need to be used in combination with other defences.

One problem that bedevils both IDSs and IPSs is that of *false positives*. In other words, the system identifies as suspicious activity that is totally innocent in reality. This defect can be surmounted by using more than one detection method simultaneously. It is particularly important that an IPS gives accurate results, because false positives may block legitimate network activity. If too many of these occurred, they would cause an organisation to lose business and would make users lose faith in the system.

8.5 Denial of Service Attacks

The aim of a Denial of Service (DOS) attack is to stop an Internet server (usually a Web server) functioning. An attacker sends multiple connection requests so as to use up all the memory in the server computer or cripple its processing power. A variation on this theme is the *Distributed Denial of Service* (DDOS) attack. Here the attacker remotely installs a hidden program on several computers (often referred to as *zombies* or *bots*—short for 'robots'), unknown to their owners. The attacker then orchestrates a combined attack from all the machines that he or she has infiltrated. There are several types of DOS and DDOS attack and in the present text, we shall discuss only a few of these.

Security is best regarded as a process rather than a finished product. New ways of exploiting vulnerabilities in software are constantly being devised. When a new exploit comes along, a *patch* (a software update) is issued. This often plugs the hole in the software but sometimes has the unfortunate effect of causing more holes. One way or the other, attackers always find new holes and exploit these sooner or

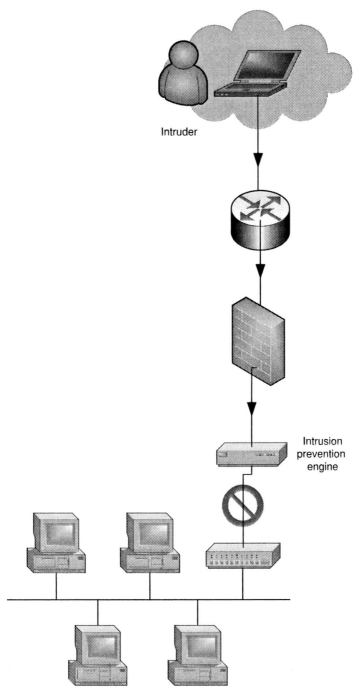

Intruder

Intrusion
prevention
engine

FIGURE 8.19. Intrusion prevention system

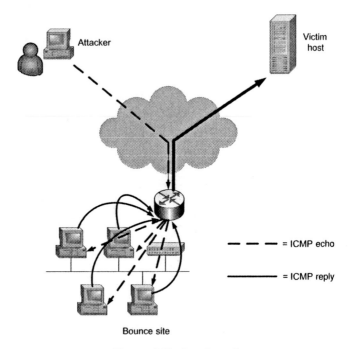

FIGURE 8.20. Smurf attack

later. Some attacks exploit vulnerabilities in operating systems, while others take advantage of vulnerabilities in applications.

8.5.1 Ping of Death/Smurf Attack

The Ping utility program was described in Section 6.1.8. An attacker can abuse it by flooding a server computer with Ping packets. The machine is overwhelmed in trying to respond to a huge number of Pings.

The Smurf attack is a variation on the Ping of Death. The attacker does not send the Pings directly to the target device. Instead, the messages are sent out as a broadcast. The packets are forged and contain the source address of the target computer. Intermediary systems that receive these packets then bombard the target with Pings. A Smurf attack is shown in Fig. 8.20. There might be thousands of Pings sent from the bounce site to the victim host.

8.5.2 SYN Flooding Attack

The three-way handshake, which is used to set up a TCP connection, was described in Section 6.2.4. The reader will recall that when a TCP client connects to another host, the two ends have to synchronise the connection and exchange initial sequence numbers. In a SYN flooding attack, an attacking source host repeatedly sends forged SYN (SYNchronise) packets to the victim host. The sending address that these SYN packets contain does not exist. So when the victim sends a SYN ACK back to this false address, there is never an acknowledgement of the SYN ACK. The result is many half-open TCP connections, which build up to such a degree that the victim host's connection queue gets full. At this point the host stops accepting all connection requests, whether legitimate or not. The attack has now crippled it. It could even run out of memory completely, which would make it crash.

8.5.3 Port Scanning

Port scanning is a method that an attacker can use to find out what TCP or UDP ports are open in a network device or a network. A port scanning tool connects to a series of ports one at a time. The response that the scan elicits shows whether a particular port is in use. The attacker can then focus his or her attack on the ports that have been found to be open and try to exploit any weaknesses to gain access.

8.6 Preventing Infection by Viruses, Worms and Trojan Horses

A *virus* spreads through networks by making copies of itself. In other words, it is self-replicating code that is attached to another file. The normal means of transmission is an e-mail attachment. However, viruses are sometimes spread via removable discs or via download from the Internet. The virus program code runs only if the user opens a file. Once the virus has been activated, it can cause serious damage to the files stored on the computer where it is run. Viruses can carry out such harmful activities as formatting hard disc drives, erasing files, sending out e-mails and making attacks on other computers. The name derives from the way a biological virus attaches itself to a cell.

A *worm* spreads itself through networks automatically, copying itself from computer to computer. It is self-replicating code, but unlike a virus it is not attached to another file. It takes advantage of vulnerabilities in systems. The aim is to infect as many computers as quickly as possible. The payload carried by worms varies. Worms can participate in DOS attacks, can deface Web sites and can delete, corrupt or steal data.

A *Trojan horse* hides itself within an apparently legitimate program. It is so named after the wooden horse in which, according to an Ancient Greek legend, Greek soldiers secreted themselves. When their enemies the Trojans brought the horse into their city, the Greek soldiers got out and opened the city gates to let the rest of their army in. A computer-software Trojan horse pretends to be a useful or interesting piece of software but is actually harmful. The gullible user is tricked into installing it. An example of a Trojan horse is a keystroke logger that captures passwords but appears to be an innocent login screen. A *backdoor* Trojan enables an attacker to gain control of a computer.

All three of these types of program are *malware* (malicious software). Anti-virus software, as long as it is kept up to date, will protect a computer against viruses, worms and Trojan horses. Common sense on the part of the user is also necessary, however. For example, it is unwise to open e-mail attachments unless one is sure that they contain nothing harmful.

8.7 Rootkits

A rootkit is a special form of remote-access Trojan horse. An intruder can use the software tools that a rootkit contains to gain complete control of a remote computer. The owner of the computer remains unaware that this has happened. *Root* is the system administrator in UNIX and UNIX-like operating systems such as Linux. A rootkit is so named because it allows the attacker to become the system administrator of the computer that he or she has infiltrated.

Software for detecting rootkits is available. This looks for hidden additions to files and changes made to the Windows registry (the database of binary files that contains system configuration information on Microsoft Windows computers). Unfortunately, the writers of rootkits are constantly refining their products to try to stay one step ahead of the defences against them.

8.8 Spam E-mail

Spam is unsolicited e-mail, much of which is caused by worms and viruses. One weapon that can be used against it is filtering. Filtering software examines the e-mail that comes into an organisation. It applies rules to the e-mail and tries to work out which e-mail is legitimate and which is not. It then filters out the e-mail that it has decided is spam. This filtering may be carried out at the company mail server. Alternatively, an outside security service can be used to filter the mail before it even reaches the company network.

One kind of filter is a simple blacklist of names or IP addresses of known sources of spam. Another type of filter looks for keywords such as 'Viagra' that often appear in spam e-mail. In *adaptive* (or *Bayesian*) *filtering*, the filter categorises the words that appear in a user's e-mail as positive, negative or neutral. Positive words are those that are normally found in the user's legitimate e-mail. Neutral words are neither associated with the user nor with spam. Negative words are those likely to be found in spam. Unlike the first two methods, adaptive filtering adapts to changes in the nature of the user's e-mail over time. This makes it more effective than simpler types of filtering.

A rather different form of defence against spam is *challenge–response*. This involves a challenge being sent to a new sender of e-mail to confirm that he or she is bona fide. Once the new sender has done this, he or she is put on a *whitelist* of legitimate sources of e-mail. However, if too many users of e-mail in the world were to start using a challenge–response system, the number of messages might overwhelm the system. An alternative strategy is to levy a small charge for sending an e-mail. The intended effect of this would be to make it too expensive to send spam.

Checking that the source IP address of an e-mail is not forged is another defence against spam. What makes this an effective measure is that spammers (those who produce spam) like to forge the 'from' address in their e-mail. This is done because it makes it difficult to find out who sent the spam. Filters can also be hoodwinked by this means. SMTP is also easily fooled.

Another measure that can be used against spam is signing legitimate e-mail with a digital signature. This also proves the integrity of the message. Sender and recipient both know that messages have not been tampered with en route.

8.9 Spyware

Spyware is software that gathers data about the way in which a computer is used. The program is installed without the user's knowledge and transmits over the Internet the information that it obtains. An example of relatively innocuous spyware is a record of visits to Web sites that is gathered for marketing purposes. An example of a rather more serious kind of spyware is that which captures personal information like credit card numbers. Anti-spyware software is available. Some anti-spyware programs prevent spyware being installed in the first place. Other programs simply scan for and remove it. Like anti-virus software, anti-spyware software needs to be updated on a regular basis to maintain its effectiveness.

8.10 Physical Security

The most basic kind of DOS attack would be if an intruder were able to enter a server room and interfere with a power cable or network cable. Server computers must be locked safely away. Preferably, an electronic key card plus a biometric system will be used instead of just a combination lock. Routers and switches too should be physically secured. Well-placed security cameras can help to deter theft and vandalism.

All equipment should be protected from environmental damage caused by floods, heat and earthquakes. Computers should be positioned away from devices that produce electromagnetic interference. Data should be protected from harm by the use of a reliable backup/archiving system. RAID systems can help to prevent data loss. Fault tolerant systems should be used where necessary.

The power to all vital network devices should be protected by an *uninterruptible power supply* (UPS). This contains a battery which will provide power for some time after the mains supply has been cut off. An UPS will also condition the electricity supply to the computers and will protect against damaging power surges.

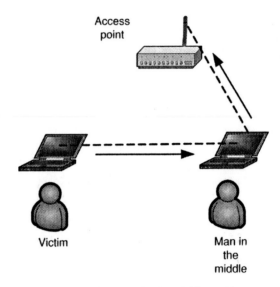

FIGURE 8.21. Man-in-the-middle attack

8.11 Wireless LAN Security

Wireless LANs were first mentioned in Chapter 4 and are described in more detail in Chapter 10. Securing such networks is especially problematic. Since wireless transmissions are not confined inside a cable, it is very easy for an eavesdropper to listen in to them. The eavesdropper may even perpetrate a man-in-the-middle attack, in which the user's messages can be modified without his or her realising this. The man-in-the-middle attack is not limited to wireless networks only, but these networks are particularly vulnerable to such attacks. Figure 8.21 shows a man-in-the-middle attack on a WLAN. The attacker, who could be sitting in the company's car park or a nearby building, is impersonating a legitimate access point (AP). All communication between the victim client and the network is going via the attacker, who is able to read and modify the messages at will.

The first security protocol that was used with WLANs was *Wired Equivalent Privacy* (WEP). The intention was that WEP would offer the same level of privacy over a WLAN as could be expected with a wired network. Unfortunately, WEP used 40-bit static encryption keys that were too easy to break. WEP was replaced by *Wi-Fi Protected Access* (WPA). WPA uses a different key for every packet of data that is transmitted. It also checks for integrity and offers authentication of clients. WPA2, the second version of WPA, uses AES encryption and is part of IEEE 802.11i, the official WLAN security standard which was agreed after WPA2. 802.11i uses the *Extensible Authentication Protocol* (EAP), which offers several different types of authentication. One of these types of authentication technology is EAP-TLS, which is PKI based. Also involved in 802.11i WLAN security is the 802.1x standard, which offers port-based network access control. In 802.1x,

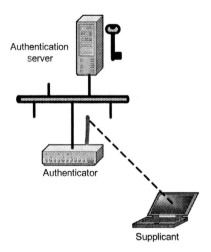

Authentication
server

Authenticator

Supplicant

FIGURE 8.22. IEEE 802.1x authentication

authentication is granted when a *supplicant* (usually a laptop computer or PDA) asks an *authenticator* (an AP) if it can be authenticated. The *authentication server* is the component that actually gives permission, though usually the AP performs this function as well as that of the authenticator. The components of IEEE 802.1x authentication are illustrated in Fig. 8.22.

8.11.1 Securing WLANs

A WLAN AP has a default password; it is not a good idea to use this. The AP is usually able to restrict access to particular MAC addresses, which is a very helpful security feature. There is often a built-in DHCP server, which can supply all clients, including any intruder, with an IP address. The DHCP server should be turned off. If a choice of security protocols is available, the best one should be used. Even WEP is better than nothing. By default, an AP broadcasts its service set identifier (SSID), which gives the network a name. SSID broadcasts should normally be turned off. There needs to be a security policy that defines the applications and protocols that are allowed to be used on the WLAN. Users should not be allowed to connect their own devices. It is a good idea to scan for open APs using the same free software that attackers use. The default access channel is usually 1, 6 or 11 and it is wise to change to a different channel. The AP should be positioned so that its signals have difficulty reaching outside the building. The middle of an office might be a better spot for the AP than an outside wall. The AP's management interface should be kept inaccessible from the WLAN. Finally, it is possible to protect a WLAN well by pretending that it is on the Internet. A firewall and a VPN can be used for maximum security.

8.12 Summary

This chapter has looked at various aspects of network security, which is an extremely important issue in today's networks. The chapter started with an explanation of several important security concepts and gave some security techniques related to these concepts. Further, the following aspects of network security were covered: VPNs; firewalls; intrusion detection and intrusion prevention systems; various kinds of attacks that may be made on networks; viruses, worms and Trojan horses; rootkits; spam e-mail; spyware; physical security and security of wireless networks.

8.13 Questions

1. When AES was devised, a competition was held to find the best encryption algorithm. Find out what criteria were used to select the winning algorithm, Rijndael. (This information is not included in this book.)
2. Why was public-key encryption developed?
3. If SSL/TLS is in use, how confident can a customer using a credit card to pay for goods from a Web site be that the transaction is secure?
4. Explain how a digital signature is produced.
5. Find two different security policy templates on the Internet and compare them. Relate their features to the list given in Table 8.1.
6. Explain the difference between the IPSec transport and tunnel modes.
7. What are the advantages of SSL/TLS-based VPNs over IPSec-based VPNs?
8. Draw a labelled diagram illustrating the exchanges that take place between client and server during the setting up of a secure, encrypted SSL tunnel.
9. The following is a router access control list:

   access-list 1 permit 172.16.0.0 0.0.255.255
   access-list 1 deny any

   What does it mean?
10. Explain how an FTP application proxy firewall works.
11. How do intrusion prevention systems differ from intrusion detection systems?
12. What is a *DDOS* attack?
13. What is a *rootkit*?
14. What is a *man-in-the-middle* attack?
15. What can be done to secure wireless LANs?

9
Network Management

As networks become more and more complex, they can become more and more difficult to maintain. The users of a network tend to rely on it heavily and will suffer if it is not running efficiently or if certain applications are unavailable when needed. So the network manager must manage the network proactively, using all the management facilities at his or her disposal.

This chapter begins with a description of the network management functional areas of the ISO network management model, which cover configuration management, fault management, performance management, accounting management and security management. Some hardware and software tools that are used for network management are then discussed. Next, some ways of troubleshooting networks are mentioned. The important Simple Network Management Protocol (SNMP), a TCP/IP Application Layer protocol that makes it easy for management information to be exchanged between network devices, is described. So is the equally important variant of SNMP, remote monitor (RMON). In the next section, the value of good network documentation is stressed. The chapter ends with a short section on LAN server administration.

9.1 ISO Network Management Model

One major goal of network management is to keep the number of problems in the network to a minimum. The other major goals are to prevent those problems that do occur causing too much inconvenience and to stop any damage spreading. ISO provides five network management functional areas to help achieve these goals. These functional areas are configuration management, fault management, performance management, accounting management and security management. We shall now examine each of the first four of these in turn. Security was dealt with in the previous chapter.

9.1.1 Configuration Management

Configuration management is concerned with monitoring and controlling normal operations in a network. When doing configuration management, network administrators attempt to understand and control how the network is configured. The administrators need to know that the components of the network exist and what their names and addresses are, as well as routing details. They need to know what the relationships between these components are and what their operational characteristics are. In order to obtain such knowledge, network managers have to collect configuration data.

9.1.2 Fault Management

Fault management is concerned with abnormal network behaviour. Fault conditions must be detected, logged, isolated and dealt with. There are three main areas of fault management: error detection, error diagnosis and error recovery. There are several ways in which errors may be detected. Ordinary users of the network may discover faults during the normal course of operations. Alternatively, special reliability tests that are carried out by network administrators may reveal faults. Error diagnosis is performed by analysing logs and running diagnostic programs. There are various ways of carrying out error recovery. The most drastic form of recovery consists of replacing faulty items of hardware or software, but fortunately it is not always necessary to go as far as that.

9.1.3 Performance Management

Performance management is concerned with the performance of various components of the network. It analyses and controls network performance. Throughput, utilisation and error rates of various components of the network are measured, analysed and controlled. The aim is to make the network perform optimally. SNMP plays an important part in performance management. SNMP is described in Section 9.4.

Establishing Baselines

So as to be able to carry out performance management, the network manager needs first to establish baselines for the various measures of performance. A baseline sets the acceptable level of performance of the network. Without a baseline, it will not be possible to tell whether performance is improving or declining. And as the network is expanded or updated, the baseline itself will need to be updated. Baselining involves measuring and recording how a network operates over a certain period of time. It can be used to find out how the network is performing currently and what the future needs are.

When performing a baseline study, the manager has to get information on all the network devices, including workstations, server computers, hubs, switches

TABLE 9.1. Hardware device record sheet

Hardware device documentation		
Type of equipment:		
Serial no.:		
Date purchased:		
Warranty expiration data:	Vendor:	Phone:
Service contract:	Vendor:	Phone:
Problems:		
Date:	Problem:	Solution:

and routers. Model numbers, serial numbers, NIC and IP addresses, protocols and network applications in use will all need to be recorded. A simple record sheet such as the one shown in Table 9.1 may be utilised, but alternatively software can be used to record the data. The manager will also need to record such figures as the average and peak network utilisation, the average and peak frame size, the average and peak number of frames per second, the number of broadcasts, the number of collisions per second, the number of CRC errors and the number of illegally short and long frames (runts and jabbers).

Useful Figures for Performance Management

Certain figures can be very useful for demonstrating current system demands and predicting future needs. Here we shall look at *mean time between failures* (MTBF), *mean time to repair* (MTTR) and *availability*.

Networks have a large number of components. If a vital component fails, it is possible that the whole network will be disrupted. The likelihood of a component failure may be known, often as the MTBF. The MTBF is the mean (average) time a device or system will operate before it fails. The MTTR is the average time necessary to repair a failure within the computer system. The availability of a component or system is the probability that the component or system will be available during a fixed time period. If we know the MTBF and the MTTR, then we can calculate availability. The formula for availability is given below.

$$\text{Availability} = \text{MTBF}/(\text{MTBF} + \text{MTTR})$$

For example, suppose that we want to calculate the availability of a network component that has an MTBF of 5000 h and an MTTR of 20 h.

$$\text{Availability} = 5000/(5000 + 20) = 99.6\%$$

If we want to know the availability of a whole system (such as a network), we will have to take into account the availability of each of its components. We must multiply the availability figures for all of the components together. Thus, if the availability of a system is A_{system}, the availability of device 1 is A_1, the availability of device 2 is A_2 and the availability of device $n = A_n$ then the formula for availability of the system is

$$A_{system} = A_1 \times A_2 \times \cdots \times A_n$$

For example, if a network sub-system consists of five components each with an availability of 0.96, what is the availability of the sub-system?

$$A_{sub\text{-}system} = 0.96 \times 0.96 \times 0.96 \times 0.96 \times 0.96 = 0.815$$

9.1.4 Accounting Management

Accounting management allows the network manager to collect data on how resources are being consumed by users and devices. From this data the manager can work out how much to charge internal cost centres for the network services that they are using. Even if the organisation does not use a cost-centre system, accounting management is still useful because it will facilitate the analysis of current network capacity and trends. Accounting management deals with such items as adding and deleting users, setting their usage quotas and granting them privileges to access resources.

9.2 Tools for Network Management

We will now examine some of the tools that are used by network managers. In the Physical Layer, *cable testers* are widely used. These vary in sophistication from a purely hardware *breakout box*, in which a light-emitting diode (LED) lights up if a wire of a copper cable has a good connection, to complex hand-held computers. Cable faults are the commonest source of errors on networks, so cable testing is very important. Testers are also available for fibre-optic cable and wireless.

Cable testers use *time-domain reflectometry* (TDR) to measure the distance along a cable to an open or shorted end. TDR works rather like radar. A pulse of energy is sent along the cable. When the pulse reaches the end of the cable or the place where there is a fault, the energy of the pulse is reflected back to the cable tester. The instrument measures the time taken for the signal to go along the cable and then be reflected back from the end. From the time taken, the tester works out the distance and displays it.

Network monitors (or *probes*) can be mounted on each segment of a network. The monitors observe and record events on the network and detect problems. They run round the clock throughout the year without human intervention. The information that the monitors provide from their captures of network traffic can be viewed from a central point. The monitors count how much the network is utilised, how many

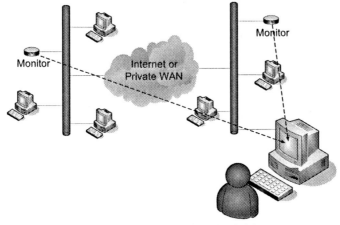

Network administrator

FIGURE 9.1. Use of network monitors

frames are sent and received by each network device and so on. Network monitors are often a part of an integrated network management system (INMS). The use of network monitors is illustrated in Fig. 9.1. These generally use RMON monitoring (see Section 9.4.5).

A *protocol analyser* (or *packet sniffer*) is able to capture and interpret network frames and packets. The protocol analyser may come in the relatively expensive form of a specialised portable computer with a built-in software. A specialised (and expensive) wireless laptop protocol analyser is illustrated in Fig. 9.2. Alternatively,

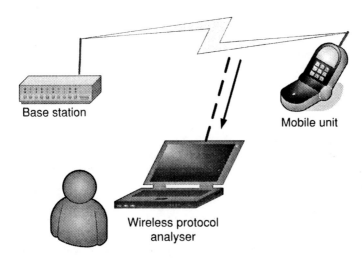

Base station

Mobile unit

Wireless protocol analyser

FIGURE 9.2. Wireless protocol analyser

the analyser may be software only and designed to run on a cheap, general-purpose computer. There are several protocol analysis software packages. Ethereal (available from http://www.ethereal.com) is an example of free protocol analysis software.

An INMS allows the network manager to monitor and control the corporate inter-network from a central point. The INMS covers all five of the ISO network management functional areas. The network administrator views the system via a graphical user interface (GUI). Software running on remote network devices gathers information that the INMS can use. SNMP (see Section 9.4) is often used in INMSs.

9.3 Network Troubleshooting

Troubleshooting involves finding out what is causing a problem on the network and sorting it out. The tools mentioned in the previous section can be used for this, along with other tools and techniques.

9.3.1 A Systematic Method for Troubleshooting

When troubleshooting, the network manager should use a systematic method for finding out the cause of problems on a network and dealing with them. We will now describe one such method, though it is not the only possible one. Firstly, the network administrator should get all the information about the symptoms of the problem together and analyse it. The problem should then be narrowed down to a particular area, for instance, a network segment or a network device. Next, the problem should be narrowed down still further, for example, to an item of software or hardware within the troublesome network device. Then the exact nature of the problem is discovered and corrected. After this has been done, the network administrator must check that the problem really has been solved. Finally, the administrator must document both the problem and what the solution to it was. All members of the network support team must be aware of what other team members have done in order to sort out the problem. The solution must be documented so the team will know what to do if a similar problem occurs again.

9.3.2 Procedures for Troubleshooting

Network testing should start with layer 1 (Physical Layer) of the OSI 7-layer model and then proceed as far up through the other layers of the protocol stack as necessary. Possible errors at layer 1 include disconnected or broken data or power cables and cables that are plugged into the wrong port on a hub, switch or router. Less easy to spot are the errors caused by intermittent cable connections or by the selection of a crossover instead of a straight-through cable or vice versa. A NIC, a router, a switch or a CSU/DSU might be faulty. The most fundamental error at layer 1 is that a device is either not plugged into the mains electricity supply or has been switched off. It is advisable to check for basic faults such as this before trying more sophisticated troubleshooting.

When troubleshooting at layer 1, indicator lights should be checked. For example, if a NIC is physically connected and working, a green light may be visible. There may also be lights that show network transmission or reception. If no green light is visible, this may be a symptom of a cable problem, but the NIC may need to be re-seated in its socket.

Potential problems at layer 2 include wrongly configured Ethernet or WAN interfaces. For example, the wrong kind of layer-2 encapsulation may have been chosen on one of the router's WAN interfaces. In the case of Frame Relay, the wrong DLCI (permanent virtual circuit number) may have been set. A layer-2 fault that can cause problems at layer 3 is one or more wrong associations between MAC and IP addresses. Purging (emptying) the ARP cache will often cure this. If a layer-2 switch is in use, VLANs may have been improperly configured, preventing communication between members of different VLANs.

There are several causes of layer-3 errors. The most common of these is an addressing error of some kind. For example, an interface on a device may have been configured with the wrong IP address or perhaps the subnet mask is wrong. For this reason, it is prudent to make sure that the addresses of router interfaces are correct before doing any further configuration. Routing protocols too can cause problems at layer 3. No routing protocol (such as RIP) may have been enabled. Or perhaps a routing protocol has been enabled but it is the wrong one.

The *Ping* utility program (described in Section 6.1.8) is a very useful tool for troubleshooting layer-3 problems. It can be used to test network connectivity over IP-based networks. The output from Ping shows the minimum, average and maximum round-trip time for a test datagram to reach the target address and be sent back to the source. From this output the network administrator can tell whether the target host can be reached, what the delays over the path to the host are and how reliable the path is. In the example given in Section 6.1.8, the ping target 193.60.1.15 replies to all four datagrams sent to it. An unsuccessful attempt at pinging a target host is shown in Fig. 9.3. This display shows that the target host is unreachable, as none of the test datagrams got to the address that they were trying to reach.

For troubleshooting at layer 7, the *Telnet* utility can be useful. Telnet, a virtual terminal protocol that works at the application layer of TCP/IP, was described in Section 7.4. Telnet is normally used to log into a remote computer and run programs on it. When used for troubleshooting, Telnet allows an administrator to check that at least one application works over a TCP/IP connection between the source and the destination. If Telnet functions OK, it shows that the whole protocol stack from Telnet downwards is working correctly. If it is not possible to Telnet to a server computer from a particular host, it might be worth trying from a router or other device. If using the name of the server does not produce a login prompt, it might be possible to get a successful result by using the server's IP address instead. The IP address may be able to be obtained by using the *nslookup* command (see below for an example). If one can still not get a response from the server, it is

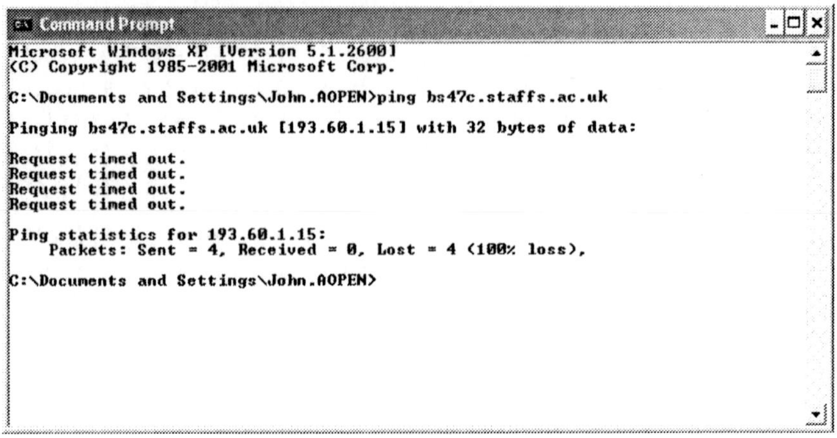

FIGURE 9.3. Unsuccessful Ping

possible that the Telnet service is not running or that, for some reason, it has been moved from its well-known port, 23.

Here is an example of the nslookup utility being used to look up the IP address(es) of www.google.co.uk. In the first line, the command is issued from the prompt on a UNIX computer called bsussoc1. The output is from the second line onwards.

bsussoc1 > nslookup www.google.co.uk
Server: bsus.staffs.ac.uk
Address: 193.60.1.17
Non-authoritative answer:
Name: www.l.google.com
Addresses: 66.102.9.147, 66.102.9.99, 66.102.9.104
Aliases: www.google.co.uk, www.google.com

The *traceroute* utility was described in Section 6.1.8. This can be employed to trace the complete route from host X to host Y. The output shows a list of all the routers that were reached. If there is a failure anywhere along the path from X to Y, traceroute will show where this occurred. An attempt at tracing a route that ends in failure is shown below. An asterisk in the output indicates failure.

Tracing route to bs47c.staffs.ac.uk [193.60.1.15] over a maximum of 30 hops:

1	12 ms	9 ms	29 ms	10.33.0.1
2	10 ms	18 ms	11 ms	gsr01-du.blueyonder.co.uk [62.31.176.129]
3	17 ms	47 ms	19 ms	172.18.4.33
4	39 ms	16 ms	19 ms	194.117.136.134

5	17 ms	28 ms	39 ms	194.117.136.146
6	16 ms	15 ms	16 ms	194.117.136.162
7	16 ms	37 ms	19 ms	janet-telewest-pvtpeer.telewest.net [194.117.147.30]
8	18 ms	17 ms	30 ms	po2-3.lond-scr4.ja.net [146.97.35.233]
9	17 ms	33 ms	17 ms	po1-0.read-scr.ja.net [146.97.33.26]
10	24 ms	20 ms	20 ms	po3-0.warr-scr.ja.net [146.97.33.54]
11	22 ms	22 ms	21 ms	po1-0.manchester-bar.ja.net [146.97.35.166]
12	33 ms	22 ms	24 ms	gw-nnw.core.netnw.net.uk [146.97.40.202]
13	25 ms	24 ms	41 ms	gw-staff.core.netnw.net.uk [194.66.25.94]
14	*	*	*	Request timed out.
15	*	*	*	Request timed out.
16	*	*	*	Request timed out.
17	*	*	*	Request timed out.
18	*	*	*	Request timed out.
19	*	*	*	Request timed out.

[etc.]

If the network manager compares the output from traceroute to a diagram of the internetwork concerned, he or she can find out where the problem area is. (In the traceroute attempt shown above, the reason for the request timing out is that the computer called bs47c.staffs.ac.uk is not directly connected to the Internet.) Traceroute also gives an approximate figure for the time taken to send an ICMP echo request and receive a response on each link. ICMP messages are sometimes filtered out by routers or firewalls at the target site, so ping and traceroute will not always work as expected.

9.4 SNMP and RMON

SNMP is used to manage networks. It was designed for use with TCP/IP, although it can work over other network protocols. SNMP has four parts. The SNMP *manager* runs on a network management station. It can query SNMP agents, get responses from these and make changes to variables by means of SNMP commands. The SNMP *agent* runs on a managed network device. It stores management data and responds to requests from the manager. The *Management Information Base* (MIB) is a database of objects (variables). These can be accessed by agents and can have

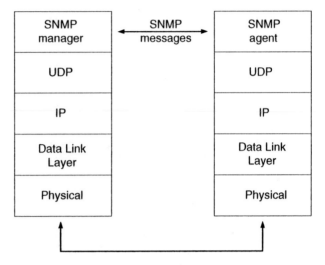

FIGURE 9.4. SNMP in the protocol stack

changes made to them using SNMP. The SNMP protocol is a TCP/IP Application Layer protocol that is used to query agents and make changes to objects. Figure 9.4 shows where the SNMP manager and agent sit in the TCP/IP stack.

9.4.1 SNMP Manager

The SNMP manager is an SNMP client program that runs on a host workstation (the management station). It can access the database of information that agents keep. For example, an SNMP agent running on a router may store totals of the number of datagrams sent and received. The SNMP manager can get these figures from the agent and compare them. By doing this it will be able to tell whether the router is experiencing congestion. The SNMP manager can also send commands to a network device by changing values in an agent's database. For example, the SNMP manager can change the device's IP address or switch a certain port on or off.

9.4.2 SNMP Agent

The agent is the SNMP server program which runs on a managed network device such as a hub, switch or router. Besides responding to the manager, it can also send out a warning (called a *trap*) to the manager about an anomalous situation. The agent's management information is stored in its MIB. The agent keeps information on various items. Examples of these items include how many virtual circuits exist and what their state is, broadcasts, error messages and so on. If the SNMP manager needs to interrogate or send commands to a proprietary (non-SNMP) agent, this can be done by making use of a proxy agent, which translates between SNMP and the proprietary software.

9.4.3 SNMP MIB

Each agent has a database (the MIB) consisting of a range of objects (variables) that can be measured, monitored or controlled. Each agent must hold a set of standard MIB objects. The MIB may also contain enterprise objects, which are specific to a particular vendor. The SNMP manager holds MIBs that correspond to those of all the agents on the network. Thus equipped, the SNMP manager and the agent can communicate with each other using the SNMP command set. A large number of MIBs exist. All MIBs have a hierarchical structure, in which the managed objects are the leaf nodes (the parts of the tree at the bottom of the hierarchy). Each managed object has a numerical identifier. The object identifiers are described using a language called Abstract Syntax Notation (ASN.1). The details of public-domain objects can be seen at http://www.ietf.org.

9.4.4 Simple Network Management Protocol

The SNMP protocol uses UDP on ports 161 and 162. SNMP is called 'simple' because it works by exchanging a limited number of types of message. The three main message types are *get, set* and *trap*. Get lets the SNMP manager retrieve MIB object values from the SNMP agent. Set allows the SNMP manager to set MIB object values at the agent. Trap lets the agent tell the SNMP manager about significant occurrences. Get and set work behind the scenes when a network manager clicks on an icon in the management station's GUI. A trap might cause an icon to turn red if, say, a connection has failed. Figure 9.5 shows the flow of SNMP messages between the manager and agent.

SNMP has evolved since it was first devised. Security was a concern in SNMPv1 and SNMPv2 because the 'community string', a field in the SNMP packet that acted as a password restricting access to managed devices, was transmitted in clear text form. The possibility of an attacker being able to control an organisation's network devices using SNMP was very worrying, so SNMPv3 supports authenticated and encrypted passwords.

When used over a WAN, SNMP traffic can slow down the response time for the normal network traffic. Further, when network devices are being interrogated using SNMP, they require extra processing. For these reasons, it is better not to poll network devices more frequently than is strictly necessary. Sometimes, a dedicated, separate network is used so that management traffic can be carried 'out of band', where it does not impede the passage of business data. One reason why the RMON MIB (see next section) was developed was to deal with the problem of monitoring network devices from a long distance away over a WAN.

9.4.5 Remote Monitor

RMON is an extension to the SNMP MIB. It was developed to facilitate the monitoring of remote sites from a central point. RMON has two parts: the hardware or software agent, usually called a *probe*, at the remote site and the client (the

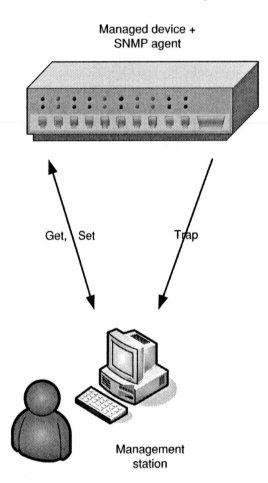

Managed device +
SNMP agent

FIGURE 9.5. Flow of SNMP messages between manager and agent

Get, Set   Trap

Management
station

manager) that displays and reports the information that the probe has collected. The probe sits on the network building up a MIB that can be sent to the manager. The probe can be either self-contained or a module on another device such as a switch. The first version of RMON worked only at the Data Link Layer. RMON 2 added support for OSI layers 3 to 7, giving the network manager more information about the network than SNMP on its own can provide. RMON can help the network manager to identify such items as where the most traffic on the organisation's internetwork is generated and which are the most heavily used routes. It makes it easier for the manager to discover if a user is making database queries that are crippling the network or spending a lot of time downloading large files. RMON can allow the manager to discover subtle changes that are occurring in the behaviour of a network. It can help the manager to decide where to place server computers and how to configure routers in the most efficient manner. Figure 9.1 (in Section 9.2) shows a network manager using RMON to monitor a network's traffic from a long distance away.

RMON has nine more MIB groups (statistical tables) than SNMP. The Statistics Group details Ethernet statistics, such as collisions and multicasts. The History Group can be used to take snapshots of the network. The Alarm Group will set off an alarm if preset parameters are exceeded. The Host Group gathers information about certain hosts. HostTopN lists the top network hosts rated according to a base statistic specified by the network management system. The Filter Group can be used to configure the probe to select individual packets for observation. The Matrix Group keeps tables of statistics about the number of packets, bytes and errors sent between two addresses, thus providing information about network traffic between users. The Packet Capture Group is used to copy packets from the filter group into buffer memory. The Event Group allows a network manager to define events for a probe, enabling it to log these events or send an SNMP trap. The advantage that this offers is that it becomes unnecessary to poll distant network devices over a WAN to discover faults. In RMON 2, 10 more groups were added. These enable the troubleshooting of applications across the network, whereas RMON 1 was restricted to viewing a single network segment at a time.

9.5 Documentation

Keeping up-to-date records of the network is of crucial importance. Unfortunately, since many people find maintaining their documentation rather tedious, they tend to forget to do it. There are many different kinds of documents that need to be kept. Some of these have been mentioned above (for example, the importance of documenting solutions to network problems was mentioned in Section 9.3.1).

General-purpose computer OSs such as Microsoft Windows have pieces of software that can be used for network management purposes built into them. Figure 9.6 shows some typical output from the msinfo32.exe program. Such information can be used to document the configuration of a workstation. Other kinds of documentation that are needed are cut sheet diagrams, wiring closet layouts and details of the software that is installed.

A cut sheet diagram indicates the path of network cables. It indicates the type of cable, the length of each cable and how it is terminated. The diagram shows where the patch panels and wall sockets are located. It also indicates the cable-labelling scheme that is in use. Diagrams of the layouts of all wiring closets should include the location of equipment racks and the equipment that is mounted in them. They should also show the configuration details of the equipment. The details of all the software installed on each computer should be recorded. This will include the standard software configuration and details of the operating system.

9.6 LAN Server Administration

If a client-server LAN (see Section 4.1.1) is in use, the network administrator has useful capabilities for control and management. The network operating system allows the network manager to set the rights that individual users or groups of users

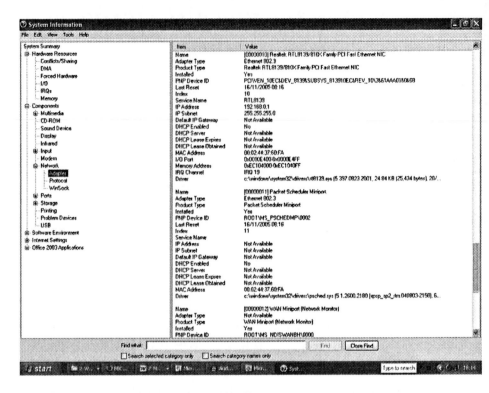

FIGURE 9.6. Typical output from msinfo.exe program

have to access particular network resources. Users can be granted such permissions as read, write, delete, print, copy and execute. The network administrator is also able to control the time periods when users or groups can access resources. The administrator can set up *profiles*, which facilitate customising of the user interface. Once set up, the profile can be used no matter which LAN workstation the user connects to the network from.

9.7 Summary

This chapter began with a description of the ISO network management model, which divides network management into configuration management, fault management, performance management, accounting management and security management. Some hardware and software tools that are used for network management were then discussed. Next, some ways of troubleshooting networks were mentioned. SNMP (a TCP/IP Application Layer protocol that makes it easy for management information to be exchanged between network devices) was then described, along with its equally important variant RMON. In the next section, the value of good network documentation was stressed. The chapter finished with a short section on LAN server administration.

9.8 Questions

1. Match the functional areas of the ISO network management model to the facts about them.

   Functional areas

   (a) configuration management
   (b) fault management
   (c) performance management
   (d) accounting management
   (e) security management

   Facts

   (i) Concerned with abnormal network behaviour.
   (ii) Analyses and controls network performance.
   (iii) Concerned with monitoring and controlling normal operations in a network.
   (iv) Concerned with access control, authentication and encryption.
   (v) Allows the network manager to collect data on how resources are being consumed by users and devices.

2. A network component has an MTBF of 10000 h and an MTTR of 12 h. What is its *availability*?

3. A network sub-system consists of four components each with an availability of 0.98. What is the availability of this sub-system?

4. Explain *time-domain reflectometry*.

5. You are a network manager. Your staff has asked for a dedicated laptop protocol analyser which is so expensive that it exceeds your budget. What reasons could you give your line manager to persuade him or her to make available enough money to buy the analyser?

6. What is an *integrated network management system*?

7. What network utility program can be used to find out an IP address from a network name and vice versa?

8. What are the parts of SNMP and what is their function?

9. Explain what the SNMP message types *get*, *set* and *trap* do.

10. Find out from books or the Internet what security algorithms are used with SNMPv3.

11. Look up the details of the standard RMON MIB objects in RFC 2819 (available from the Internet). According to this RFC, what does a probe have to do in order to implement the MIB?

10
Wireless Networks

Wireless networks have become more and more popular, in business and industrial environments, in the home and in *hotspots* in public places such as airports and hotels. Wireless networks can be classified in a variety of ways. In this chapter, we classify them as follows: personal area networks (PANs), home area networks (HANs), wireless LANs (WLANs), cellular radio networks (for mobile phones) and wireless technologies for replacing the wired analogue local loop. We start with a mention of some technical aspects of transmission. The chapter finishes with a short discussion on Radio Frequency Identification (RFID).

Certain aspects of WLANs were covered in previous chapters and the reader is encouraged to refer back to these. Infrared and microwave transmission (including satellites) were mentioned in Section 2.10.3. The WLAN access point and radio (the wireless NIC) were described in Section 4.1.3. The particular security problems posed by WLANs were covered in Section 8.11.

10.1 Spread Spectrum Wireless Transmission

This book is not the place to go into a detailed explanation of radio transmission. However, it is worth mentioning two related examples of transmission techniques that are commonly used in wireless networks. As we saw in Section 8.11, wireless networks pose a security problem. Direct sequence spread spectrum (DSSS) and frequency hopping spread spectrum (FHSS) are two transmission techniques that are used to help to alleviate this. In DSSS, each data bit is encoded as a group of bits that are transmitted simultaneously on a number of different frequencies. The individual transmissions are at such a low power level that an intruder has difficulty distinguishing them from the normal background noise. The IEEE 802.11b WLAN is an example of a wireless network that uses DSSS transmission.

FHSS uses more powerful signals that are transmitted in a pseudo-random sequence on several different frequencies. The receiver has to ensure that it is on the same frequency as the transmitter at exactly the same time. Bluetooth is an example of a wireless technology that uses FHSS transmission over a very short range.

10.2 Personal Area Networks

PANs, or *piconets* as they are sometimes called, permit communication between devices that belong to a single owner. The distances involved are very short, about 10 metres or less. The devices that are connected together can include mobile phones, portable computers, personal digital assistants (PDAs), printers, televisions and so on. PANs resemble small-scale WLANs. The most important PAN standard is Bluetooth.

10.2.1 Bluetooth

Bluetooth (IEEE 802.15.1) uses microwave radio to communicate. Infrared transmission (see Section 2.10.3) would be unsuitable because it is highly directional and cannot pass through obstructions. Bluetooth uses FHSS transmission in the same frequency band (2.4 GHz) as microwave ovens and many WLANs. It avoids interfering with the signals sent by other systems by transmitting at very low power levels. Nevertheless, the signals are still able to travel through the interior walls of a house. FHSS helps Bluetooth devices resist interference from other devices that use the same frequency band. Because the frequency changes regularly, any interference only affects a small part of the data. This small part is sent again if there was interference.

Bluetooth devices communicate with each other automatically whenever they come within range of each other. The devices arrange themselves into a piconet consisting of one master device and one or more slaves. The master has a clock that gives timing for the piconet. The slaves use this clock signal to synchronise with the frequency hopping sequence of the master. The piconet might be as simple as a mobile phone communicating with a headset or a more complex arrangement such as that illustrated in Fig. 10.1.

The device shown at the top of Fig. 10.1 is a PDA. This is a small, handheld portable computer, which possesses many of the capabilities of larger machines. Its functions are often combined with those of a mobile phone in a single device.

10.2.2 Wireless USB and Ultra-Wideband

The aim of wireless USB (WUSB) is to provide a wireless replacement for wired USB. WUSB is based on ultra-wideband (UWB). UWB transmits streams of very short pulses of energy, which are spread over many frequencies simultaneously. It needs only very low power levels and resists interference well. It works well inside buildings. It can support data rates of several hundreds of megabits per second. Security is good because the energy pulses are so short that they are difficult to intercept. The range is short (potentially up to 100 metres, but usually less) but this is not a problem if it is used to replace wired USB.

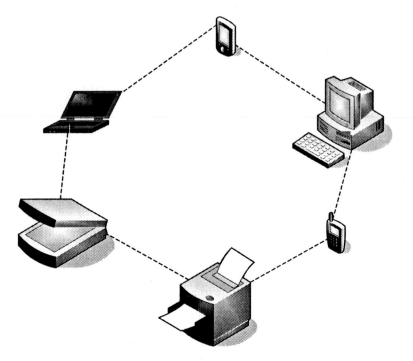

FIGURE 10.1. Bluetooth piconet

10.3 Home Area Networks

A house may have in it several remotely controlled devices. It would be convenient if the multiple remotes that are needed could be replaced by just one. A device that did not need a line of sight would also be convenient. ZigBee offers remote control of this nature.

10.3.1 ZigBee

ZigBee is based on the IEEE 802.15.4 standard and was designed to be used in wireless control and sensing networks. It uses DSSS transmission and can operate in the unlicensed 2.4-GHz band, like Bluetooth and some wireless fidelity (Wi-Fi) networks. The data rate is low (up to 250 kbps) and the range is limited (up to 30 metres). As a consequence, power consumption is very low. Batteries will last for years, rather than just a few hours, as with IEEE 802.11x WLANs or Bluetooth devices. ZigBee can be used in other applications besides home automation. For example, it can be used in toys as well as in industrial automation and building control.

10.4 WLANs

The aim of a WLAN is to provide exactly the same features as a wired LAN does but without the impediment of cables. WLANs can completely replace a conventional LAN or can be used to extend one. In all wireless networks, the atmosphere is the medium through which the signal travels. It is possible to use infrared transmission (see Section 2.10.3) but radio is far more popular because it offers greater range and higher data rates. The 2.4- and 5-GHz frequency bands are used because these do not need a licence in most parts of the world.

10.4.1 Benefits of WLANs

Although the data rate offered by WLANs tends to be lower than that of wired LANs, they possess many advantages. WLANs offer the possibility of users and devices being able to move about much more freely than is the case with wired LANs (*roaming* capability). Another advantage that WLANs possess over wired LANs is that it is possible to expand them fast and easily. The fact that there is no cabling to put in also means that WLANs are much easier and quicker to install in the first place. WLANs offer a much more flexible system than conventional LANs.

10.4.2 Drawbacks of WLANs

Data rates are often lower than can be obtained with a wired LAN. As we will see in the following section, the data rates that vendors claim for WLANs tend to be exaggerated. Line-of-sight obstructions, such as a metal cabinet or a partition in an open-plan office, can obscure the radio signals. Signals can also be reflected by walls and furniture. Another disadvantage of WLANs is that there is some concern about microwave radiation from transmitting WLAN devices.

10.4.3 802.11x WLAN Standards

The main standards for WLANs belong to the IEEE 802.11x family. 802.11x is a generic term that is used to refer to the whole family. An alternative name for 802.11x is Wi-Fi. The first really popular WLAN standard was IEEE 802.11b. This offered a nominal data rate of 11 Mbps in the 2.4-GHz band. The IEEE 802.11g standard provides a nominal 54 Mbps in the same frequency band. 802.11n is claimed to be about ten times as fast as 802.11g. 802.11n uses Multiple Input, Multiple Output (MIMO) aerial technology. Each 802.11n device has several aerials and each of these aerials is connected to a separate transceiver (transmitter/receiver). This means that multiple signal paths can carry multiple, independent streams of data, thus increasing the overall data rate. Unfortunately, the claimed data rates for 802.11x WLANs are never reached in practice. For example, an 802.11b WLAN usually gives about half its claimed 11 Mbps.

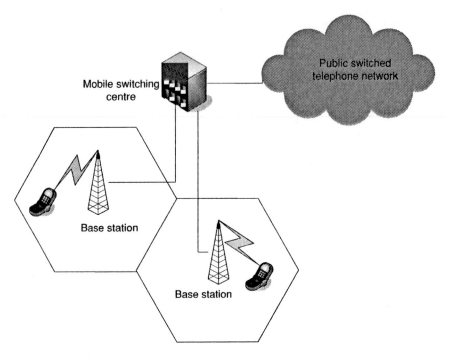

FIGURE 10.2. Mobile phone network

10.4.4 WLANs Between buildings

Fig. 2.37 in Chapter 2 shows how an optical link can be made between LANs in two buildings. Microwave wireless bridges can be used in a similar way to extend a WLAN between buildings or even to join together LANs that are several miles apart. This kind of solution usually works out much cheaper than using a leased line.

10.5 Cellular Radio Networks

Mobile telephone networks use cellular radio. As can be seen in Fig. 10.2, the mobile unit (whether a phone or a computer) communicates with a *base station*. The base station is the equivalent of the access point in a WLAN and consists of a transceiver (transmitter/receiver) and a base station controller. The coverage area of a base station is called a *cell*. Cells are really circular, but in diagrams are usually shown as hexagonal, as in Fig. 10.2. There are many base stations in a cellular network. Fibre optic or point-to-point wireless links connect the base stations to a *mobile switching centre* (MSC)—a special telephone exchange for mobile applications. The MSC connects calls from fixed-line phones to mobile phones and switches calls between cells as the mobile devices move from one cell to another (*handoff* or *handover*). The same radio frequency can be used in more than one cell, as long as those cells are not next to each other. Reusing frequencies in this fashion increases the capacity of the phone network without causing interference between cells.

10.5.1 Mobile Telephone Technologies

It is possible to classify mobile telephone technologies by comparing the way in which the medium is shared out among users. Both frequency division multiplexing (see Section 2.8.2) and time division multiplexing (see Section 2.8.1) have been used for mobile phone systems. The first cellular mobile telephone networks were analogue. These used Frequency Division Multiple Access (FDMA). The cells were divided into separate channels and different users used different frequencies for their calls. So-called second generation (2G) mobile phone networks use Time Division Multiple Access (TDMA). In these systems, different users are given different time slots on a channel. Global System for Mobiles (GSM) is the most widely used kind of 2G mobile phone system.

General Packet Radio Services (GPRS)—sometimes referred to as 2.5G—is based on GSM. However, the data is chopped up into packets instead of a continuous stream of bits being sent down a switched circuit as in GSM. GPRS gives an 'always on' service, in which the user appears to be constantly connected to the network. It also offers higher data rates than does GSM.

Third generation (3G) mobile phone systems generally use some form of Code Division Multiple Access (CDMA). This is very different from FDMA and TDMA, where the bandwidth is divided into many narrow channels. In CDMA, in contrast, every station constantly transmits over the whole frequency spectrum. A transmission channel can carry many signals from different users at the same time without interference between the users because different users are allocated different codes to provide access to the system. The signal that carries the information is multiplied with another signal that is faster and has a wider bandwidth—a pseudo-noise (PN) sequence. The resulting mixed signal closely resembles a noise signal. The receiver extracts the information by using the same PN sequence as the transmitter did. Signals from different users are distinguished by their use of different PN sequences. A good analogy for CDMA is a room that contains many people who are communicating in many different languages at the same time. The overall volume of noise is high, but one can still easily pick out someone speaking in the same language as oneself. CDMA is based on the DSSS transmission method (see Section 10.1). Wideband CDMA (WCDMA) is a variant of CDMA that can support multimedia communications at higher speeds than were previously possible. This is used in Universal Mobile Telecommunications System (UMTS) 3G networks. High-Speed Downlink Packet Access (HSDPA) and High-Speed Uplink Packet Access (HSUPA) are add-ons to the standard 3G infrastructure that support faster data rates. Fourth generation (4G) mobile phone systems offer still faster data rates.

10.5.2 Integration Between Wi-Fi and Mobile Phone Networks

A service that integrates Wi-Fi and a mobile phone network is possible. When a subscriber to such a service moves within the range of a WLAN hotspot, he or she may be switched over from the cellular radio network to the WLAN automatically. The advantage of this is that the WLAN provides a bandwidth greater than the phone network and is likely to be cheaper to use. If a laptop computer is equipped with a suitable PC-card, it can switch between a mobile phone network and a WLAN when occasion demands.

10.6 Wireless Local Loop

As we saw in Section 5.2, the local loop is the telephone line between the customer's premises and the local exchange. It is usually composed of twisted pair copper cable and is normally analogue. The local loop is a bottleneck for data communications. DSL (see Section 5.7) is one technology that has been used to speed up the local loop. There are also several wireless technologies that may be used to replace the copper local loop.

10.6.1 Satellite

A brief description of satellite technology was given in Section 2.10.3. With a satellite service, there is always more latency (delay) than with other options for replacing the local loop. This is caused by the distance the satellite is from the earth's surface. The data rates offered by satellite services tend to be high. So, satellites are good for downloading large files (because of the high data rate) but not at all good for VoIP (because of the high latency).

10.6.2 Worldwide Interoperability for Microwave Access

Worldwide Interoperability for Microwave Access (WiMAX) is a microwave radio-based technology that can be used to replace the local loop. A base station offers about 70 Mbps, though that bandwidth has to be shared out among all the users of the base station. The coverage of a base station is a radius of 2–10 km. A base station can reach a broadcast tower up to 48 km away if there is a line of sight. WiMAX uses a transmission technique called orthogonal frequency division multiplexing (OFDM). OFDM, which is also used in 802.11a and 802.11g WLANs, reduces the need for a line of sight. Without a line of sight, the range of WiMAX is reduced. In addition, the further the signal has to travel, the lower the data rate that can be achieved. The fixed wireless WiMAX standard is IEEE 802.16-2004. There is also a standard for mobile WiMAX, IEEE 802.16e. WiMAX offers QoS guarantees for users. As can be seen in Fig. 10.3, the uses of WiMAX are not limited to local loop replacement.

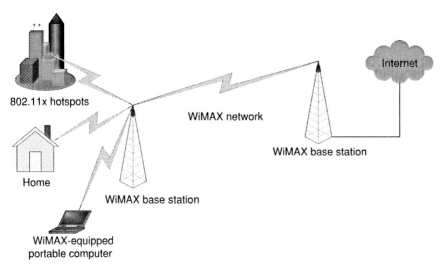

802.11x hotspots

WiMAX network

Internet

WiMAX base station

Home

WiMAX base station

WiMAX-equipped
portable computer

FIGURE 10.3. WiMAX

10.7 IEEE 802.20

The aim of IEEE 802.20, which also uses OFDM transmission, is to facilitate a wireless network with data rates high enough to provide Internet access about as good as that available from cable modems. The result is rather like a 3G mobile phone service, in that users can access it from almost anywhere while travelling at even high speeds. However, the network is accessible by portable computers such as laptops as well as mobile phones.

10.8 Radio Frequency Identification

RFID is a form of automatic identification technology. In an RFID system an ID number is transmitted wirelessly by an RFID *tag* (or *transponder*). A tag can be interrogated remotely about the information that it contains. Various radio technologies can be used to communicate with the tag, but it will normally consist of a microchip and a miniature radio aerial inside a mounting of some kind. Tags can be attached to items in supermarkets, factories or warehouses. The movements of such items can then be tracked. *Passive* tags need no internal power source, but *active* tags do need a power source.

10.9 Summary

This chapter started with a mention of some technical aspects of transmission. We investigated various kinds of wireless networks, both fixed and mobile. We saw how PANs can be set up, using such technologies as Bluetooth or WUSB.

We looked at ZigBee, a HAN technology. We explored some aspects of WLANs that were not covered in Chapter 4. Various types of cellular radio networks for mobile phones were described. We found that satellite networks, WiMAX and IEEE 802.20 are all technologies that can replace the wired analogue local loop, although this is not the only possible use for these. The chapter finished with a short discussion of RFID.

10.10 Questions

1. Explain the differences between DSSS and FHSS wireless transmission techniques.
2. In UWB transmission, extremely short pulses of energy are spread over many frequencies simultaneously. What is a potential problem with such a transmission method?
3. Discuss the advantages and disadvantages of WLANs.
4. How can users of 802.11x LANs be authenticated? (You may find it helpful to refer back to Section 8.11.)
5. Ethernet LANs do not use acknowledgements but 802.11x LANs do. Why is this?
6. A wireless access point (AP) has been set up as follows:

   SSID = 24HillSt
   Channel = 6
   SSID Broadcast = enabled
   Security = WEP

   Comment on what changes to the above configuration may be advisable.
   (You may need to refer to Section 8.11 as well as the current chapter to answer this question.)
7. In what circumstances is wireless transmission required? (This question is an opportunity for reflection; a complete answer cannot be derived from this text only.)
8. Explain the role of *base stations* in a mobile phone network.

Appendix A

This appendix contains diagrams illustrating some TCP/IP packet formats. Figure A.1 shows the format of the IPv4 datagram header. Figure A.2 shows the IPv6 datagram format. Figure A.3 shows the IPv6 base header format. Figure A.4 shows the TCP segment format.

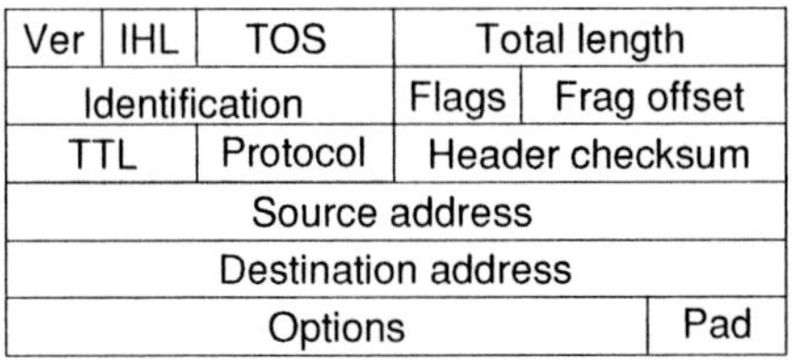

Ver	IHL	TOS	Total length	
Identification			Flags	Frag offset
TTL		Protocol	Header checksum	
Source address				
Destination address				
Options				Pad

FIGURE A.1. IPv4 datagram header format

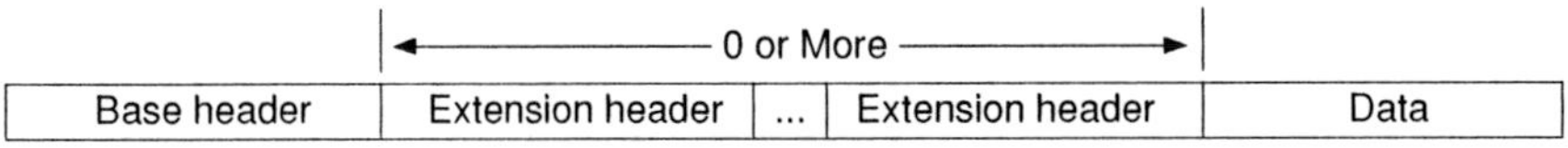

Base header	← Extension header	...	Extension header →	Data

FIGURE A.2. IPv6 datagram format

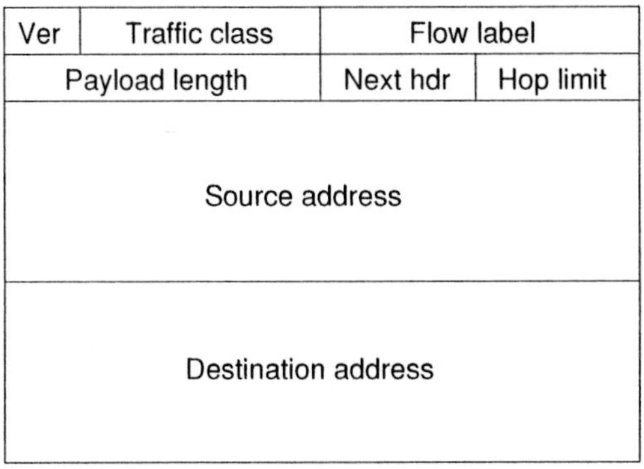

Ver	Traffic class	Flow label	
Payload length		Next hdr	Hop limit
Source address			
Destination address			

FIGURE A.3. IPv6 base header format

177

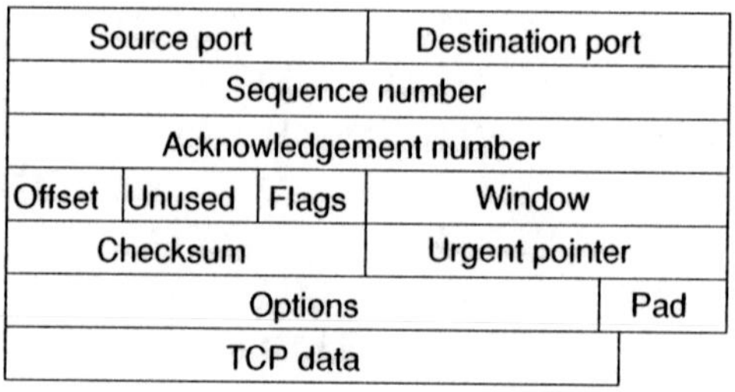

Source port	Destination port		
Sequence number			
Acknowledgement number			
Offset	Unused	Flags	Window
Checksum		Urgent pointer	
Options			Pad
TCP data			

FIGURE A.4. TCP segment format

Appendix B: Glossary

10 GbE. See 10-Gigabit Ethernet.

10GBASE-ER. A 10 GbE Ethernet variant.

10-gigabit Ethernet. Ethernet standard offering a nominal data rate of 10,000 Mbps.

2.5G. See GPRS.

2G. See second generation mobile phone network.

3G. See third generation mobile phone network.

4G. See fourth generation mobile phone network.

ABR. See available bit rate.

abstract syntax notation. A formal language mainly used to specify data used in protocols.

access control list. In networking, a packet filter that controls traffic in and out of a router interface.

access point. Hardware or software that allows users of wireless devices to connect to a wired LAN.

accounting management. An ISO network management functional area.

ACK. See positive acknowledgment.

acknowledgment. A signal that informs a transmitting device whether the receiver has successfully received data or not.

active RFID tag. An RFID tag that needs an internal power source.

ad hoc. See Peer-to-Peer.

adaptive filtering. An E-mail filter that adapts to changes in the nature of the user's e-mail over time.

address. A unique value that dentifies a computer.

address resolution protocol. A protocol that allows a source host to discover the data-link address of the destination.

advanced encryption standard. A secret-key encryption algorithm.

AES. See Advanced Encryption Standard.

aggregation. See route summarisation.

AH. See Authentication header.

always on. A service where the user is constantly connected to a network.

AM. See amplitude modulation.

American National Standards Institute. The organisation that administers and coordinates the US standardisation and conformity assessment system.

amplitude modulation. A technique for encoding digital information by manip-ulating the amplitude of an analogue carrier signal.

analogue leased line. A leased line that uses analogue signalling.

analogue network. A network that uses analogue signalling.

analogue signalling. Signalling that uses continuously varying electrical waves.

analogue transmission. Transmission that uses continuously varying electrical waves.

anonymous FTP. An FTP service for which the user does not need an account on the remote host.

ANSI. See American National Standards Institute.

anti-spyware software. Software that combats spyware.

anti-virus software. Software that combats viruses.

AP. See access point.

API. See application programming interface.

Application Layer. The highest layer in the OSI 7-layer model; the environment where user programs operate and communicate.

application programming interface. An interface that an application provides so as to allow other applications to request its services and to allow data to be exchanged.

application proxy firewall. A firewall that prevents network traffic from passing directly between external and internal networks.

ARP request. A broadcast to all devices in a network.

ARP. See Address Resolution Protocol.

ARP table. A table that contains correspondences between IP and MAC addresses of devices on a network.

ARQ. See automatic repeat request.

ASCII transfer mode. The mode of operation used in FTP to transfer plain text files.

ASN.1. See Abstract Syntax Notation.

asymmetric DSL. A form of DSL in which the downstream data rate is greater than the upstream data rate.

asynchronous transfer mode. A point-to-point, switch-based and cell-based network technology, which was designed to be suitable for multimedia traffic.

asynchronous transmission. Transmission where the unit of transfer is a single character and no clock signal is supplied to the terminal.

at command set. A language for controlling modems developed by the Hayes modem company.

ATM. See Asynchronous Transfer Mode.

attenuation. The weakening of a signal.

authentication. A procedure for checking that someone or something is who or what he/she/it claims to be.

authentication header. An IPSec packet header that supports authentication and data integrity.

authentication server. In 802.1X, a server that authenticates supplicant devices.

authentication server. In Kerberos, the server that keeps the database of encrypted user identities.

authenticator. In 802.1X, a component that grants authentication.

authorisation. A procedure that allows network managers to control who can have access to which network resources.

automatic repeat request. A procedure in which a receiver automatically asks for a retransmission of any erroneous data block.

availability. The probability that a component or system will be available during a fixed time period.

available bit rate. An ATM class of service that gives minimal bandwidth guarantees.

B channel. See bearer channel.

backdoor Trojan. A Trojan horse that enables an attacker to gain control of a computer.

bandwidth (analogue). The difference between the highest and lowest frequencies contained in a signal.

bandwidth (digital). See data rate.

base header. The basic IPv6 header.

base station. An element of a mobile phone network that consists of a transceiver and a base station controller and covers a cell.

base station controller. The element that provides the intelligence for a base station.

base64. The commonest standard method for encoding binary e-mail messages.

baseband transmission. Transmission that uses just one unmultiplexed channel.

baseline. Sets the acceptable level of performance of a network.

basic rate interface. An ISDN service that provides two 64-kbps B-channels and a 16-kbps D-channel.

Bayesian filtering. See adaptive filtering.

bearer channel. A 64-kbps ISDN channel that can carry voice or data traffic.

best-effort delivery. A form of packet delivery in which the network tries its best to deliver the data but does not guarantee that it will be delivered.

binary exponential backoff algorithm. The algorithm that computers on a CSMA/CD Ethernet network use after a collision has occurred.

binary transfer mode. The mode used in FTP to transfer binary files.

biometrics. The use of a physical characteristic such as a fingerprint to authenticate a user.

bit stuffing. A process in HDLC which ensures that the flag bit-pattern is not transmitted inside a data frame.

blacklist. A kind of anti-spam filter.

bluetooth. A microwave transmission standard for PANs.

bonding. A mechanism for combining two ISDN B-channels.

BOOTP. See Bootstrap Protocol.

Bootstrap Protocol. A mechanism for IP address assignment.

bot. See Zombie.

breakout box. Test equipment used for diagnosing cabling problems.

BRI. See Basic Rate Interface.

bridge. A device that can be used to connect LAN segments.

broadband. The use of a wide band of frequencies to transmit signals over more than one channel at the same time.

broadcast. A transmission sent to all hosts on a network at once.

broadcast address. The address used to send data to all hosts on a network at once.

buddy list. See Contact List.

burst error. A consecutive sequence of erroneous bits.

bus. A single piece of cable to which all the computers in a bus network are attached.

CA. See Certificate Authority.

cable modem. Device that modulates and demodulates computer data for transmission and reception over a cable TV system.

carrier. A telecommunications company that provides long-distance links.

carrier Ethernet. A service that uses Ethernet technology to provide longhaul links that offer the same performance and availability as standard WAN services.

carrier sense multiple access/collision detection. The MAC protocol that nonswitched variants of Ethernet use.

carrier signal. A signal that is sent across a network and is manipulated to encode data.

CAT 5e. See category 5e.

category 5e. A form of UTP copper cable.

CBR. See Constant Bit Rate.

CCITT. See Consultative Committee on International Telegraph and Telephone.

CDMA. See Code Division Multiple Access.

cell. A short, fixed-length packet (used in ATM).

cell. The coverage area of a wireless base station.

cellular radio. Provides a mobile telephone service by using a network of cells.

certificate authority. Issues digital certificates.

challenge–response. A defence against spam e-mail in which a challenge is sent to a new sender of e-mail to confirm that he or she is bona fide.

challenge–response system. An authentication system in which users have to supply an encrypted number that is the same as the one that a server has generated.

channel service unit/data service unit. DCE device that connects to a digital leased line; performs conversion between LAN and WAN data frames.

checksum. A method for detecting transmission errors by adding up the bytes of the message.

CIDR. See classless interdomain routing.

ciphertext. Encrypted text.

CIR. See Committed Information Rate.

circuit switching. Communication in which a dedicated circuit is established for as long as the transmission lasts.

cladding. Material that surrounds the core of a fibre optic cable.

classful addressing. The original Internet addressing scheme, using address classes A, B, C, D and E.

classless interdomain routing. An addressing scheme for the Internet which is more efficient than the older, classful scheme.

client–server LAN. A LAN that consists of one or more server computers (where shared files and programs are kept) and many client workstations.

client–server scheme. A scheme in which the client requests services and the server provides services in response to the client's requests.

cloud. See Network Cloud.

coaxial cable. A kind of cable formerly used in Ethernet networks.

code division multiple access. A mobile telephone technology.

collision. What happens on a CSMA/CD Ethernet network when two computers try to transmit at the same time.

colon hex. See Colon Hexadecimal.

colon hexadecimal. The standard notation used for IPv6 addresses.

committed information rate. The guaranteed data rate that a carrier commits to provide to a customer.

compact flash. A small, removable, flash-based storage device.

confidentiality. The process of ensuring that information can be accessed only by those authorised to have access to it.

configuration management. An ISO Network Management functional area.

connectionless working. A form of working where no dedicated end-to-end connection is set up; data is simply sent out in the hope that it will arrive at the destination.

connection-oriented working. A form of working in which when devices need to communicate with each other, they must first set up a connection.

constant bit rate. An ATM class of service.

Consultative Committee on International Telegraph and Telephone. The former name of the ITU-T.

contact list. A list of people (contacts) with whom one wants to exchange instant messages and who are logged into the instant messaging system.

continuous RQ. An ARQ scheme in which the sender can continue to transmit data blocks, even though no acknowledgements may have been received for previously transmitted blocks.

control field. In an HDLC frame, indicates the type of the frame.

convergence. The state of an internetwork when all the routers that belong to it possess the same knowledge of routes through it.

core. The innermost region of a fibre optic cable.

CRC. See Cyclic Redundancy Check.

crossover cable. A cable that is used to connect two computers directly to each other without a hub or switch.

crosstalk. Electromagnetic interference between the signals carried on adjacent wires of a copper cable.

CSMA/CD. See Carrier Sense Multiple Access/Collision Detection.

CSU/DSU. See Channel Service Unit/Data Service Unit.

custom subnet mask. A mask that is used for subnetting.

cut sheet. A record sheet that indicates the path of network cables.

cut-through mode. A mode of operation of a layer-2 switch.

cyclic redundancy check. An efficient error detection method.

D-channel. See Delta Channel.

DAD. See Duplicate Address Detection.

daemon. A UNIX process that runs in the background without human intervention.

data circuit terminating equipment. Communication equipment that connects to a carrier's network, for example a modem.

data compression. A technique that enables devices to transmit the same amount of data using fewer bits than without compression.

Data Link Layer. The OSI layer that transforms the raw transmission facility provided by the physical layer into a communication channel that appears to be free of errors.

Data over Cable Service Interface Specification. Defines the standards for transferring data using a cable modem system.

data rate. The amount of data transferred per second.

data terminal equipment. A computer that connects to a network.

datagram packet switching. A form of packet switching in which each packet contains the destination address.

data-link connection identifier. The virtual circuit identifier in a frame relay frame.

DCE. See Data Circuit Terminating Equipment.

DDOS. See Distributed Denial of Service.

de facto standard. A standard supported by more than one vendor but with no official status.

DECnet. Network architecture of the Digital Equipment Corporation (now defunct).

decryption. The inverse of encryption.

dedicated link. A link provided for the exclusive use of an organisation.

default gateway address. The address of the router that a computer will use to access another network by default.

delta channel. The ISDN signalling channel.

demilitarised zone. A network area between an organisation's trusted internal network and an external network such as the Internet.

denial of service. An attack with the aim of stopping an Internet server (usually a Web server) functioning.

dense wavelength division multiplexing. Similar to ordinary wavelength division multiplexing but offers greater data rates.

destination address. An address that identifies the receiving computer.

destination. The receiving computer.

deterministic network. A network technology which guarantees that the maximum waiting time before gaining access to the network will not be above a certain figure.

DF flag. See Don't Fragment flag.

DHCP. See Dynamic Host Configuration Protocol.

dial-up modem. A modem used with the analogue PSTN.

digital certificate. A user's public key that has been digitally signed.

digital subscriber line. A technology which offers high data rates over ordinary copper telephone lines.

direct sequence spread spectrum. A wireless transmission technique in which each data bit is encoded as a group of bits that are transmitted simultaneously on a number of different frequencies.

distance-vector routing protocol. A routing protocol in which a router regularly sends copies of its routing table to its neighbours.

distributed denial of service. A DOS attack mounted from many computers at once.

distributed system. A system consisting of many processors linked together and acting as one computer under the control of one copy of the operating system.

DIX. The original Ethernet standard, developed by the Digital, Intel and Xerox companies.

DLCI. See Data-Link Connection Identifier.

DMZ. See Demilitarised Zone.

DNS. See domain name system.

DOCSIS. See Data over Cable Service Interface Specification.

DOD. The US Government Department of Defense.

domain. A group of computers that belong together for some reason.

Domain Name System. The system that automatically translates domain names into IP addresses.

Don't Fragment flag. A bit in an IP datagram that if set tells a receiving router not to fragment the datagram.

DOS. See Denial of Service.

dotted decimal. The standard notation for IPv4 addresses.

download. To transfer files from a remote host (server) to the local host (client).

DSL access multiplexer. A device that allows multiple subscriber lines to be multiplexed together for long-distance transmission over a high-speed leased line.

DSL. See Digital Subscriber Line.

DSLAM. See DSL Access Multiplexer.

DSSS. See Direct Sequence Spread Spectrum.

DTE. See Data Terminal Equipment.

dumb terminal. A terminal with no processing power.

duplicate address detection. A feature of IPv6.

dynamic address assignment. A system in which a server can give a host an IP address on request.

dynamic host configuration protocol. A protocol used for automatic address assignment.

E3. A digital leased line standard that offers a data rate of 34.368 Mbps.

EAP. See Extensible Authentication Protocol.

EAP-TLS. An authentication protocol.

E-carrier. A digital leased line service available in Europe and much of the rest of the world.

echo message. A type of ICMP message.

echo reply. A type of ICMP message.

echo request. A type of ICMP message.

EIA. See Electronic Industries Alliance.

EIA/TIA-232. A physical-layer protocol.

Electronic Industries Alliance. A standards body.

encapsulating security payload. An IPSec header that offers privacy using encryption.

encapsulation. The packaging of data into a suitable form to be transmitted over a network.

encryption. The process of encoding data so as to make it unreadable by anybody except the intended receiver of the data.

envelope. A part of an e-mail message that encapsulates the message itself and contains the necessary information for transporting the message.

error control. Error detection and error correction.

error correction. Error control that allows a receiver to correct a message that has been corrupted during transmission.

error detection. Error control that allows a receiver to detect errors in a message that it has received.

ESMTP. See Extended SMTP.

ESP. See Encapsulating Security Payload.

Ethernet address. The address of an Ethernet NIC.

Ethernet II. A synonym for DIX Ethernet.

Ethernet interface. An Ethernet NIC.

Ethernet switch. A layer-2 switch used on an Ethernet network.

ETSI. See European Telecommunications Standards Institute.

European Telecommunications Standards Institute. A standards body.

even parity. A parity bit added to a character to make the number of 1 bits an even number.

extended SMTP. Allows much longer messages than normal SMTP.

Extensible Authentication Protocol. An authentication protocol used on WLANs.

Extensible HyperText Markup Language. A markup language similar to HTML but with a more tightly defined syntax.

Extensible Markup Language. A markup language used to describe many different kinds of data.

Extension Header. An optional IPv6 header.

Extranet VPN. A VPN that allows a business to share data with partners, suppliers, customers and other businesses.

false positive. The misidentification by an IDS or IPS of innocent activity as suspicious activity.

fault management. An ISO network management functional area.

FCS. See frame check sequence.

FDDI. See fiber distributed data interface.

FDM. See frequency division multiplexing.

FDMA. See frequency division multiple access.

FEC. See Forward Error Correction.

FHSS. See Frequency Hopping Spread Spectrum.

fiber-distributed data interface. A large-scale, ring-based token passing system, with built-in fault tolerance.

fibre channel. A high-speed fibre optic network technology.

fibre-optic cable. A glass (or plastic) fibre that carries a beam of light.

File Transfer Protocol. A protocol used to transfer files to or from an FTP server.

firewall. Software or hardware that restricts access to an organisation's computers.

fixed wireless. A term referring to the use of wireless technologies with devices that do not move.

flag field. The field that delimits an HDLC frame.

flow control. A mechanism for speeding up or slowing down the rate at which a source is sending data, according to how much buffer space the receiver has available.

flow label. A field in the IPv6 base header used to forward datagrams along a prearranged path.

FM. See Frequency Modulation.

formal standard. A standard issued by an official standards body.

forward error correction. An error control mechanism that allows a receiver to correct errors without having to ask for a retransmission.

fourth generation mobile phone network. A mobile phone system offering high data rates.

FRAD. Frame relay access device.

fragmentation. An IP mechanism for dividing a large datagram into smaller ones.

fragment-free mode. A mode of operation of a layer-2 switch.

frame check sequence. The CRC field in a data-link layer frame.

Frame Relay. A WAN technology which uses virtual circuits.

frame. The data-link layer protocol data unit.

frame trailer. Extra data placed at the end of a frame.

free space optics. The use of lasers for computer communications through free space (without a cable).

frequency division multiple access. A technique used in analogue mobile phone systems for sharing out bandwidth.

frequency division multiplexing. A technique for dividing up an analogue link into several frequency bands, with each frequency band carrying one channel.

frequency hopping spread spectrum. A microwave wireless transmission technique in which signals are transmitted in a pseudo-random sequence on several different frequencies.

frequency modulation. A modulation technique, involving manipulation of the frequency of the carrier signal, that can be used in modems.

frequency. The number of times a wave goes up and down per second (measured in Hertz).

FTP. See File Transfer Protocol.

full duplex. A form of working in which data is transmitted in two directions at the same time.

general packet radio services. A mobile phone service in which the data is transmitted in packets.

geosynchronous orbit. The usual orbit for communications satellites, synchronised with the rotation of the earth.

gigabit Ethernet. The 1000 Mbps version of Ethernet.

global system for mobiles. The most widely used kind of 2G mobile phone system.

go-back-N. An ARQ retransmission scheme in which all blocks from the erroneous block onwards are retransmitted.

GPRS. See General Packet Radio Services.

GSM. See Global System for Mobiles.

half duplex. A form of working in which data can be transmitted in two directions but not in both directions at the same time.

HAN. Home Area Network.

handoff. The transfer of a mobile device from one base station to another as the device moves from one cell to another.

handover. See Handoff.

handshake. An exchange between sender and receiver used to negotiate the parameters of a communication.

hashing algorithm. An algorithm to which the input is a long message and the output is a short binary string.

Hayes. A modem company (defunct).

HDLC. See High-level Data Link Control.

head-end. The place where a cable company is connected to the Internet and where it receives television channels.

header. In an e-mail, contains control information such as sender, recipient, subject etc.

header. The information that precedes the data in a packet.

Hertz. A unit used to measure frequency (cycles per second).

hierarchical topology. An alternative term for a tree topology.

High-level Data Link Control. A data-link protocol used in WANs.

high-speed downlink packet access. An add-on to the standard 3G infrastructure that supports faster downlink data rates.

high-speed uplink packet access. An add-on to the standard 3G infrastructure that supports faster uplink data rates.

home page. The site a Web browser first goes to when it is started (can also signify the main page of a Web site).

hop count. A measure of the number of hops (networks) between one router and another.

host. A computer that is connected to a network.

host field. That part of an IP address which indicates an individual host on a network.

host-based IDS. An IDS that is mounted on a host computer.

HSDPA. See High-Speed Downlink Packet Access.

HSUPA. See High-Speed Uplink Packet Access.

HTML. See HyperText Markup Language.

HTTP GET command. A command used to download data from a Web server to a browser.

HTTP POST command. A command that can be used to upload data to a Web server from a browser.

HTTP PUT command. A command that can be used to upload data to a Web server from a browser.

HTTP. See HyperText Transport Protocol.

hub. A central device that can be used to connect all the computers in a network.

HyperText Markup Language. A markup language used to make Web pages and cause them to appear on screen in a particular way.

HyperText Transfer Protocol. A protocol used to transfer pages on the World-Wide Web.

ICMP echo request. A message that sends a packet of data to a host and expects the data to be sent back in an Echo Reply (underlies the Ping utility).

ICMP. See Internet Control Message Protocol.

idle RQ. An ARQ scheme in which the sender waits for the receiver to acknowledge receipt of a data block before sending the next block.

IDS. See Intrusion Detection System.

IEEE 1000BASE-T. A twisted-pair variant of Gigabit Ethernet.

IEEE 100BASE-T. A twisted-pair variant of 100 Mbps-Ethernet.

IEEE 802.11a. A 54-Mbps wireless LAN standard.

IEEE 802.11b. An 11-Mbps wireless LAN standard.

IEEE 802.11g. A 54-Mbps wireless LAN standard.

IEEE 802.11i. An official WLAN security standard which was agreed after WPA2.

IEEE 802.11n. A high-speed wireless LAN standard that uses MIMO technology.

IEEE 802.11x. A generic term used to refer to the 802.11 family of WLAN standards.

IEEE 802.15.1. The Bluetooth standard.

IEEE 802.15.4. The standard that ZigBee is based on.

IEEE 802.16-2004. A fixed-wireless WiMAX standard.

IEEE 802.16e. A mobile WiMAX standard.

IEEE 802.1p. A prioritisation standard for IP telephony.

IEEE 802.1q. A standard that supports virtual LANs.

IEEE 802.1X. An authentication standard for LANs.

IEEE 802.20. A high-speed mobile wireless standard.

IEEE 802.3. An Ethernet standard.

IEEE. A standards body. See Institute of Electrical and Electronics Engineers.

IETF. See Internet Engineering Task Force.

IKE. See Internet key exchange.

IM. See instant messaging.

IMAP. See Internet Message Access Protocol.

information frame. An HDLC frame that carries data.

infrared. A part of the electromagnetic spectrum that can be used for short-distance wireless communications.

INMS. See Integrated Network Management System.

instant messaging. A form of messaging that allows real-time written communications over the Internet.

Institute of Electrical and Electronics Engineers. An American standards body.

integrated network management system. A system that allows a network manager to monitor and control the corporate internetwork from a central point.

integrated services digital network. An all-digital telephone network that can offer integrated services of various kinds.

intermediate system-to-intermediate system. A routing protocol.

International Organisation for Standardisation. A standards body.

International Telecommunication Union Telecommunication Standardisation Sector. A standards body.

Internet control message protocol. The protocol that IP uses to report errors and carry informational messages.

Internet Engineering Task Force. A standards body.

Internet. A global internetwork that uses TCP/IP protocols.

Internet key exchange. A protocol that is responsible for transfer of encryption keys in IPSec.

Internet Message Access Protocol. A protocol for retrieving e-mail from a server.

Internet Protocol. A layer-3 protocol used on all TCP/IP networks, including the Internet.

Internet Service Provider. A company or organisation that offers access to the Internet.

Internet Small Computer System Interface. A protocol that carries SCSI commands over an IP-based Ethernet SAN.

Internet telephony. See Voice over IP.

internetwork. Two or more computer networks connected together.

intrusion detection system. A system that automatically detects intrusion attempts.

intrusion prevention system. A system that automatically prevents intrusion attempts.

IP address. A layer-3 32-bit (IPv4) or 128-bit (IPv6) address given to a computer that uses TCP/IP.

IP security protocol. A framework of open security standards that was developed by the IETF.

IP. See Internet Protocol.

IP telephony. See Voice over IP.

IP version 6. Version 6 of IP, designed to improve upon IPv4 in various ways.

IPS. See Intrusion Prevention System.

IPSec. See IP Security Protocol.

IPSec transport mode. An IPSec mode in which routers use the original IP header.

IPSec tunnel mode. An IPSec mode in which the whole source packet, including the original header, is authenticated and encrypted and is given a new IP header.

IPv4. Version 4 of IP; uses 32-bit addresses.

IPv6. See IP Version 6.

iSCSI. See Internet Small Computer System Interface.

ISDN D-channel. See Delta Channel.

ISDN. See Integrated Services Digital Network.

IS-IS. See Intermediate System-to-Intermediate System.

ISO. See International Organisation for Standardisation.

ISP. See Internet Service Provider.

ITU-T. See International Telecommunication Union Telecommunication Standardisation Sector.

jabber. An illegally long Ethernet frame (alternatively, a malfunctioning device).

jack. A socket into which a plug fits.

jitter. Variation in delay.

jumbo frame. A large Ethernet frame.

Kerberos. A server-based authentication system.

key. A value used to encrypt and decrypt a message.

keystroke logger. Software that captures a user's keystrokes.

label. An extra four bytes added to packets as they enter an MPLS network.

LAN. See Local Area Network.

LAPB. See Link Access Procedure Balanced.

LAPD. See Link Access Procedure D-channel.

LAPF. See Link Access Procedure for Frame Mode Services.

latency. Delay.

layer-2 switch. An internetworking device used to connect network segments.

layering. The organisation of networks as a series of layers or levels.

leased line. A permanent, dedicated, point-to-point link that is leased from a telecommunications carrier.

length field. The field in an IEEE 802.3 frame that contains the length of the data.

LEO. See Low Earth Orbit.

line filter. A device that can be used instead of an ADSL splitter.

link access procedure balanced. An HDLC-type protocol used in X.25.

link access procedure D-channel. An HDLC-type protocol used in the ISDN D channel.

link access procedure for frame mode services. An HDLC-type protocol used in frame relay.

link-state advertisement. In link-state routing, a small packet that is broadcast to all the other routers in the internetwork whenever there is a change in the state of a link.

link-state routing protocol. A routing protocol in which each router in an internetwork keeps a map of the topology of the whole internetwork.

LLC field. The field for logical link control in IEEE 802.3.

Local Area Network. A network spanning a small geographical area.

local loop. The telephone line between the customer's premises and the local exchange.

localhost. An alternative term for Loopback Address.

location bar. The place where a Web browser shows the URL of the Web page that is being viewed.

logical connection. An alternative term for a virtual circuit.

logical link control. The upper sub-layer of IEEE 802 LAN protocols; controls the setting up of a link using an HDLC-type protocol.

logical topology. How the transmission medium can be accessed by the computers on the network.

loopback address. The address 127.0.0.1 (in IPv4), used for testing IP software.

low earth orbit. An alternative orbit to the geosynchronous orbit.

MAC address. The unique hardware address of a NIC.

MAC. See Media Access Control.

malware. Malicious software.

MAN. See Metropolitan Area Network.

management information base. The database of objects (variables) used in SNMP.

Manchester encoding. An encoding scheme used in 10-Mbps Ethernet.

man-in-the-middle attack. An attack in which a user gets between a sender and receiver and is able to read and modify the messages passing over the network at will.

maximum transmission unit. The largest packet that can be sent over a network.

mean time between failures. The mean time for which a device or system will operate before it fails.

mean time to repair. The average time necessary to repair a failure within a computer system.

media access control. Control of access to the network medium (for example, a cable).

media player. A streaming audio and/or video client.

media. The plural form of medium.

media server. A streaming audio and/or video server.

medium. The path along which data travels (often a cable).

mesh topology. A topology in which every computer is directly connected to every other one.

message digest. The output from a one-way hash function.

message switching. The switching of complete messages from router to router.

message transfer agent. Software that transfers e-mail messages from one computer to another.

metafile. A file that contains data describing another file.

metric. A way of measuring how good routes are.

metropolitan area network. A network that can span an entire city and its suburbs.

MIB. See Management Information Base.

microwave radio. The commonest form of wireless transmission; consists of ultra-high, super-high or extremely high frequency radio waves.

MIME. See Multipurpose Internet Mail Extensions.

MIMO. See Multiple Input, Multiple Output.

mobile IP. A feature of IPv6; allows mobile computers to keep their network connections while roaming.

mobile switching centre. A special telephone exchange for mobile applications.

modem. MOdulator/DEModulator; encodes digital information so that it can be carried over an analogue system.

modulation. Refers to ways of encoding information onto a carrier signal – amplitude, frequency or phase modulation.

modulo-2 arithmetic. A kind of arithmetic in which there are no carries and no borrows and there is no difference between addition and subtraction.

monitor. See probe.

Moving Picture Experts Group. A working group that develops video and audio encoding standards.

MP3. See MPEG-1 Audio Layer 3.

MPEG. See Moving Picture Experts Group.

MPEG-1 Audio Layer 3. An encoding and compression format for digital audio.

MPLS. See Multiprotocol Label Switching.

MSC. See Mobile Switching Centre.

MTA. See Message Transfer Agent.

MTBF. See Mean Time Between Failures.

MTTR. See Mean Time To Repair.

MTU. See Maximum Transmission Unit.

multicast. The same message sent to a group of hosts.

multimode fibre. Optical fibre in which multiple wavelengths of light take multiple paths through the fibre core.

Multiple Input, Multiple Output. Microwave wireless technology that uses several aerials (antennae) at once.

multiplexer. A communications device that combines several signals for transmission over a single line.

multiport repeater. A repeater with several ports (a hub).

multiprotocol label switching. An efficient way of doing routing, based upon a four-byte label.

multipurpose internet mail extensions. A standard way of encoding and decoding non-text e-mail attachments.

NAK. See Negative Acknowledgement.

NAT. See Network Address Translation.

negative acknowledgement. A signal that informs a transmitting device that the receiver has not successfully received data.

network access layer. A layer in the TCP/IP model that carries out the functions of the OSI Data-link and Physical layers.

network adaptor. See Network Interface Card.

network address translation. A technique that allows many devices on an internal network to use only one external IP address.

network architecture. A set of layers and protocols that work together.

network cloud. A term that is often used to refer to a WAN when we are not interested in its internal details.

network. Consists of a number of interconnected, autonomous computers.

network interface card. A circuit board that lets a computer connect into a network.

network operating system. The operating system that runs on the server computer in a client-server LAN.

network troubleshooting. The process of finding out what is causing a problem on a network and sorting it out.

network-based IDS. An IDS in which sensors monitor traffic on each network segment.

NIC. See Network Interface Card.

node. A device connected to a computer network.

noise. Interference (usually electromagnetic).

non-deterministic network. The inverse of a deterministic network.

non-repudiation. A procedure for preventing the sender or receiver of a message from denying that the message has been sent.

non-return-to-zero. A digital encoding scheme.

NOS. See network operating system.

notary service. A trusted third-party system that provides non-repudiation.

NRZ. See non-return-to-zero.

nslookup. A network utility program that can be used to look up the IP address corresponding to a URL or vice versa.

OC-192. Optical Carrier level 192: a SONET standard for transmission over optical fibre.

octet. A group of eight bits (a byte).

odd parity. A parity bit added to a character to make the number of 1 bits an odd number.

OFDM. See Orthogonal Frequency Division Multiplexing.

open shortest path first. A link-state routing protocol.

open systems interconnect. A network architecture devised by ISO.

optical fibre. Glass (or plastic) fibre used to connect devices in a network.

orthogonal frequency division multiplexing. A microwave transmission technique that reduces the need for a line of sight.

OSI 7-layer reference model. See Open Systems Interconnect.

OSI. See Open Systems Interconnect.

OSPF. See Open Shortest Path First.

P2P. See peer-to-peer.

packet sniffer. See Protocol Analyser.

packet spoofing. The constructing of a packet with a false sender address by an attacker.

packet switching. A technology in which messages are divided into packets before they are transmitted; the packets are then sent individually, possibly reaching the destination via different routes.

packet. A unit of information suitable for travelling between one computer and another.

packet-filtering firewall. A kind of firewall in which a router blocks certain IP addresses, subnets or TCP or UDP port numbers by means of access control lists.

PAN. See Personal Area Network.

parallel data transfer. A procedure in which multiple wires are used to transfer whole units of data simultaneously.

parity. An error detection technique in which an additional bit is appended to a character to give either an even or an odd number of 1 bits.

passive RFID tag. An RFID tag that does not need an internal power source.

patch. A software update.

patch panel. A piece of hardware that acts like a small switchboard and is a convenient means of connecting various pieces of networking equipment together.

path MTU discovery. A technique for finding out the maximum size of data that can be sent all the way from source to destination in one packet.

PC-card. A standard for 16-bit add-on cards for laptop computers (formerly called PCMCIA card; the 32-bit standard is called CardBus).

PCI. See Peripheral Component Interconnect.

PCMCIA. See Personal Computer Memory Card International Association.

PDA. See Personal Digital Assistant.

peer processes. The entities comprising the corresponding layers of a network architecture such as OSI or TCP/IP on different machines; these appear to communicate directly with each other.

peer-to-peer file sharing. Sharing files over the Internet without a central server.

peer-to-peer LAN. A LAN in which none of the computers has control over the LAN and they act as client or server computers as necessary.

performance management. An ISO Network Management functional area.

peripheral component interconnect. A PC expansion bus standard.

permanent virtual circuit. A virtual circuit set up by an administrator for repeated use between the same two devices.

Personal Area Network. A network that permits communication between devices that belong to a single owner over very short distances.

Personal Computer Memory Card International Association. The organisation responsible for the PC card standard.

personal digital assistant. A small, handheld portable computer which possesses many of the capabilities of larger machines.

phase modulation. A technique for encoding digital information by manipulating the phase of an analogue carrier signal.

Physical Layer. The OSI layer concerned with the transmission of bit patterns over a communications channel.

physical topology. The physical configuration of a network.

piconet. See Personal Area Network.

Ping of Death. An attack in which the attacker tries to overwhelm a server computer by flooding it with Ping packets.

Ping. A utility program used to check for reachability of a host.

PKI. See Public Key Infrastructure.

plaintext. The message used as input to an encryption algorithm.

PM. See Phase Modulation.

PN sequence. See Pseudo-Noise Sequence.

point-to-point link. A link from one place to one other place.

POP. See Post Office Protocol.

POP3. POP version 3.

port. A number that TCP and UDP use to map incoming data to an application running on a computer.

port. A physical interface.

port mapping table. A table used by a NAT router to tell it which device on the internal network is sending or receiving data via the external address at any one time.

port scanning. A method that an attacker can use to find out what TCP or UDP ports are open in a network device or a network.

positive acknowledgement. A signal that informs a transmitting device that the receiver has successfully received data.

Post Office Protocol. A protocol for retrieving e-mail from a server.

Preamble. The first field in an Ethernet frame; warns stations on the network that a frame is coming.

Presentation Layer. The OSI layer that deals with data formatting, data compression and data encryption.

PRI. See Primary Rate Interface.

primary rate interface. A form of ISDN that offers thirty 64-kbps B channels (23 in North America) and a 64-kbps D channel.

private IP address. An address that can be used only within a private network.

private-key encryption. See Secret-key Encryption.

probe. An RMON agent that reports the information that it collects from a network segment.

proprietary standard. A standard devised by a vendor for use with the company's products.

protocol. A set of rules for communication.

protocol analyser. Special software or hardware that is able to capture and interpret network frames and packets.

protocol stack. A set of protocols that work together.

proxy server. An intermediary system involved in VoIP call setup when the SIP protocol is in use. (More generally, a server that lets clients make indirect network connections to other network servers.).

pseudo-noise sequence. A signal used in CDMA mobile phone systems.

PSTN. See Public Switched Telephone Network.

public key infrastructure. The legal, organisational and technical framework used to support public key cryptography.

public switched telephone network. The ordinary, fixed-line telephone network that has been in use for a century or so.

public-key encryption. An encryption system in which different keys are used for encryption and decryption – a public key that everybody knows and a private key that only the recipient of the message knows.

PVC. See Permanent Virtual Circuit.

QoS. See Quality of Service.

Quality of Service. The capability of a network to provide a guaranteed throughput level.

radio. A microwave transmitter/receiver that allows a device (computer, phone etc.) to access a wireless network.

radio frequency identification. A form of automatic identification technology.

RAID. See Redundant Array of Independent Disks.

RARP. See Reverse Address Resolution Protocol.

real-time streaming protocol. A protocol that is often used to control the delivery of streamed data over a network.

real-time transport protocol. A protocol for transmitting real-time data such as audio and video over the Internet.

reassembly. The process of putting back together a fragmented IP datagram.

redundant array of independent disks. A system that uses two or more hard drives in combination to give fault tolerance and/or better performance.

Reed–Solomon code. An error-correcting code.

registered jack-45. An eight-wire connector for twisted-pair cable, often used to connect computers to a LAN.

remote control. A method of remote access to a LAN in which the user's PC on the LAN does the processing but is under the control of the remote PC.

remote monitor. An extension to the SNMP MIB that allows the monitoring of remote sites from a central point.

remote node. A method of remote access to a LAN in which the remote computer acts as a node or workstation on the LAN.

remote-access VPN. A VPN that allows home workers to gain secure access to their company's network.

repeater. A hardware device that regenerates a digital signal.

request–response protocol. The type of protocol used in a client server system, in which a client requests services and the server provides services in response to the client's requests.

requests for comments. Documents that contain technical and organisational notes about the Internet, including definitions of Internet standards such as protocols.

reverse address resolution protocol. A mechanism for IP address assignment.

RFC. See Requests for Comments.

RFID. See Radio Frequency Identification.

RFID tag. A very small microchip that can be interrogated by radio and can transmit its ID number.

RFID transponder. See RFID Tag.

ring. A network topology.

RIP. See Routing Information Protocol.

RJ-45. See Registered Jack-45.

RMON. See remote monitor.

roaming. The ability of a WLAN device to move from one WLAN AP coverage area to another with no interruption to the service.

rootkit. A special form of remote-access Trojan horse that can give an intruder complete control of a remote computer.

route summarisation. The ability to represent a block of addresses by just one summary address using CIDR.

router. A computer that can make decisions about where an incoming network packet should be sent next, using information contained in its routing table.

router configuration file. A file containing rules and instructions to control the way in which data packets flow through a router.

router discovery request. A procedure that a host that has not been configured with a default gateway uses to find out available routers.

router solicitation request. An ICMP message that is the first step in the router discovery procedure.

routing information protocol. A distance-vector routing protocol.

routing protocol. A protocol that allows routers to inform each other about networks that they know about without human intervention.

routing table. A table that contains a router's knowledge about open paths through networks.

RS232-C. The former name of EIA/TIA-232.

RTCP. See RTP control protocol.

RTP control protocol. A control protocol that works together with RTP.

RTP. See real-time transport protocol.

RTSP. See real-time streaming protocol.

runt. An illegally short Ethernet frame.

SAN. See Storage Area Network.

screened twisted pair cable. A form of twisted pair cable in which there is an outer braided or foil shield.

SCSI. See Small Computer System Interface.

ScTP. See Screened Twisted Pair Cable.

SDH. See Synchronous Digital Hierarchy.

SDSL. See Symmetric DSL.

second generation mobile phone network. A digital mobile phone network that uses TDMA (or rarely CDMA); GSM is the most widely used kind.

secret-key encryption. A form of encryption that uses the same mathematical key for encryption and decryption.

secure shell. A protocol and program that includes all the functionality of Telnet, but is secure.

secure single sign-on. A system that requires users to log into a network once only and thus get access to all the resources that they are allowed to use.

secure sockets layer/transport layer security. Two very similar protocols that provide secure communications on the Internet.

security management. An ISO Network Management functional area.

security policy. A document that gives rules for access, states how policies are enforced and explains the basic architecture of a security environment.

security policy specification language. A special language for writing security policies devised by the IETF.

segment. A portion of a larger network.

segment. The TCP protocol data unit.

selective retransmission. An ARQ retransmission system in which only the blocks that have errors are retransmitted.

sequence number. A number given to a frame or segment of data when it is transmitted.

serial data transfer. A method of data transfer where only one wire carries the data and only one bit is transmitted at a time.

serial interface. A port on a computer for serial transfer.

serial interface. A port on a router used to connect to a WAN.

server. A server-class computer, more powerful than mere workstations.

server. Software that provides services in response to a client's requests.

service set identifier. A unique name, 32 characters long and attached to all packets on a wireless network, to identify the packets as belonging to that network.

session initiation protocol. A TCP/IP application-layer protocol that can establish, modify and end multimedia sessions, including VoIP calls.

Session Layer. An OSI layer that deals with the establishment, maintenance and termination of a session (a communication path) between two users.

shielded twisted pair. A twisted pair cable with shielding added to give more protection from interference both from inside and outside the cable.

shielding. Metal mesh or aluminium foil that helps to prevent electromagnetic interference.

shortest path first. A link-state routing algorithm.

Simple Mail Transfer Protocol. The standard protocol for sending electronic mail over the Internet.

Simple Network Management Protocol. A TCP/IP application-layer protocol that makes it easy for management information to be exchanged between network devices.

single point of failure. Any component of a system which if it fails will cause the whole system to stop working.

single-mode fibre. A fibre the diameter of whose core is just sufficient for one wavelength of light.

SIP location server. A SIP proxy server with which users are able to register their location.

SIP request. A SIP message used during call set-up and release.

SIP. See Session Initiation Protocol.

site-to-site VPN. A type of VPN that connects remote offices over the Internet.

sliding window. A flow control mechanism.

Small Computer System Interface. An interface standard and command set for attaching peripheral devices to computers and transferring data.

SMTP. See Simple Mail Transfer Protocol.

smurf attack. A DOS attack in which a network connected to the Internet is swamped with replies to pings that it did not send.

SNMP agent. Software that runs on a managed network device; it stores management data and responds to requests from the manager.

SNMP community string. A field in the SNMP versions 1 and 2 packet that acted as a password, transmitted in clear text.

SNMP get. An SNMP message type that lets the SNMP manager retrieve MIB object values from the SNMP agent.

SNMP manager. Software running on a network management station that can query SNMP agents, get responses from these and make changes to variables by means of SNMP commands.

SNMP MIB. A database of objects (variables) that can be accessed by agents and can have changes made to them using SNMP.

SNMP. A TCP/IP application layer protocol that is used to query agents and make changes to objects.

SNMP. See Simple Network Management Protocol.

SNMP set. An SNMP message type that allows the SNMP manager to set MIB object values at the agent.

SNMP trap. An SNMP message type that lets the agent tell the SNMP manager about significant occurrences.

SONET. See Synchronous Optical NETwork.

source. A sending computer.

source address. Identifies the sending computer.

spam filter. Software that applies rules to e-mail and tries to classify it as legitimate or illegitimate.

spam. Unsolicited e-mail.

spammer. A person who produces spam e-mail.

splitter. In ADSL, separates the DSL signal from the analogue telephone service.

spread spectrum. A microwave wireless transmission technique.

SPSL. See Security Policy Specification Language.

spyware. Software, installed without the user's knowledge, which gathers data about the way in which a computer is used.

SSH. See Secure Shell.

SSID. See Service Set Identifier.

SSL/TLS. See Secure Sockets Layer/Transport Layer Security.

standards body. A body that issues formal standards (standards relevant to computer networking and telecommunications in this instance).

star topology. A network configuration in which the computers are connected to a central hub or switch.

start bit. In asynchronous transmission, a bit that alerts the receiving device to the fact that a character is about to be transmitted.

start frame delimiter. In 10-Mbps IEEE 802.3 Ethernet, a byte that indicates the end of the timing bits.

start–stop transmission. See Asynchronous Transmission.

stateful inspection firewall. A firewall that can keep track of the connections traversing it.

static address assignment. A form of IP address assignment in which a person has to enter the host's IP address manually.

static route. A route that a network administrator configures manually.

stop bit. In asynchronous transmission, a bit that tells the receiver that no more bits will be sent for a while.

stop-and-wait RQ. See Idle RQ.

storage area network. A special network that is dedicated to storage.

store and forward. In a packet-switching network, packets are briefly stored at every switch in the communication path before being passed on to the next switch.

store-and-forward mode. A mode of operation of a Layer-2 switch.

STP. See Shielded Twisted Pair.

straight-through cable. The standard twisted-pair copper cable used for connecting a computer to a hub or switch.

streaming audio. A client-server technology that permits an audio file to begin playing before the entire file has been transmitted.

subnet mask. A mask that allows an IPv4 network to be subdivided.

subnet. On a TCP/IP network, a subnet (subnetwork) consists of all devices whose IP addresses have the same prefix.

subnetting. A technique that is used to make the most efficient use of IPv4 addresses by dividing them into subnets.

supernetting. An alternative term for Route Summarisation.

supervisory frame. An HDLC frame that deals with flow control and error control.

supplicant. In the 802.1X LAN security standard, a device that requires authentication.

SVC. See Switched Virtual Circuit.

switched virtual circuit. A virtual circuit that is set up temporarily when needed.

symmetric DSL. A form of DSL where the upstream and downstream data rates are the same.

symmetrical encryption. See Secret-key Encryption.

SYN. A packet used in TCP to synchronise the initial sequence numbers on two computers that are initiating a new connection.

SYN flooding attack. An attack in which an attacking source host repeatedly sends forged TCP SYN packets to the victim host.

synchronous digital hierarchy. The ITU standard equivalent of SONET.

synchronous modem. A modem suitable for use on an analogue leased line.

synchronous optical network. A Physical Layer standard for fibre-optic transmission systems.

synchronous transmission. A transmission technique in which data is sent as a continuous stream at a constant rate.

T3. A T-carrier digital leased line that offers a data rate of 44.736 Mbps.

tag. In 802.1q, a four-byte label inserted into an Ethernet frame to indicate to which VLAN the frame belongs.

tag. In HTML, a label used to mark up the text.

tag. In RFID, a transponder.

tape library. A storage device which consists of at least one tape drive and a mechanism for loading tapes automatically.

T-carrier. A digital leased line service available in North America and Japan.

TCP. See Transmission Control Protocol.

TCP/IP suite. The protocol stack used in the Internet.

TDM. See Time Division Multiplexing.

TDMA. See Time Division Multiple Access.

TDR. See Time Domain Reflectometry.

Telecommunications Industry Association. A standards body.

Telnet. A client-server terminal emulation protocol and program for TCP/IP networks.

terminal adaptor. A device used to connect a computer to the ISDN network.

terminal type. In Telnet, the type of terminal emulation that a computer uses.

TFTP. See Trivial File Transfer Protocol.

third generation mobile phone network. A digital mobile phone system able to support faster data transfer speeds than second generation networks; generally uses some form of CDMA.

three-way handshake. A procedure used to open and close a TCP connection and to synchronise both ends of the connection.

throughput. The amount of data successfully transferred from one place to another in a given time (unlikely to be such a high figure as the notional data rate).

TIA. See Telecommunications Industry Association.

TIA/EIA-232. A Physical-Layer standard for serial data communications.

ticket. In Kerberos, authenticates a Kerberos client as an authorised user.

time division multiple access. A mobile phone technology in which different users are given different time slots on a channel.

time division multiplexing. A type of multiplexing in which bits (or bytes) from several sources are interleaved.

time-domain reflectometry. A technique used for cable testing.

Time to Live. A value in the IP datagram header that limits the number of routers that a datagram is allowed to pass through before it is discarded.

timeout. The length of time that a sender will wait for an acknowledgement from the receiver before giving up.

time-synchronous authentication system. An authentication system in which an intelligent token must be synchronised with the authentication server.

TLS. See Secure Sockets Layer/Transport Layer Security.

token. A pattern of bits which constantly circulates around a token ring and is used to give permission to transmit.

token. In computer security, a piece of software or hardware that generates a one-time password.

token. In data compression, a short bit pattern that is used to replace a longer bit pattern.

Token Ring. A type of LAN that uses a token to grant access.

top-level domain. The last part of an Internet domain name.

topology. The configuration (physical or logical) of a network.

total internal reflection. A phenonemon that keeps a light beam within the core of an optical fibre.

traceroute. A utility program that allows one to trace the complete route from one host to another.

trailer. See Frame Trailer.

transmission control protocol. One of the most important protocols in TCP/IP networks; allows two hosts to establish a connection and exchange data.

transmission medium. The medium along which data is transmitted (often, but not always, a cable).

transponder. A radio transceiver that automatically transmits an identifying signal when it receives a signal from elsewhere, for example an RFID tag.

transponder. A receiver and transmitter in a communications satellite that relays the signals it receives back to the ground.

Transport Layer. The OSI layer responsible for end-to-end connections between hosts.

tree. A network topology (alternative name: hierarchical topology).

Trivial File Transfer Protocol. A simpler file transfer protocol than FTP.

Trojan horse. A form of malware that hides itself within an apparently legitimate program.

TTL. See Time to Live.

tunnelling. A networking technology in which packets belonging to a private network are encapsulated and sent over a public network.

two-factor authentication. An authentication protocol that demands two independent ways of verifying identity.

Type field. In Ethernet II, a field containing a value that indicates which higher-layer protocol is being carried in an incoming frame.

UA. See User Agent.

UBR. See Unspecified Bit Rate.

UC. See Unified Communications.

UDP. See User Datagram Protocol.

ultra-wideband. A wireless transmission technique in which streams of very short pulses of energy spread over many frequencies are transmitted.

UMTS. See Universal Mobile Telecommunications System.

unicast. Packet delivery in which packets are delivered to only one address.

unified communications. The integration of several different forms of communication, letting users send and receive all kinds of messages from a single interface.

Uniform Resource Locator. A World Wide Web address.

uninterruptible power supply. A device that contains a battery which will provide power for some time in the event of a power cut.

universal mobile telecommunications system. A technology used for 3G mobile phone systems.

unnumbered frame. An HDLC frame that carries line setup information.

unshielded twisted pair. Twisted-pair cable consisting of four pairs of copper wires with no shielding.

unspecified bit rate. An ATM class of service that gives no guarantees as to if or when transmitted data will arrive at the destination.

uploading. The process of moving files from the local client to a remote server.

UPS. See Uninterruptible Power Supply.

URL. See Uniform Resource Locator.

user agent. An e-mail client.

user datagram protocol. A connectionless alternative to TCP in the TCP/IP protocol stack.

UTP. See unshielded twisted pair.

UWB. See ultra-wideband.

variable bit rate. An ATM class of service for LAN-type traffic.

variable-length subnet mask. Allows an organisation to use more than one subnet mask inside the same network address space.

VBR. See Variable Bit Rate.

VDSL2. See Very High-Speed Digital Subscriber Line 2.

vertical cabling. The network cabling that runs between floors of a building.

Very High-Speed Digital Subscriber Line 2. A high-speed version of DSL.

video on demand. A system that allows users to choose and watch video over a network.

virtual circuit. A connection between two devices that appears to be a physical path, though the actual physical path along which successive packets travel may vary.

virtual circuit number. A number that identifies a virtual circuit.

virtual communication. The apparently direct communication that seems to take place between two peer processes in the higher layers of a network architecture.

virtual LAN. A LAN that does not exist physically, but consists of a logical group of devices or users, selected from the devices or users on an actual, physical LAN.

virtual private LAN service. A service that securely connects two or more Ethernet LANs over an MPLS network.

virtual private network. A service that provides the equivalent of a private network but runs over a public network.

virus. Self-replicating code that is attached to another file.

VLAN. See Virtual LAN.

VLSM. See Variable-Length Subnet Mask.

Voice over IP. Hardware and software that allows people to use IP networks to carry telephone calls.

VoIP. See Voice over IP.

VPLS. See Virtual Private LAN Service.

VPN. See Virtual Private Network.

W3C. See World Wide Web Consortium.

wake on LAN. A facility on a NIC that allows the host computer to be switched on by sending it a special packet over the network.

WAN. See Wide Area Network.

wavelength division multiplexing. A technique that allows data from different channels to be carried at very high rates over a single strand of optical fibre.

WCDMA. See Wideband CDMA.

Web browser. A program that presents data from the World Wide Web.

Web page. A document on the World Wide Web, usually formatted in HTML or XTML.

well-known port number. A port number (below 1024) that is used for a standard TCP/IP application.

WEP. See Wired Equivalent Privacy.

whitelist. A list of legitimate sources of e-mail.

Wide Area Network. A network that connects computers over long distances.

wideband CDMA. A variant of CDMA that can support multimedia communications at high speeds.

Wi-Fi protected access. A security protocol for WLANs.

wi-fi. See Wireless Fidelity.

wildcard mask. A mask whose bits define the scope of a router's access control list address filter.

WiMAX. See Worldwide Interoperability for Microwave Access.

window advertisement. An indication of how many bytes of buffer space a TCP receiver has available.

window size. The number of outstanding, unacknowledged bytes in a sliding window system.

windowing system. A flow-control mechanism.

wired equivalent privacy. The first security protocol that was used with WLANs.

wired LAN. A LAN that uses cables as its transmission medium.

wireless bridge. A device that can be used to extend a WLAN between buildings or to connect LANs over a distance of up to several miles.

wireless communication. Communication without cables.

wireless fidelity. An alternative term for 802.11x WLANs.

wireless LAN. A LAN that does not use cables as its transmission medium.

wireless local loop. The use of a wireless technology to replace the copper local loop.

wireless USB. A wireless replacement for wired USB, based on UWB technology.

wiring closet. A walk-in cupboard that contains racks of network hardware.

WLAN. See wireless LAN.

World Wide Web. An easily accessible information service offered over the Internet.

World Wide Web Consortium. A standards body that develops specifications and software for the World Wide Web.

worldwide interoperability for microwave access. A microwave radio-based wireless technology which has fixed and mobile versions.

worm. Malware that can spread itself through networks automatically, copying itself from computer to computer.

WPA. See Wi-Fi Protected Access.

WPA2. The second version of WPA.

WUSB. See wireless USB.

X window. A client-server system that offers a windowing environment on UNIX and Linux computers.

X.25. A standard protocol suite for packet-switching WANs.

xDSL. A generic term for all forms of DSL.

XHTML. See Extensible HyperText Markup Language.

XML. See Extensible Markup Language.

ZigBee. A short-range wireless communication standard with low power demands that is based on the IEEE802.15.4 standard.

Zombie. A computer that is under the control of an attacker, who can make use of it in a DDOS attack.

Index

Please note: Bold text is used to indicate section and subsection headings.

Printed in the United Kingdom
by Lightning Source UK Ltd.
118322UK00002B/22-24